A World
Made by Men

*In the midst of thick
darkness enveloping the
earliest antiquity, so remote
from ourselves, there shines
the eternal and neverfailing
light of a truth beyond all
question: that the world of
civil society has certainly
been made by men, and that
its principles are therefore
to be found within the
modifications of our own
human mind.*

—Vico, *The New Science*,
331.

A World
Made by Men

Cognition and
Society, 400-1200

Charles M. Radding

The University of

North Carolina Press

Chapel Hill and London

© 1985 The University of North Carolina Press

All rights reserved

Manufactured in the United States of America

Library of Congress Cataloging in Publication Data

Radding, Charles.

A world made by men.

Includes index.

1. Civilization, Medieval. 2. Cognition and culture
—Europe—History. 3. Civilization, Medieval—12th
century. I. Title.

CB353.R33   1986   940.1   85-1111

ISBN 0-8078-1664-7

Contents

A Note on Vico

Introducing me to Vico was one of Peggy Brown's many contributions to this book. The parallels between Vico's ideas and those of Piaget had already been the subject of wide discussion, and I could further see that Vico's reading of certain periods closely fitted those I had reached in my own work. But what struck me most forcibly was Vico's insistence that human intelligence actively created the social world. His articulation of that principle greatly stimulated my thinking about the relationship between cognition and society, and I came to see that issue as a central theme of this book.

The title of this book—which of course does not exclude women as makers of the world—points toward this theme. For cultural history it marks the difference between studying traditions and studying what people *do* with traditions. Thus there will be little said about traditions of any kind, and readers should not expect to find discussions of the influence of Augustine, Boethius, or any other figure. More generally the title reminds us of the essential dignity of humans. The effects of social, and even material, circumstances are not unvarying, because human activity, guided for good or bad by human consciousness, alters the impact of these outside forces. This book is a history of people who tried, in different ways, to understand their world and sometimes made it over according to the model of their understanding.

Acknowledgments

In the ten years between the beginning of this project and the manuscript's final departure from my hands, I have benefitted enormously from the help of many scholars who have read drafts and shared with me their comments. Those who have read and commented on the whole manuscript include C. R. Hallpike, Rosalind Hays, Donald LePan, Lester Little, Gabrielle Spiegel, Teofilo Ruiz, Laetitia Ward, and Charles Wood. Several other scholars read sections and chapters. John Bollweg helped with the computerization of part of the book. My thanks to them all.

Thanks of a different sort are due to the National Endowment for the Humanities for a Fellowship in 1979–80; the leisure from a heavy teaching load afforded by that fellowship permitted me to research and write the book in much less time than otherwise would have been needed. Publication of the book was supported by a subvention from Loyola University of Chicago. The epigraphs from Vico's *New Science* are reprinted from *The New Science of Giambattista Vico: Unabridged Translation of the Third Edition (1744) with the addition of "Practice of the New Science"*, translated by Thomas Goddard Bergin and Max Harold Fisch. Copyright 1948 Cornell University. Used by permission of the publisher, Cornell University Press.

Very special thanks, finally, are due to three individuals. From the very beginning, Elizabeth Brown sustained me with encouragement when I needed it, all the while pressing me—as only she could do—to think through the really difficult issues, to write the book that the subject demanded to be written, whether I wanted to or not. The book would have been finished sooner, and have been much the worse for the haste, without her. Robert Lerner has been the skeptical voice close at hand, demanding more proof, asking new questions, but also guiding me into areas with which I previously had been too little familiar; I always knew I had something good when he was pleased. Finally, to Maureen Flanagan, my wife and a fine historian in her own right, I owe thanks—not for typing or indexing or keeping the children out of my hair (for she did none of those things)—but for being the first to hear, the first to read, *x*   and for not letting me be the prima donna all writers secretly wish to be. Though her efforts did not speed the writing of the book, they improved it immeasureably, and prevented me from running up even more arrears to my family than I eventually did.

Abbreviations

CCCM Corpus Christianorum, Continuatio Mediaevalis (Turnhout)

CSEL Corpus Scriptorum Ecclesiasticorum Latinorum (Vienna, 1866–)

MGH   Monumenta Germaniae Historica
    AA   Autores Antiquissimi (Berlin, 1877–)
    Cap.   Capitularia Regum Francorum, Legum Sectio ii (1883)
    Conc.   Concilia, Legum Sectio iii (1893–)
    Epist.   Epistolae Merovingici et Karolini Aevi (1892–)
    Leges   Legum Sectio i (Hanover, 1888–)
    SRM   Scriptores Rerum Merovingicarum (Hanover, 1884–)
    SS   Scriptores (Hanover-Leipzig, 1826–)

PL   Patrologie cursus completus, series latina, ed. J.-P. Migne (Paris, 1844–1864)

RS   Rolls Series, 99 vols. (London, 1858–96)

To facilitate reference to works that exist in numerous editions, especially classical and patristic works and law codes, I have cited by book (in lower case Roman numerals) and chapter, e.g. viii.7. I have used the abbreviations c. and cc. to cite chapters and *capitulae*.

PART I

Introduction

Here is revealed the origin of duels, which as they were certainly celebrated in the last barbarian times, so they are found to have been practiced in the first barbarian times. . . . The duels they practiced were appeals to certain divine judgments. They called on God as witness and made God judge of the offense, and accepted with such reverence the decision that was given by the fortune of combat that even if the outraged party fell vanquished he was considered guilty. . . . This natural barbarian sense can only be grounded in the innate concept which men have of that divine providence in which they must acquiesce when they see the good oppressed and the wicked prospering.

—The New Science, 27.

ONE

Historians and the Study of Culture

Curiosity—that inborn property of man, daughter of ignorance and mother of knowledge—when wonder wakens our minds, has the habit, wherever it sees some extraordinary phenomenon of nature, a comet for example, a sundog, or a midday star, of asking straight way what it means.

—The New Science, 189.

One day shortly after my daughter Sarah turned five, it happened that she found a long green bamboo stake. Noticing that the end of the stake was above her head as she stood holding it upright, I asked her, "Why is that stick taller than you?" Though an adult who overheard looked at me as if I had lost my senses, Sarah thought my question perfectly reasonable. And she knew the answer: "Because it is older."

My question did not come out of the blue; it was reported by Jean Piaget, who had heard one child ask it of another; and the incident as a whole illustrates several aspects of children's reasoning whose importance Piaget was the first to understand. The question itself, as others that belong to the category of "whys" with which all parents of young children are familiar, stems from the young child's belief that the universe is perfectly ordered so that all facts have a cause. Thus, the expression "it happened," which I used in my first sentence, would not be used by a child under six or seven because young children do not yet accept the existence of chance. Sarah's answer is typical of young children's tendency to assimilate external phenomena to themselves, in this case by attributing growth to a stick and assuming that age correlated with height. But the most important lesson, and one which Piaget stressed in all his work, is the independence of children's thought

3

from that of adults. Sarah's ideas did not come from me or any other American adult. They were her own response to the world, and only the acquisition of new ways of reasoning as she grew up would bring her ideas into line with those of the society around her.

A Piagetian anecdote about a child may seem an arbitrary way to begin a book of history. Piaget is famous for his studies of children, but there is little obvious relationship between the kinds of questions he asked his subjects—about why boats float or where names come from—and the concerns of historians. Yet while Piaget's materials are remote from those that historians customarily deal with, the issues he sought to address about the processes of learning and thought are not. In the course of doing historical research, historians inevitably suppose certain answers to the questions of how people learn, what relationship exists between ideas and the environment, and what indeed is the nature of thought. Historians' assumptions about such epistemological issues are usually unspoken and often (one suspects) unconscious, but they are not the less important for that. They direct us to the evidence on which we do our research, prompt us to ask certain questions of that evidence, and suggest explanations for historical phenomena.

To determine what assumptions are in use by historians and how those assumptions limit our ability to understand medieval culture I propose to consider how historians have studied medieval ordeals. The history of ordeals is not one full of dramatic events or controversies. The use of ordeals to determine guilt became common in the wake of the Germanic invasions without attracting any comment, ordeals were widely used for centuries without provoking complaints, and the turn of opinion against them in the twelfth century has more the character of a mopping-up action than a sharply contested battle. Yet there are three reasons why ordeals are suitable for my immediate purposes. First, although the history of ordeals is one of the lesser paths through the Middle Ages, it traverses terrain that is very important indeed. The role of divine providence in human life; conceptions of the miraculous and the natural; attitudes toward human society; the idea of justice: all these concerns, central ones in the Middle Ages, had their impact on the fate of the ordeal. Second, since ordeals were used to decide the fate of people's lives, property, legal status, and orthodoxy, we can be sure that had doubts been widespread the loser in the proceedings would have expressed them. Third, and in some ways most important, is the fact that ordeals have generated a body of historical literature that goes back to the nineteenth century and continues to grow today. In this literature one can perceive with exceptional clarity the epistemological premises that underlay the different methods which historians use to understand the past.

Ordeals and the Problem of Culture

The word ordeal derives from the Germanic word for *judgment* (modern form = *Urteil*) and describes a wide variety of tests known in the early middle ages as judgments of God *(judicia Dei)*. In the ordeals of boiling water and glowing iron, burns were inflicted on a subject who might be either the person whose case was at issue or a substitute. The burned areas were sealed for three days and the case was lost if there were signs of infection when the bandages were removed. The ordeal of cold water required the subject be immersed, usually while bound; if the water rejected the subject—that is, if he or she floated—the case was lost. All these ordeals had their roots in Germanic custom. Also of Germanic origin were judicial duels and compurgatory oaths, which also were ordeals in our sense because they shared the belief that their results revealed a divine judgment on the question at issue. In compurgation, for example, the swearers claimed no special relevant knowledge—they were not even character witnesses—and the oaths they swore were verbal formulas that had to be repeated faultlessly for the oath to succeed.[1]

Despite the pagan origins of these tests, the early medieval church was far from opposed to their employment, and priests often presided at their administration. One formulary, for example, has the iron heat in the fire for as long as it takes the priest to say mass. The priest is then to take communion and give it to the subject; sprinkle the iron with holy water; invoke the blessing of

1. For ordeals in general, see H. Nottarp, *Gottesurteilstudien*, Bamberger Abhandlungen und Forschungen no. 2 (Munich, 1956); Jean Gaudemet, "Les ordalies au moyen âge: doctrine, législation, et pratique canonique," *Recueils de la Société Jean Bodin pour l'histoire comparative des institutions*, 18 (1965): *La Preuve*, 2: 99–135; and, for England in particular, Paul R. Hyams, "Trial by Ordeal: The Key to Proof in Early Common Law," in *On the Laws and Customs of England: Essays in Honor of Samuel E. Thorne*, ed. Morris S. Arnold et al. (Chapel Hill, N.C., 1981), pp. 90–126. For compurgation see Frederick Pollock and F. W. Maitland, *History of English Law*, 2d ed. (Cambridge, 1898), 2: 600; Katharine Fischer Drew, *Notes on Lombard Institutions*, Rice Institute Pamphlet, vol. 48 no. 2 (Houston, 1956), pp. 6–8.

the Trinity on the judgment; and place the iron in the subject's hand for him or her to carry it nine feet. Other ordeals distinctly show their origins in Christian theology. In the Carolingian ordeal of the cross, the litigants held their arms out from their shoulders to form the shape of the cross; the first to let fall his or her arms lost the case. During the church reform movement of the eleventh century, suspected simoniacs were often required to prove their innocence by taking the Eucharist—inability to swallow it proved guilt—or recite the Lord's Prayer.

Judgments of God were not the only proofs admissable in early medieval courts, but whenever documentary evidence or testimony of witnesses was lacking or ambiguous (and these cases may have been in the majority), courts commonly accepted as decisive the verdict of some form of ordeal, and participants do not appear to have experienced much doubt that the ordeals revealed divine judgment. This expectation of divine intervention is perhaps nowhere more vividly apparent than in the criticism directed against ordeals by Agobard, a ninth-century bishop of Lyon. Agobard questioned, not whether God was present at *judicia Dei*, but whether one could be sure of interpreting the judgment correctly. A subject might receive punishment for a sin other than the case being tried, for example, or the just side might lose in a trial by battle since "Christian soldiers conquer by dying not by killing."[2] Evidently Agobard's contemporaries did not share his concern that the inscrutability of God rendered ordeals useless, for Hincmar of Reims writing a little later in the ninth century cited the inscrutability of God as an argument in favor of ordeals.[3]

This confidence in ordeals was scarcely shaken by 1100—as late as the last quarter of the eleventh century Gregory VII contemplated putting his dispute with Henry IV to ordeal—but in the twelfth century doubts began to multiply.[4] In England, Henry II's distrust of ordeals is apparent in his legal reforms: he punished those accused by their neighbors of breaking the peace by exile even if they succeeded at the water ordeal (if they failed he had them executed); and he denied *diffamati* (notorious) individuals

2. *Adversus legem Gundobadi et impia certamina quae per eam geruntur,* PL 104: 117, 118, 119.
3. "De divortio Lothari," PL 125: 665; cited in Gaudemet, "Ordalies," p. 109.
4. Colin Morris, "Judicium Dei: The Social and Political Significance of the Ordeal in the Eleventh Century," *Studies in Church History* 12 (1975): 95–111.

any right at all to prove their innocence by ordeal. Henry also offered trial by jury as a substitute for trial by battle in property cases, through the grand assize, the writ of novel disseisin, and the other petty assizes. *Glanvill*, at the end of the reign, was full of praise for these innovations because they avoided "the doubtful event of the duel" which "scarcely if ever" elicited justice.[5]

Compared to Henry's decisive actions, the reservations of trained legists appear quite timid. Gratian collected canons both authorizing and condemning the use of ordeals, and he included in the *Decretum* a passage from Numbers describing an ordeal of bitter waters to test whether wives had been adulterous. Gratian's conclusion left open the question of the licitness of ordeals, and subsequent canonists generally followed his example: either they approved some forms of ordeal while condemning others, or they pronounced ordeals acceptable where conclusive proof otherwise would be lacking. Uncompromising positions were taken only by Peter of Blois, who felt ordeals tempted God regardless of where they were employed, and Huguccio, who denounced all forms of ordeals on the narrow (and historically inaccurate) ground that they were useless novelties.[6]

In the midst of these muted debates, Peter the Chanter stands forth with refreshing clarity. Peter's writings, all from the last decades of the twelfth century, display scholarly interests that were extremely wide: he produced commentaries on all the books of the Bible; his *questiones* were collected into a *Summa* on the sacraments and on cases of conscience; and his *Verbum Abbreviatum* set forth his views on moral theology in a popular format. Peter's position as chanter of the cathedral of Paris enabled him to attract students and disseminate his opinions to a wide audience, but this does not entirely account for the popularity his works enjoyed. Equally important was the Chanter's own forceful personality, which won the respect of his contemporaries who often chose him to serve as judge or arbitrator and which led Peter himself on one

5. *Tractatus de Legibus et consuetudinibus regni Anglie qui Glanvilla vocatur*, ii.7, ed. and trans. G. D. G. Hall (London, 1965), p. 28. W. Stubbs, *Select Charters*, 9th ed., rev. R. W. C. Davis (Oxford, 1913), pp. 170–73, 179–81; Donald W. Sutherland, *The Assize of Novel Disseisin* (Oxford, 1973), pp. 35–36, Hyams, "Trial by Ordeal," pp. 117–24.
6. For this and what follows, see John W. Baldwin, "The Intellectual Preparation for the Canon of 1215 against Ordeals," *Speculum* 36 (1961): 613–36, later summarized in Baldwin, *Masters, Princes and Merchants: The Social Views of Peter the Chanter and His Circle* (Princeton, 1970), pp. 323–32.

occasion to lecture Philip Augustus on how he should govern France.

Much of this vigor passed into his writings, and it is nowhere more apparent than in his frequent and unqualified denunciation of ordeals.[7] We can trace Peter's campaign against ordeals without difficulty, since it is a theme for which he found a place in all his works. Discussing penance in his *Summa*, for example, Peter used the conviction of an innocent person by ordeal to illustrate how sin can accrue indirectly, in this case to the thief who permits another to be punished for his crime.[8] At another place in the *Summa* Peter recounted how Alexander III was embarrassed to have a holy vessel recovered from one man after another man, convicted of its theft by ordeal, had paid him compensation. "Good Jesus," the pope said, "what devil deceived me that I might be used so miserably by that judgment!"[9] As a Biblical commentator, the Chanter endeavored to demonstrate that the Bible offered no support for the practice of ordeals. This was an important task since supporters of ordeals justified their reliance on divine judgments by pointing to the ordeal in Numbers—this Peter dismissed as a concession of God to the "malice of the Jews"—as well as to Biblical stories of miraculous rescues of the good and punishments of the wicked. Peter, in response, denied categorically that the wonders worked by a few holy men provided a precedent for procedures that could be invoked by nearly anyone. "If you read of the three boys, who were led unconsumed from the furnace of fire, . . . if you assert Jonah escaped unharmed from the belly of the whale, and Daniel from the lion's den, and John from the jar of boiling oil, and much else in this fashion, nevertheless you cannot cause miracles by your blessings of water or iron, since you are not Daniel, or the three innocent boys."[10]

Peter devoted much effort to preparing his arguments and collecting his stories of ordeals that misfired, and we may well ask why an important and busy cleric undertook such a time-consuming project. As a theologian Peter felt that for men to use ordeals was to presume outrageously on their relationship with God. To be sure, God could conceivably intervene in an ordeal to reveal inno-

7. The works of Peter the Chanter are published in *PL* 205, and *Summa de Sacramentis et Animae Consiliis*, ed. Jean-Albert Dugauquier, Analecta Mediaevalia Namurcensia nos. 4, 7, 16, 21 (Louvain and Lille, 1954–67).
8. *Summa* 2: 254.
9. Cited in Baldwin, "Intellectual Preparation," p. 627 n. 97.
10. *PL* 205: 548D.

cence or guilt, but this would happen only through God's own
volition; neither the priest's words nor his office have any power
over God, and priests act foolishly when they put God to the test
by commanding a miracle. Peter clearly believed it was a serious
offense for a cleric to tempt God in this fashion—in one place he
declares he himself would prefer the eternal anathema of the
Church to consecrating water or iron for an ordeal—but this theme
had been enunciated before in discussions of ordeals without decisive effect. Original with Peter, however, was his insistence that it
was not only impious but foolish to expect justice from ordeals. He
reminded his audience that there was nothing extraordinary in water causing light objects to float while heavier ones sink, or in hot
iron burning flesh; success at the ordeal of hot iron may depend on
how calloused one's hands are, or whether one is the first or third
person to carry the iron after it is removed from the fire.[11] Again,
the Chanter had an example to nail down his point in a story of a
Parisian who faced an ordeal of cold water at which his inheritance
was at stake. He prepared for the ordeal by immersing each of his
sons in a cask of water in an experiment to determine which of
them would pass the ordeal. The first two floated, but when the
third hit the bottom of the cask the old man rejoiced: "Blessed be
the day I begot you, my son, since 'it is you who restore my inheritance to me.' (Psalm xv) Notice," the Chanter concluded, "the old
man did not place as much confidence in miracles as in natural
buoyancy."[12]

Peter the Chanter's open skepticism stands in sharp contrast to
the easy and frequent invocation of divine judgment by reformers a
hundred years earlier, and the trend was definitely with Peter. In
1215, fewer than twenty years after Peter's death, the Fourth Lateran forbade clerics to bestow their blessing on the implements of
ordeals; and while the ban was not immediately effective, the end
of clerical participation seriously undercut the claim of these tests
to divine inspiration. In England, the jury quickly took over most
of the areas where ordeals had still been used, the exception being a
few procedures where a form of compurgation survived to test the
ingenuity of lawyers at avoiding it.[13] Elsewhere it was most often
the Roman inquest that was pressed into service. But either way, the
path was cleared for the judicial proofs we still use today.

11. Baldwin, "Intellectual Preparation," p. 627 n. 97.
12. PL 205: 548D.
13. The form of compurgation that survived in church courts should not

One can, without undue simplification, divide the historical problem posed by ordeals into three categories: How did ordeals establish themselves in European law at the expense of the proofs of
Roman law? Why did generations of Europeans find ordeals a satisfactory means of settling their disputes? What were the causes of
the turn against ordeals in the twelfth and thirteenth centuries? Of
these questions, the first has perhaps received less attention than it
deserves because the invasion of the Germanic tribes appears to
offer a full explanation. I myself am not persuaded that this is the
whole story, for some procedures resembling ordeals were becoming common even before the invasions, and the eagerness with
which postinvasion Christians employed ordeals in their own disputes suggests conviction more than surrender to superior force.
But since our concern here is less with ordeals themselves than with
the methods that have been used to study them, the bulk of our
discussion must be devoted to the use and disappearance of ordeals.

In the nineteenth century, when the first serious research was
done on ordeals, the Enlightenment tradition of historiography was
still in the ascendant and no one felt embarrassed to describe ordeals as superstitions. They belonged to the Dark Ages, a period
when rational thought was less common than it later became—a
period, in fact, with many similarities to primitive societies of the
nineteenth century—and there accordingly was a great inclination
to place ordeals in the perspective of world history. Henry Charles
Lea, among others, pointed out that nearly every society had employed ordeals at some time in its development, just as there were
many societies in which the practice of witchcraft was common.
Lea believed that the rejection of ordeals, as of witchcraft, was an
instance of the emancipation of reason "from the cruel and arbitrary domination of superstition and force."[14] The use of ordeals
was thus explained as irrational, and the disappearance of ordeals
as a consequence of the progress of enlightenment.

Lea himself was chiefly interested in discovering the range of
forms ordeals could take and did not attempt to understand what
were the characteristics of superstitious thought. This task was

---

be confused with Germanic compurgation because the objective was not to
repeat verbal formulas but to testify to the character of the accused. Cf.,
R. H. Helmholz, "Crime, Compurgation and the Courts of the Medieval
Church," *Law and History Review* 1 (1983): 1–26.

14. *Superstition and Force* (Philadelphia, 1892), p. 590.

taken up fifty years later, when Paul Rousset tried to place ordeals
in their cultural context. Rousset observed that reliance on ordeals was only one example of a belief in immanent justice that was widespread in the Middle Ages. Raoul Glaber, for example, explained a famine as a punishment of human sins; Herman of Reichenau described the triumph of the Normans in Italy as a "hidden judgment of God"; the *Miracles of Saint Benedict* tells how a drought was a response to sin.[15] This widespread disposition on the part of medieval people to seek supernatural explanations for everyday events, moreover, Rousset found an expression of what anthropologist Lucien Lévy-Bruhl described as the primitive mentality, although he explicated this mentality by reference not to African or Australian tribesmen but to children. "This feudal man . . . cannot imagine a world inert and indifferent, acts without meaning, words and thought without efficacy. . . . He knows that evil exists and that it does not succeed, that good, right and virtue triumph in the end. . . . The need for immediate justice, the will to ignore the delays of history and suppress space and time, the paradoxes of faith and superstition, charity and cruelty—all this reveals a child's sensibility and imagination, an intelligence in development."[16]

Rousset argued, in short, that ordeals had to be understood as expressions of a mindset that experienced the world differently from modern Westerners. Yet when Rousset wrote, the tide was already turning against this kind of explanation. In place of the Voltairian willingness to label some beliefs as superstitious or childish there had come in the early twentieth century the doctrine of cultural relativism. This position, as put by one recent student of ordeals, is that

> if, instead of pursuing the myth of reason triumphing over
> unreason, we accept what seems to be a perennial factor in
> observable human societies, namely a sustaining tension be-
> tween cognitive and affective processes, the rational and irra-
> tional elements in medieval judicial procedures, as in our
> own, can be treated as constituent parts of one system and ex-
> plained in terms of their particular social context. . . . Reason
> and unreason, like rational and irrational, are value terms,

15. "La croyance en la justice immanente a l'époque féodale," *Le moyen âge* 54 (1948): 226–43.
16. Ibid., pp. 247–48.

and much misunderstanding has been generated by their indiscriminate use.[17]

The horrors of the twentieth century certainly had much to do with the success of this doctrine: no survivor of the era of the world wars and the death camps could be unreservedly confident of the superiority of Western Civilization or doubt the dangers of racism.

At the time cultural relativism arose, it provided a badly needed answer to the claims that had been made that Western men (though not Western women) had intelligence superior to the rest of humanity and were therefore entitled to take other races into tutelage.[18] But the effect of the doctrine has been not just to discourage invidious comparisons but also to assert, as a point of faith, that cognitive processes are in everyone more or less identical. Thus Maitland could explain the Anglo-Saxon practice of bequeathing land with the phrase, "I give this to you after I die," by observing that it was possible only because "men do not . . . apply the dilemma, 'Either you give at this moment, in which case you cease to have any right in the land, or else you only promise to give, in which case the promisee acquires at most the benefit of an obligation.' "[19] Today, however, cultural relativists have made the moral implications of such statements so daunting that most people, historians included, now instinctively shy away from making them.

In practice, the impact of cultural relativism has been heightened and to some extent directed by the rise of social science. The passage just quoted, for example, shows the influence of Freud in the equation of the irrational with the emotional, and the influence of sociology and anthropology in the assumption (whose lineage goes back to Durkheim) that morality and culture are to be explained solely in terms of social context. One effect of this marriage of cultural relativism with the social sciences has been to give premises of the social sciences immunity from criticism. Another is that instead of seeing ideas as leading to institutions and behavior, as had the Victorians, we prefer to study the social and cultural conditions that impressed ideas into people's minds. One exaggerates only slightly by saying that whereas for Lea and Maitland, intelligence had formed culture, for us culture forms intelligence.

17. Rebecca B. Colman, "Reason and Unreason in Early Medieval Law," *Journal of Interdisciplinary History* 4 (1974): 572.

18. For the brain measurers and other scientists who sought to place Caucasians at the top of an evolutionary ladder, see Stephen J. Gould, *The Mismeasurement of Man* (New York, 1981).

19. Pollock and Maitland, *History of English Law*, 2: 317.

The consequences of this shift are apparent in recent historical writing about ordeals; the requirement that we view people as identically rational has made it necessary to explain not why ordeals made sense to medieval people, as Rousset had tried to do, but (as the author I quoted above meant to imply by making a parallel between medieval and modern justice) why they might make sense to us. Some scholars have tried to accomplish this task by arguing that the tests were effective instruments of justice. They suggest, for example, that psychological pressures weighing on those about to face God's infallible justice must have caused many guilty parties to compromise or abandon their cases, and that fear of punishment for perjury deterred others from lying under oath. These historians assume people sincerely believed in God's participation in ordeals—why else should they feel anxiety? But their arguments for the efficiency of ordeals must be doubted. Psychological pressures may have lain as heavily on the innocent as on the guilty. And while fear of perjury may have deterred some people from lying, this fear was never so widespread that clerics ceased to preach with great regularity against false swearing. Oaths in any case could be manipulated, as was the oath in the thirteenth-century poem *Tristan*: Iseult swore that no man had come between her legs save her husband and the old pilgrim who had carried her on his back to the ordeal, when the pilgrim was in fact Tristan in disguise.

If historians have failed to offer an account for the use of ordeals compatible with the presumption of universal reason, they have not been noticeably more successful in explaining the turn against ordeals. Neither the spread of formal education nor the recovery of classical texts had a direct impact on ordeals: we have noticed how Peter the Chanter launched a vigorous attack on ordeals based entirely on the Bible and what seems just common sense, while canonists, the beneficiaries of major innovations in method and texts, generally treated the issue with the care they would use walking on eggs. The growth of towns, moreover, the focus of much of the social change of the period, similarly had little obvious effect on ordeals. Florence, already a large town in the eleventh century, was the scene of one of the most spectacular ordeals of the movement for church reform, Pietro Igneo's walk between two walls of flame to prove the bishop of Florence a simonist.[20] Henry II, on the other hand, certainly no townsman, was one of the early movers against ordeals, and Henry's great uncle William Rufus had, before

20. Morris, "Judicium Dei," pp. 105–7.

1100, expressed the opinion that certain ordeals which had acquitted forest offenders were a judgment of men, not of God. [21]

The difficulties of these traditional interpretations have recently led historians Rebecca Colman and Peter Brown independently to adopt functionalist interpretations of culture that were developed by anthropologists and sociologists to explain primitive societies. The basic tenet of functionalism is that rituals that to outsiders appear senseless are to be understood as accomplishing socially necessary ends, in most cases preserving the cohesion of the community. Brown and Colman accordingly contend that ordeals were invoked, not because people believed in them, but because they permitted communities to impose settlements on disputes that threatened to lead to internal warfare. As Brown put it, "What we have found in the ordeal is not a body of men acting on specific beliefs about the supernatural; we have found instead specific beliefs held in such a way as to enable a body of men to act."[22]

The strength of functionalist method is its close attention to context, and this is amply shown in different ways by both Brown and Colman. But as explanation, as opposed to description, both articles suffer from the inablity to prove their main point: that communities actually controlled the judgment. Brown tries to do this by arguing that the indeterminacy of, for example, burns (his source is Peter the Chanter of all people) enabled the community to project its unconscious judgment as if in a Rorschach test. Colman, more radically (and on the basis of even less evidence), suggests that the conditions of some ordeals could be manipulated in advance. Doubtless both these things happened. But neither Brown nor Colman considers ordeals such as compurgation, battle, or the Carolingian ordeal of the cross where there would seem to be little room for tampering with the results. Because the different forms of ordeal were often regarded as interchangeable, this gap in the inter-

---

21. Eadmer, *Historia Novarum*, RS 81: 102. "Ad hoc quoque lapsus est, ut Dei iudicio incredulus fieret iniustitiaeque illud arguens, Deum aut facta hominum ignorare aut aequitatis ea lance nolle pensare astrueret." Ordeals had acquitted all of fifty accused forest offenders and, Maitland comments, "the king did well to be angry." Pollock and Maitland, *History of English Law*, 2: 599 n. 2.

22. Peter Brown, "Society and the Supernatural: A Medieval Change," *Daedalus* (Summer, 1975): 140; Colman, "Reason and Unreason." I discuss these theories in greater detail in my article, "Superstition to Science: Nature, Fortune, and the Passing of the Medieval Ordeal," *American Historical Review* 84 (1979): 945–69.

pretation—an apparently unavoidable one—is enough to make the whole, rather shaky structure collapse.[23]

Although it might be possible to develop a functionalist interpretation of ordeals along lines different from Brown's and Colman's, certain problems appear inescapable. First, functionalist theory depends on the conception that primitive societies such as those of the early Middle Ages act as cohesive social organisms; without this hypothesis, it would not be possible to explain institutions solely as instruments of social cohesion. How the needs of society are communicated to its members, however, who may have interests of their own, is something that functionalists have never adequately explained. In the case of the ordeal it is far from obvious that everybody in society had the same interest. Defeated litigants and their families, at the very least, stood to gain property if not life itself by discrediting the verdicts. We could assume these individuals were so completely and perfectly socialized that they sacrificed their own survival to preserve community solidarity, but altruistic self-denial scarcely seems a dominant trait in the turbulent communities of the early Middle Ages. This was, after all, the age of the bloodfeud.

Functionalists must also claim to know better than their subjects what their subjects mean, a risky business for any historian. Participants in ordeals claimed to be inviting the presence of supernatural forces and to be willing to accept the judgment revealed by the ceremony. Functionalists, in effect, deny that anyone could act on the basis of such nonsense, and assert that people went through the

23. A related issue is the lack of rigor in the concepts of social cohesion and social context, which make it easy for the researcher to discover what he or she sets out to find. Ernest Gellner observes: "It may be that the sympathetic, positive interpretations of indigenous assertions are not the result of a sophisticated appreciation of context, but *the other way around*: that the manner in which the context is invoked, the amount and kind of context and the way context itself is interpreted, depends on prior tacit determination concerning the kind of interpretations one wishes to find. . . . After all, there is nothing in the nature of things or societies to dictate visibly just how much context should be described." Since it is easy for someone with a functionalist orientation to explain any apparently irrational belief as functional in some terms or other, Gellner concludes that functionalism as an approach is too charitable in the sense that it simply rules out the possibility of finding that beliefs are irrational or unempirical. Gellner, "Concepts and Society," in *Rationality*, ed. Bryan Wilson (New York, 1970), p. 33. For a general critique of functionalist interpretations, see I. C. Jarvie, *Functionalism* (Minneapolis, 1973).

motions of ordeals in order to impress or reach agreement with their neighbors: instead of a solemn appeal to supernatural judgment, ordeals become a bizarre theatrical performance in which it is hardly possible to distinguish the actors from the audience. A theory that began as an attempt to acquit poor primitives from accusations of superstition thus ends up denying that consciousness really matters at all.

I have devoted this space to ordeals and their handling by historians because the doctrine of uniformity of reason, so apparent in the historiography of ordeals, has been sufficiently pervasive that virtually all historians who study culture or mentalities treat reason as a constant shaped by external forces. Their methods fall into four main categories: the history of ideas and its close relative, the history of education; Marxist and other approaches that look for the economic and material bases of culture; psychoanalytic history that studies the emotional origins of ideas; and ethnographic history that regards society and its needs as the source of culture. These methodologies differ among themselves about the factors that most powerfully influence human thought and action, and these differences sometimes erupt into violent historiographical debates. But they are all agreed that intelligence itself is to be regarded as passive if, in fact, it is to be regarded at all.

Historians of ideas or of education seek the origins of an individual's ideas in external sources: a text, a school, or occasionally, in cases of striking novelty, foreign cultures. This research can be extremely valuable when it reveals the context in which individuals worked and wrote; thus, John Baldwin's work on the intellectual preparation for the ban on ordeals was an invaluable source for the history I presented above. But the effort to pin down influences often encourages a belief that ideas create people rather than the other way around, and when this happens two kinds of errors can result. The first comes when the search for influences leads historians to forget that their subjects may have any original ideas of their own. Gordon Wood aptly described this approach to history as believing that "ideas, emanations from great thinkers, are more or less poured into empty vessels that apparently are the minds of more ordinary people."[24] But even this assessment is only partially correct; the historian who traces Madison's ideas back to Locke or Hume will, in dealing with Locke or Hume, seek to trace their

24. *New York Review of Books* (2 April 1981): 16.

sources in turn. This not only interferes with our ability to see the originality of many interesting thinkers. It also leads to the preoccupation with labels, such as "augustinian," "platonic," or "machiavellian," which have so many potential meanings that they can actually obstruct our ability to think clearly about what the subjects of our inquiries actually thought.[25]

The preoccupation with influences can also lead historians of ideas to the error of creating schools or traditions whose members have nothing in common except the opinion under study. An example of this kind of mistake is Baldwin's grouping of Agobard of Lyons with Peter the Chanter in a "theological tradition" of opposition to ordeals because they both relied upon the Bible to justify their postion. In reality, Peter's ideas have very little in common with those of Agobard who, though he thought ordeals were difficult to interpret accurately, shared his contemporaries' belief that God was present at the judgment and that God intervened frequently in everyday life. (Agobard opposed the claims of magicians to control the weather because "it is obvious that God sends thunderstorms over those he judges worthy of punishment.")[26]

If historians of ideas see intellectual traditions as major influences on people, a second group of historians regards ideas as rationalizations or instruments of an individual's economic interests. Not all practitioners of this approach are Marxist—some indeed are outspokenly anti-Marxist—but all share the Marxist expectation that ideas express the interest of some class or social group. Although this method can be quite useful in studying political conflict, where it is possible to make a careful analysis of who gains and loses in a specific historical situation, it is harder to assess materialist interpretations of ideas that are concerned with class experience broadly defined instead of economic interest in a narrow sense. Jacques Le Goff, for example, attributes the modern conception of time as composed of discrete units to medieval merchants. They, unlike priest or peasants, were concerned less with the natural rhythms of weather and seasons than with calculating the length of the workday, the duration of a voyage, or the prob-

25. For a good treatment of this problem, see M.-D. Chenu's essay on the varieties of twelfth century platonism in *Nature, Man and Society in the Twelfth Century*, ed. and trans. Jerome Taylor and Lester K. Little (Chicago, 1968).
26. *PL* 104: 151, *Liber contra insulsam vulgi opinionem de grandine et tonitruis*, "apparet . . . hominum Dominum mississe grandine super eos, quos talo flagello dignos judicavit."

able value of goods or money at some time in the future; according
to Le Goff this calculating and rationalizing mentality led ultimately to the measurement of time by clocks.[27] Le Goff's theory
would seem to require showing that merchants personally initiated
the invention of clocks, participated in the creation of the new
sense of time, or at least that towns provided the environment in
which clocks were invented. Apart from the interest shown by four-
teenth-century merchants in using clocks to regulate the hours of
work and trade, however, Le Goff offers no evidence that directly
connects merchants to measureable time. In fact, although Le Goff
makes a point of contrasting the time of the merchant to the time
of the church, the cleric Gerbert discussed the problem of measur-
ing uniform hours in the late tenth century,[28] the first known evidence of an escapement mechanism is found on a sketch of a device
intended to turn an angel on a church so that the angel's finger
followed the path of the sun,[29] and David Landes has recently
argued that the first timing devices were invented by monks who
needed to wake for prayers.[30] Impressive as is the vision that Le
Goff presents, therefore, his essay is chiefly of interest for epito-
mizing the difficulties of linking intellectual trends to material
conditions.

The view that ideas are essentially instruments of some ulterior
purpose also appears in psychoanalytic history, though here the
motive to be uncovered is emotional, not economic. The American
Revolution, the French Revolution, and the Nazi movement are
among the phenomena for which psycho-historical interpretations
have been offered, despite the uniqueness of each person's child-
hood that might seem to stand in the way of a truly psychoanalytic
account of groups or collective mentalities.[31] This difficulty has

27. "Au Moyen Age: Temps de l'Eglise et temps du marchand," *Pour un
autre Moyen Age* (Paris, 1977), pp. 46–65 [now translated as chapter 2 of
Time, Work, and Culture in the Middle Ages (Chicago, 1980)].
28. Epistle 161 in Harriet Pratt Lattin's numbering, *Letters of Gerbert*
(New York, 1961), pp. 189–91.
29. A. C. Crombie, *Medieval and Early Modern Science*, 2d ed. (New
York, 1959), p. 211. Le Goff cites this work in his essay but, curiously,
does not mention this important piece of evidence.
30. *Revolution in Time* (Cambridge, Mass., 1983), pp. 58–66.
31. See, among others, Peter Shaw, *American Patriots and the Rituals of
Revolution* (Cambridge, Mass., 1981); Fred Weinstein and Gerald Platt,
The Wish to Be Free: Society, Psyche, and Value Change (Berkeley and Los
Angeles, 1969); George Forgie, *Patricide in the House Divided: A Psychological Interpretation of Lincoln and His Age* (New York, 1979); Peter

been overcome in various ways—not the least common is ignoring the existence of a problem—and the presumption that infantile experience explains all adult behavior of any importance has never met general acceptance. The notion that ideas are shaped by unconscious forces does, however, appear with some frequency in the discussions of primitive magic: thus Keith Thomas suggests that "ignorance of the future encouraged men [in early modern England] to grasp at omens or to practice divination as a basis for making decisions. . . . Correspondingly, the decline of magic coincided with a marked improvement in the extent to which environment became amenable to control."[32] We have seen that virtually the same argument was applied to the use and subsequent disappearance of judicial ordeals, which occurred 500 years before the period Thomas studied.

The last method of studying mentalities we need to consider borrows the methods of ethnography. Functionalism is one such approach; another is the "thick description" used by Clifford Geertz; a third looks back to Durkheim and Mauss. At their best these methods can use sources on rituals and festivals, superstitions, the physical environment, or the rhythms of work to restore our sense of everyday life. Both Brown and Colman do this admirably, each in a different way, in their articles on ordeals. Yet while this accomplishment is often justly praised, two negative consequences of this choice of material frequently escape notice. First, in attending primarily to minor details of social behavior, historians fall into the assumption that all who acted in a certain way did so for the same reason. This error homogenizes all those who lived at a certain time and place; and it can also disguise the pace of cultural change. Can one assume the ritual of vassalage meant the same thing in the twelfth century it had in the tenth, any more than the continuity of English coronation ceremonial means that the monarchy has the same role today as it had in the seventeenth century? Second, as we have seen in our discussion of functionalism, by studying what people do rather than what they think, ethnographic history often ends by portraying the subjects of its study less as thinking individuals than as participants in socially ordained rituals. Durkheim for one would not have shrunk from this conclusion and many of the *Annales* historians who have adopted his

Loewenberg, "The Psychological Origins of the Nazi Youth Cohort," *American Historical Review* 76 (1971): 1457–1502.
32. *Religion and the Decline of Magic* (New York, 1971), p. 650.

methods do not either. And though English-speaking historians are less likely to rely on concepts as abstract as Durkheimian "représentations mentales," when they engage in functionalist ethnography they employ a conception of society that ultimately allows no more room for thinking human beings.

I do not mean to suggest that these established methods are inevitably useless. No one would deny that reading and instruction do influence what people think, that the pressure of circumstances often moves them to give thought to one set of issues instead of another, and that strong emotional impulses sometimes persuade individuals to go against their training and best interests. Yet by concerning themselves exclusively with influences external to the conscious mind, historians, even historians of ideas, have let themselves forget that people think, sometimes with novel results, and that people act on the basis of what they think, sometimes with revolutionary consequences. It may well be, therefore, that what David Hackett Fischer called the "apathetic fallacy" of "treating rational men as if they were not rational,"[33] is far and away the most common methodological error historians impose on their subject.

We shall see shortly that Piaget provides the basis for a theoretical correction of this error. But my present point is the practical one: by regarding reason as a constant, historians have rendered some simple problems difficult and some difficult ones impossible. Baldwin cannot explore the important and obvious differences in reasoning between Agobard of Lyon and Peter the Chanter because he does not admit they exist; and Le Goff does not look for the development of a new idea of time arising in a clerical milieu because for him the only possible source of new ideas is the pressure of external and especially economic circumstances. Their errors are not caused by lack of skill, but result from a blind spot in their methods. Barred by the doctrine of cultural relativism from investigating whether historical peoples reasoned differently than we ourselves do, they can neither comprehend practices that are based on beliefs widely at variance with our own, nor make sense of social changes that arise when people come to think differently about their world and then reform the institutions that do not fit with their new ideas.

Here again ordeals provide a case in point. For the assumption of most modern writers has been either that belief in immanent justice

33. *Historians' Fallacies* (New York, 1970), p. 193.

is so little rational that exceptional circumstances must be adduced to explain its existence, or (and here I am thinking especially of historians of ideas) that one believes or disbelieves in immanent justice entirely as a matter of education and conditioning. Piaget, however, found that even in societies where adults do not endorse the idea of immanent justice, a lengthy learning process is needed to root it out. This was demonstrated by an associate of Piaget who told 167 French children a story about a child who stole apples from an apple orchard, and, while running away over a rotten bridge, fell into the water. When asked what they thought of the story, most of the youngest children (under age eight) said that the child would not have fallen in the water if he had not taken the apples.

> DEP (6) "What do you think of this story?" *"It serves him right. He shouldn't have stolen. It serves him right."* "If he had not stolen the apples, would he have fallen into the water?" *"No."*[34]

Children somewhat older tended to feel he would have fallen in anyway, but that he did so because he had stolen; only those near the age of ten were troubled by the contradictions between these two explanations. Finally, at about the age of ten or twelve, Piaget's subjects discarded the idea of immanent justice in favor of mechanical chance: the thief fell because the bridge was rotten and would have fallen in even if he had not taken the apples.[35]

Parallels can also be noted to the process by which Europeans came to distrust ordeals in the twelfth century. Colin Morris has

34. J. Piaget, *The Moral Judgment of the Child,* trans. Marjorie Gabain (New York, 1948; orig. pub. 1932), p. 253. Since the English translations of Piaget's works vary considerably in the format they employ in quoting Piaget's interrogatories, I have standardized them as follows: the child's name, where given, is in capitals; the number in parenthesis gives the child's age in years and months; the child's comments are given in italics and those of the interviewer in roman, both in quotes.

35. Ibid., pp. 251–52. In this connection readers might recall something similar to the taunt "cheaters never prosper" which my colleague Lew Erenberg learned as a child in California. It was chanted after a dispute, for example over whether a ball was fair or foul, when the replay proves to benefit one's side. One Chicago variant of the saying, according to my students, is "cheater's proof," and there are several other versions from other parts of the country. But what is important is that the clear meaning of the phrase is that one's position in the argument was vindicated by subsequent events. The replay, in effect, becomes a spontaneous schoolyard ordeal.

commented that believers in ordeals had no very clear ideas of how they worked. "If we ask by what mechanism this judgment was thought to operate we encounter almost complete silence."[36] In contrast, Peter the Chanter was acutely interested in the means by which the ordeal was supposed to work, as we have seen in his concern with the way God's participation was invoked and in his treatment of frauds. The Chanter also commented on a kind of dual causality assumed by participants in the ordeal. "In trial by battle the participants invariably choose their champions according to their skill in arms. Why do they not choose decrepit men . . . to demonstrate clearly the miracle."[37] Piaget similarly observed that concern with the causal mechanism of immanent justice only appears among "those who no longer believe the physical universe functions like a policeman"; younger children, as we have seen in the story of the bridge, are quite willing to propose two mutually independent explanations of a single event.[38]

The parallels I have drawn between the development of reasoning in children and the history of medieval ordeals may appear to be a return to those habits deplored by cultural relativists, of treating medieval adults as "child-people." But there is a deeper issue to be explored. For if children believe in immanent justice though raised in a society where adults do not, then it is apparent that it is not enough to know what a person is taught or how he or she lives to understand that individual's thought. Individual cognition has its own role to play in interpreting these influences, and it is as a guide to understanding that role that Piaget has much to offer.

Socialization, Learning, and Cognition

Before Piaget, psychologists' conceptions of intellectual development were remarkably similar to those we have found historians still using. Learning theorists, dating back to Locke, held that there was nothing in the intellect that was not first in the senses. A baby's mind was assumed to be a clean slate—a *tabula rasa*—on which was written the perceptions and experiences of everyday life: conceptions of number, for example, developed in response to countable objects; ideas of good and evil grew out of sensations of plea-

36. Morris, "Judicium Dei," p. 101.
37. Baldwin, *Masters, Princes and Merchants*, pp. 327–28.
38. *Moral Judgment*, pp. 257–58.

sure and pain. Allied to the Lockean view, at least in placing the sources of knowledge outside the individual, were various schools stressing the role of social conditioning through pleasant or painful experiences. But whereas Lockean empiricists had been interested mainly in sensory impressions as the origins of scientific knowledge, conditioning theories stressed the role of society in shaping children to the roles they would fill as adults. These theories, rather like functionalism, tend to regard individual members of society as so many interchangeable parts, rather like cookies stamped out by the same cutter, and to see any innovation as evidence of poor adaptation. The last main interpretation of thought, that of Freud and his followers, was primarily concerned with the relationship between cognitive and affective components of personality. Though Freud did occasionally discuss primitive myths and rules as expressions of unconscious wishes and fears, he never elaborated a theory of learning in any great detail. He had more to say about moral reasoning, which he believed began when children resolved the conflict between their love for and their fear of their parents by identifying with their parents. The internalized or introjected parent became, as the superego, an integral part of the children's own personality and perpetuated the parents' ideas and values.

Piaget began to formulate his own theory of cognition around 1920, when he was given the job of analyzing children's responses to the questions of the Binet intelligence tests. The wrong answers particularly interested him, and he adapted the free-flowing examining procedures he had learned at Bleuler's psychoanalytic clinic to the study of the reasoning by which children arrived at them. Pursued over the next decade Piaget's research into the development of language and thought persuaded him that children's reasoning led them to beliefs that they could not have learned from adults and that often were opposed by adult ideas. He concluded that children do not imitate or internalize the ideas or reasoning of adults; they reconstruct them following a definite sequence of stages.

Piaget developed these themes for over fifty years in wide-ranging research of often elegant design, but none comes closer to the materials familiar to students of culture than his early investigation of a boys' game of marbles. The game itself constituted, as Piaget remarked, "a well-marked social reality 'independent of individuals' (in Durkheim's sense) and transmitted, like a language, from one generation to another." Yet Piaget's primary concern was not, as an anthropologist's might have been, what the rules were but what individual children made of them.

We simply asked ourselves (1) how the individuals adapt themselves to these rules, i.e., how they observe rules at each age and level of mental development; (2) how far they become conscious of rules, in other words, what types of obligation result . . . from the increasing ascendancy exercised by rules.[39]

In other words, the study addressed the question both of the interactions between cognition and a well-defined external culture, and between thought and action.

The first stage of playing the game belonged to the outlook Piaget called egocentric because of the children's inclination to assume theirs is the only way of seeing the world. In the case of the game of marbles, egocentrism meant that children just learning the game believed that they were playing like the others, although in fact they followed only rules of their own choosing. Even boys who regularly played together described different rules, and when playing with each other often paid little attention to what their playmate was doing. The egocentrism of the first stage was also expressed in what Piaget called psychological realism—the attribution to ideas of an existence independent of thought. Thus the children, when asked, made it clear that they regarded the rules as sacred and established by high authority: parents, God, or (the study was made in Geneva) "the Gentlemen of the Commune." Indeed, the game was not only invented by superiors but the children saw themselves as powerless to change it.

We asked Leh quite simply if everyone played from the coche [shooting line] or whether one could not (as is actually done) put the older ones at the coche and let the little ones play close up. "No," answered Leh, *"that wouldn't be fair."* "Why not?" *"Because God would make the little boy's shot not reach the marbles and the big boy's shot would reach them."*

39. *Moral Judgment*, p. 24. The entire study is presented over pp. 13–108. Piaget conducted this study by having children explain the game while playing with him, by watching them play with each other, and by eliciting their ideas by means of interrogatories similar to those we already encountered in the materials on immanent justice. Piaget's style of presenting this material (first the data and then the conclusions) owed much to his early training as a natural scientist; thus, he treated the practice of rules separately from the consciousness of them, although the subjects in each case were the same. I have merged this data for clarity in a much shorter discussion.

In other words, divine justice is opposed to any change in the rules of marbles, and if one player, even a very young one were favored in any way, God Himself would prevent him from reaching the square.[40]

Even whatever innovations occurred as a result of the children's imagination were regarded as a complementary addition to the initial revelation. "Thus Geo . . . believes the rule invented by him to be directly due to a divine inspiration analogous to the inspiration of which the Gentlemen of the Commune were the first recipients."[41]

These theoretical ideas were only gradually and belatedly altered in the second stage, but the practice of rules showed more substantial development. The key feature is the fact that boys of this stage (around 10 years old in Piaget's sample) did manage to play together and compete according to the same rules. Yet the quality of this agreement should not be exaggerated. "Boys of 7 to 10 do not ever succeed in agreeing amongst themselves for longer than the duration of one and the same game; they are still incapable of legislating on all possible cases that may arise, and each still has a purely personal opinion about the rules of the game."[42] Thus, queried separately, boys from the same class used to playing together described different rules and were unfamiliar with rules known by their classmates. "It is only when they are at play that these same children succeed in understanding each other, either by copying the boy who seems to know most about it, or, more frequently, by omitting any usage that might be disputed."[43]

It is with the third stage that appears a genuine interest in legislation and with it a new conception of what the rules mean. Not only do the boys who play together agree on every aspect of the rules, so that the rules in force have a life beyond the individual game, "but also—and this undoubtedly is something new—they seem to take a peculiar pleasure in anticipating all possible cases and codifying them."[44] This interest in tinkering with the rules, moreover, is ac-

40. Ibid., p. 58.
41. Ibid., p. 61.
42. Ibid., p. 46.
43. Ibid., p. 42.
44. Ibid., p. 50. Readers will perhaps remember from their own experience something like what Piaget described as "the extraordinary behavior of eight boys of 10 to 11 who, in order to throw snow-balls at each other, began by wasting a good quarter-of-an-hour in electing a president, fixing the rules of voting, then in dividing themselves into two camps, in deciding

companied by a new consciousness on the part of the boys that they are the author of the rules by which they play.

> "Could one change the rules?" "Yes." "Could you?" "Yes, I *could make up another game. We were playing at home one evening and we found out a new one.*" [He shows it to us.] "Are these rules as fair as the others?" "Yes." "Which is the fairest, the game you showed me first or the one you invented?" "*Both the same.*"[45]

The experience of reaching agreement at the level of practice thus eventually alters the way the rules are perceived at the level of ideas, so that law ceases to be external to the mind and becomes a matter of convention whose force depends on the conscious agreement of the players.

For Piaget, there were two main lessons to be learned from the game of marbles. The first was that morality consists not of rules taught and learned but of ways of reasoning about rules. Indeed, though viewed anthropologically, the existence of the rules cannot be doubted, "psychologically, the same rule is a completely different reality for the child of 7 who regards it as sacred and untouchable and for the child of 12 who, without interfering with it, regards it as valid only after it has been mutually agreed upon."[46] The rules themselves, therefore, cannot be said, except in a very superficial way, to be the main influence on how the boys played. The second lesson was that cooperation between peers is the chief —if not the only—cause of the development of moral thought. Unilateral respect, the attitude of the inferior to the superior, whether in the society of children or adults, can only result in the attitudes that hold the rules external and immutable. It is only when, through interaction with their peers, children learn to act out of feelings of mutual respect that they give their full consent to the rules and try to live according to the spirit and not the letter of the law.

The concepts Piaget used to analyze the rules of the game are typical of those he found in cognitive development in general. Psychological realism, for example, is just one aspect of egocentric

---

upon the distances of the shots, and finally in foreseeing what would be the sanctions to be applied in cases of infringment of these laws." Ibid.
45. Ibid., p. 67.
46. Ibid., pp. 96–97.

reasoning. Others are the privileged place of appearances (as when
a child assumes water poured from one container to another has changed in quantity because it has changed in shape); the expectation that events have meaning and order; and a belief that properly performed rituals can manipulate external reality. Learning to take into account the perspectives of others—one of the solvents of the egocentric attitude toward rules—is a specific case of the ability to perform mental operations on phenomena by imagining situations that do not actually exist. Piaget believed that learning is not simply a matter of passively taking in facts. Facts are always molded to fit the operatory schema a given individual has available at a given time. Thus while children can learn by rote the words of a song or the steps of a dance, repetition alone will not suffice to teach them to recognize the operation of chance or to evaluate actions by considering the intention of the actor. To think in cognitively sophisticated ways about nature or morality also requires cognitive skills such as the ability to take account of perspectives different from one's own and to consider multiple variables at one time. Not every person develops all these capacities, and we shall see, when we turn to our analysis of historical sources, that there are important differences even between adults.

It should already be apparent why Piaget's influence on theories of culture has been so slight. On the one hand, by insisting that there exist different kinds of reason, his work runs counter to cultural relativism as well as the tendencies explicit in much sociology and anthropology and implicit in most twentieth-century history. On the other, by pointing out that children are not influenced by external reality, in this case the rules, without adapting that reality to their own mental structures, Piaget's theory requires us to see intelligence as *by its nature* active. This is precisely what twentieth-century social scientists and the historians who have borrowed their methods have been most unwilling to admit.

Though Piaget's occasional asides show his interest in the problem, he himself never tried to spell out a theory of culture.[47] But given thought, the implications of his developmental psychology are quite clear, and anthropologist C. R. Hallpike, in his *Foundations of Primitive Thought* (Oxford, 1979) reached essentially the

47. For a survey of Piagetian approaches to culture, see Elizabeth Brown's review of R. Howard Bloch, *Medieval French Literature and Law* in *History and Theory* 19 (1980): 319–38.

same conclusions that I shall be spelling out here. Because anthropological approaches to culture parallel historical ones in many ways, historians may find much of interest in Hallpike's lucid and finely argued theoretical exposition. Medievalists will additionally discover that many early medieval habits of thought and action have exact parallels in societies where the same kind of cognition dominates.

For our present purposes, the essential point is that if our own children reason differently from us (and I do not think any critique of Piaget can shake this finding), then it is necessary for us as historians to redefine what we believe to be the relationship between individuals and their culture. Any assumption that culture somehow exists in society as a whole and that each member of society (or of a given class in society) is imprinted with the culture is untenable, not simply because thought goes on in people's heads and not elsewhere, but because the people's understanding of the rules they live by, of the books they read, of the religion they practice, of the physical world they live in—of all, in short, that constitutes "culture"—depends as does the game of marbles on the logical structures into which they integrate their experience. To ask, as many historians do, what people are taught in their homes, schools, and churches without also asking how they interpreted and applied those teachings is to ignore the mentalities that give sense to tradition and shape to societies. I would argue, therefore, that humans must instead be seen as living in a dialectical relationship with their traditions, influenced by the values and ideas they are taught but also, and at the same time, bending those traditions to fit their minds. Culture, therefore, should be regarded not as an entity distinct from human intelligence but as the interaction of cognition and tradition.

The second point is related to the first: if each individual's logical structures are created through a lengthy developmental process and not stamped out of an identical mold, then it follows that some exceptions to the norm of any given society are to be expected, that one cannot assume without investigation that even members of a society with similar background and education reasoned in identical ways about religion, politics, or daily life. This fact does not preclude generalization, because it is possible for certain kinds of reasoning to be dominant in terms of numbers or influence. But it does lead us away from the *Annales* or Geertzian conception of *mentalité* as that which is shared among all members of society. In discussing what is common to, say, Aquinas and a French peasant

of his time one severs beliefs from intellectual processes in a way
that seriously distorts the ideas of both.[48]

The third consequence of the importance of cognitive structures
is that the social environment can affect culture by impeding or
encouraging cognitive development. Piaget's stages are not matura-
tional in the sense of being biologically determined. Children do
not proceed through the stages simply because they get older, but
by dealing with the intellectual issues posed by their experiences.
Thus an individual may not attain the highest stages unless the
external environment stimulates him or her to do so.

Such stimulation may come from many directions.[49] One of
them is certainly a diversity of social experience, so that people
have to learn to explain themselves to others of a different background. As Hallpike notes:

> to be born into a society whose basic institutions are simply
> accepted without question as the only proper ones, since they
> often rest on word and symbolic foundations, is a powerful
> disincentive to the development of the critical, analytical, and
> generalizing faculty in very extensive areas of social life. One
> has only to reflect on the continuing debate on forms of gov-
> ernment which have been a feature of Western European civi-
> lization since the last Tarquin was expelled from Rome, and
> the political and constitutional theorizing of the Greeks, to
> appreciate the force of this distinction.[50]

Because in a city dealings with those of different backgrounds and
occupations—friends and tradespeople as well as strangers—will
be more numerous than in rural society, it is doubtless this factor,
more even than wealth, that accounts for the importance of cities
to any cognitively sophisticated culture. Another, less obvious, is

48. The same point is made by Carlo Ginzburg, *The Cheese and the Worms*, trans. John and Anne Tedeschi (Baltimore, 1980), p. xxiii.
49. Piagetian cross-cultural studies are difficult to conduct, and the field is still developing, but see P. R. Dasen, "Cross-cultural Piagetian Research: A Summary," in *Culture and Cognition: Readings in Cross-Cultural Psychology*, ed. J. W. Berry and P. R. Dasen (London, 1974); Michael Cole and Sylvia Scribner, *Culture and Thought: A Psychological Introduction* (New York, 1974); and the works cited in notes 9 and 26 of the appendix.
50. *Primitive Thought*, p. 124. The early Middle Ages constitutes an important exception to Hallpike's comments about Western civilization, and we shall see that one of the subtle accomplishments of the Carolingian period was to reintroduce an element of tension about what were the proper forms of social organization.

the quality of interpersonal and especially peer relationships, not only among children but among adults, for these can provide an important stimulus to breaking out of the habit of regarding rules and ideas as fixed. A third is the extent to which the general culture supports or challenges egocentric conceptions of the world. For example, experiences such as those Piaget found in the game of marbles must be common in all societies, but those lessons can be reinforced or negated depending on whether adults and social institutions expect children to judge by intention and see themselves as makers of the rules. On the other hand, methods of childrearing such as psychoanalytically oriented historians often study will not concern me here, because these have more to do with personality than cognition.

My final point concerns the relations between ideas and action. Whatever the charitable impulses that inspired the doctrine of cultural relativism, one of its costs has been to encourage us to see people as passive in the face of external pressures. Society molds them, economics makes them rich or poor, religions provide them with rituals, and except for the domain of winks and gestures wherein personal eccentricity is possible they must submit to all these forces. Too easily it has been forgotten that these forces are not impersonal but simply other people, acting on the basis of ideas about right and wrong or profit and loss that are by no means immutable. Taking ideas seriously enables us to see this, to recognize that culture and institutions are only what people make of them, and that sometimes—and the century between 1050 and 1150 is one of those times—when their ideas change, people remake their societies.

The Scope of the Work

The subject of this book is the medieval culture from the end of classical civilization to the beginning of the thirteenth century. The problems posed by this subject are essentially the same as those already encountered with ordeals: Why did certain concepts disappear from ancient culture, well before the Germanic invasions? Why was early medieval culture, with its belief in supernatural forces and its tolerance of political and economic underdevelopment, persuasive to generations of Europeans? What in the eleventh and twelfth centuries caused the shift away from those ideas with the result that European society for the first time took on many of the features that continue to characterize western civilization in our own time? There is nothing novel in this list of questions; some of our greatest historians, from Gibbon on, have addressed them. But I shall be approaching them in a way that has not been attempted before by asking about cognitive processes instead of cultural products, how people reasoned about their traditions instead of what those traditions were. Generalizations about cognition I shall refer to as mentalities, although my use of this term should not be taken to mean I believe that society as a whole has a "mind" that is capable of development or evolution. I would not wish anyone to mistake my argument in this book for one that medieval society "grew up" like children do. I am discussing changes in reasoning of real men and women over generations of history.

Acknowledging the importance of individual cognition and the likelihood of variation within a society does make the selection of evidence a particularly serious problem for the historian of mentalities. In this book I shall be using two types of sources. First, I study reasoning of individuals who were widely accepted as intellectual leaders by their contemporaries. Not all of these individuals are those we would today consider the most profound thinkers of their time, though many of them are; I selected them because their popularity is the best evidence available that their contemporaries shared their approach to problems. In many cases, moreover, the esteem of their contemporaries resulted in lasting influence for their works. Augustine, for example, is of interest both for what he tells us about late imperial culture, and because in the early Middle Ages his works were often the most readily available source of classical ideas. Second, in order to reach beyond the numerically small segment of medieval society that was literate, I shall investigate certain institutions that required wide support at least among social elites to operate effectively. It is often difficult to be sure one has grasped the reasoning underlying religious, legal, and political practices, but I believe that if this kind of evidence is used carefully it can shed a great deal of light on the difficult subject of what illiterate people thought about themselves, their society, and the world. By thus casting my net widely, I believe I can make generalizations about the cognitive processes in use during the Middle Ages, and about changes in cognition with as great an accuracy as possible.

In approaching these sources, I shall be looking particularly at the issues whose cognitive dimensions were investigated by Piaget and his associates. The appendix explains how Piaget himself dealt with these issues, and those particularly interested in testing the historical evidence against psychological theory will wish to look there before proceeding.

In the moral and social realms, I shall be asking: How did people apply their laws? Why did they accept the authority of those who ruled them? Whom did they believe made the laws? In applying rules, did they make their judgments on the basis of the external consequences of the action or the intention of the actor? Finally, I have asked how people saw their society, whether as a group of autonomous individuals, as subordinates to a common superior, or as members of a coherent community.

In examining ideas about the physical world, the danger for the historian is to study verbal definitions (which can be copied from books) instead of how these ideas were put into practice. I have therefore asked whether people saw the physical world as a moral force, as in ordeals, or as following its own rules regardless of human actions. When do writers suggest natural causes for physical occurrences, and when do they prefer to see the action of demons, the saints, or God? What kinds of reasoning are used to support allegations of miracles? Are rituals believed to be magical tools for manipulating reality? When do medieval chroniclers account for events as an expression of divine judgment, and when by fortune or chance? The last question is particularly important, for only when the concept of chance begins to supplant the egocentric expectation of order can minds doubt that all events have an ultimate or supernatural meaning and begin inquiries to determine which do.

In the chapters that follow I shall be asking how medieval sources handled these issues, and how the handling of these issues changed in the Middle Ages. Yet I do not wish it to seem that investigating cognition is chiefly a matter of matching the comments of medieval people (or people of any period) against those of Piaget's subjects. The essential point is that in all of these concepts the component provided by an individual's own logical capacities is very high. And because these concepts have a strong logical component, analyzing them requires us to pay attention to how the concepts are used in practice.

One final comment. I shall at certain places in the following chapters have occasion to compare the reasoning of medieval adults to that of modern children. I by no means intend to imply by this comparison that those adults were in other respects childlike or that they were in any way children. Similarities or differences in reasoning apart, adults are distinguished from children by their emotional development, their ability to have sexual relations and raise families, and their general experience of the world. I could argue that Homer shared many of children's attitudes toward nature, chance, and morality without in any way gainsaying the mastery of rhythm, language, and imagery that assures his place as one of the greatest poets of Western civilization. Nor, should I add, does the fact that one person reasons at a cognitively more advanced stage than another person prove that the first is a morally better person or a wiser one than the second. People can be honest or dishonest in terms of their stages depending on whether they have the will and integrity to do what they think is right. My purpose in this book is to attempt to make sense of the culture and society of the Middle Ages by studying the reasoning people then used. Readers who translate the results of this investigation into judgments that some people were better or wiser than others should be aware that it is they, not I, who make these judgments.

PART II

The Early Middle Ages

For everywhere violence, rapine, and murder were rampant, because of the extreme ferocity and savagery of these most barbarous centuries. Nor . . . was there any efficacious way of restraining men who had shaken off all human laws save by the divine laws dictated by religion.

—*The New Science,* 105.

TWO

Pygmies in the Shadows of Giants

Intellectuals of the Early Middle Ages

*But as the popular states
became corrupt, so also did
the philosophies. They
descended to skepticism.
Learned fools fell to
calumniating the truth.*

—*The New Science*,
1102.

Between 400 and 600 the character of Western society, already different from that of classical times in 400, completed its evolution toward the forms that would be typical of the early Middle Ages. Many of the influences that gave direction to this transformation are well known: the growing weight of imperial bureaucracy, the declining productivity of the ancient economy, the conversion to Christianity, the Germanic invasions. But none of these factors was entirely independent of the changing cognition of the times. Both government and economy were shaped by what officials thought were the problems of society and what remedies they could imagine to solve them. The ideas of theologians depended on how they perceived the relationship of humans to God and the action of supernatural forces in the world. And the shape that Christianity took in general depended on how its precepts were integrated into the cognitive processes of individual Christians.

One theme of this chapter, then, is the role of cognition in the creation of early medieval society. Another, and equally important, is the effect of changing cognition on the survival of classical culture. For one of the central historical issues of the period is why, in a society that continued to admire and read classical works of scholarship, the concepts routinely employed in those works fell out of use. This phenomenon, not to my knowledge paralleled in any other period, becomes more intelligible when one realizes that intellectuals of the later empire reasoned differently from those of 37 classical times, and that the difference in cognition itself posed a major barrier to understanding.

I shall begin with a careful examination of Augustine of Hippo. Far from being typical, Augustine was both the most accomplished Latin intellectual of his time and the man who exercised the greatest influence over the centuries to come. His cognitive processes will therefore serve to mark the difference between the cognition of the late empire and that of classical times, while in his contemporaries it will be possible to notice still more clearly some of the characteristics of the mentality of the early Middle Ages. Our attention will then turn to the intellectuals of the period following the Germanic invasions, in whose writings that mentality reached full expression.

Augustine and the World of Late Antiquity

Augustine's career was a long one, stretching from his conversion to Catholicism in the 380s to his death in 430 as Hippo was besieged by Vandals, and throughout it was shaped by the controversies of his time.[1] He wrote first against the Manichees, a group to which he once belonged, then the Donatists, then both the Pelagians and the pagans who took the defeats Rome endured at the hands of the Germans as an indictment of Christianity itself. Because of these origins in controversy, his doctrines developed piecemeal, one in answer to one opponent, another in response to a different challenge, often with the various elements never systematically related to each other. But our concern in what follows is not just with Augustine's formally expressed ideas but with the cognitive processes by which he interpreted his experiences and organized his ideas. These reveal themselves, as we shall see, in the concepts he employed over and over again in his arguments and in the issues that he felt it important to address in the course of defending his doctrines.

1. For Augustine in general see Peter Brown, *Augustine of Hippo* (Berkeley and Los Angeles, 1967); for his education H.-I. Marrou, *Saint Augustine et la fin de la culture antique* (Paris, 1938); Pierre Courcelle, *Late Latin Writers and Their Greek Sources*, trans. Harry E. Wedeck (Cambridge, Mass., 1969), pp. 165–94. Augustine's works are available in numerous editions so for him, as for the other Church Fathers, I have cited book and chapter. However translations, where I have used them, are specifically noted.

Augustine's *Confessions* can serve as a point of departure. Its very structure is worth noticing. Because a confession requires an author to convey his or her ideas in a manner that takes account of the perspective of both a human and a divine audience, it is an inherently fragile form; anyone who doubts the difficulty of making it work should read the memoirs of the twelfth century's Guibert of Nogent who found the illusion impossible to maintain even with Augustine's example before him. But underlying Augustine's achievement in holding to the framework was the cognitive ability to take simultaneous account of the differences in the perspectives of two people. Even writing less complex in form than the *Confessions* requires this ability to a certain extent, because authors must—at minimum—cope with the difference between what they and their audience know. We shall see below that by the sixth century this capacity is far from common.

But this ability is not only necessary for the clear presentation of facts. It is also, as Piaget showed, essential for moral reasoning that finds value in good intentions instead of in actions that conform to a rule. Augustine himself was keenly aware of the difference, noting in the *Confessions* that

> Many actions . . . which seem disreputable to men are, according to your testimony, to be approved, and many actions that are praised by men are, in your sight, to be condemned. The appearance of the act, the mind of the person who does the act, and the secret promptings of the occasion are all capable of great variations.[2]

Augustine is not here stating the obvious; Piaget and many others have shown that judgment by intention is an early sign of moral reasoning that looks beyond reliance on rules and external behavior. His care in stating this principle of judgment by intention, both here and elsewhere,[3] suggests that the majority of the educated

2. *Confessions*, iii.9. Except where noted I have used the translation of Rex Warner (New York, 1963).
3. For example, in the *Enchiridion*, he made a point of explaining that the gravity of lies depends on the intention of the liar, not the truth of what is said. "No one, of course, is to be condemned as a liar who says what is false believing it to be true, because such a one does not consciously deceive, but rather is himself deceived . . . [And] the man who unwittingly says what is false, thinking all the time that it is true, is a better man than the one who unwittingly says what is true, but in his conscience intends to deceive." *Enchiridion* xviii, J. F. Shaw, trans. (Chicago, 1961). For Piaget on lies, see *Moral Judgment*, pp. 139–74.

Christians for whom the *Confessions* were written were perhaps themselves tending to judge by objective outcomes. Indeed, there may well have been cognitive differences between Augustine and his later adversary Pelagius that led them to disagree on the relative importance of actions and intentions.[4] Thus one of Augustine's treatises against the Pelagians was entitled *On the Spirit and the Letter.*

Intentionality is one aspect of moral reasoning that we shall have frequent occasion to notice in the pages that follow. Conceptions of institutions and society are another, because they reveal the terms in which an individual perceives his or her experience and the level of abstraction manipulated in addressing problems. There are several levels of abstraction: society seen as composed of autonomous individuals, of interpersonal relationships, or as a whole—the social perception necessary for concepts such as the state. These social perceptions are constructs, in the sense that they are created mentally instead of simply internalized, so they do not necessarily correspond directly to reality as it would be experienced by another person. Just because one has contact with, for example, the administration of a university does not mean that one will necessarily recognize the institutional imperatives that influence the actions of individual administrators. Until the concept of *administration* has been constructed, their actions will be thought of as resulting from their individual personalities.[5]

As a theologian, Augustine's ideas about politics tended to be expressed as asides in writings devoted to other subjects, most especially in the *City of God* which was written to refute pagans who blamed the empire's defeats by the Germanic tribes on the adoption of Christianity. Naturally enough, his views on politics grew out of his theological concerns. Conceiving of humans as fallen, he therefore believed, as Deane put it, that "the peace and order which the State maintains are supremely important and, at the same time,

4. Pelagius, for example, writes of "laying down rules of behavior and the conduct of a holy life," *Ad Demetriadem* 2 *(PL* 30: 17B), cited in Brown, *Augustine of Hippo,* p. 342. Brown himself notes that "For one person, a good action could mean one that fulfilled successfully certain conditions of behaviour, for another, one that marked the culmination of an inner evolution. The first view was roughly that of Pelagius; the second, that of Augustine."

5. For more on the relationship between cognition and social perceptions, see Kohlberg's works, cited in the appendix, and Gale Stokes, "Cognition and the Function of Nationalism," *Journal of Interdisciplinary History* 4 (1974): 525–42.

highly precarious. Augustine is so sharply aware of the need to impose a system of order on the conflicting wills of sinful men . . . that the maintenance of peace is the primary function of the state. He is willing to settle for this one great accomplishment and to ask for relatively little in the way of positive benefits from the political system."[6]

This summary is entirely adequate as an account of the relationship between Augustine's political thought and his theology. But Deane, like many other scholars, makes a significant error when he uses terms like "state" and "political system" to describe Augustine's views. For Augustine did not write, and probably did not think, in terms of such abstractions. R. A. Markus has well observed that Augustine tended to write "in a vocabulary of persons rather than institutions. Although he did have at his disposal words such as *imperium* or *res publica*, which may suitably be rendered in abstract political terminology, these are not the words he uses for this purpose. He will speak of emperors rather than empire, of kings and magistrates rather than of state or government."[7] An example of what Markus means can be found in a sermon in which Augustine defended the imperial order confiscating the property of heretics. Whatever man possesses, Augustine wrote, he has through human right, that is, "by the right of the emperors. . . . Do not say, What have I to do with the king? as in that case what have you to do with the possessions? It is by rights derived from kings that possessions are enjoyed."[8]

Some scholars attribute such language to deliberate policy or simple indifference to worldly affairs. Indeed, if Augustine wrote in some contexts of persons and in others of institutions, it might be correct to suppose the differences resulted from conscious choice. Yet to employ concepts such as the *state* an individual must create a mental abstraction out of the concrete materials of his or her experience. Not everyone does this. Augustine's choice of words, not only with regard to the state but throughout his writings, is entirely in accord with cognitive processes that think in terms of interper-

6. Herbert A. Deane, *The Political and Social Ideas of St. Augustine* (New York, 1963), p. 240; see also Brown's essay in *Trends in Medieval Political Thought*, ed. Beryl Smalley (Oxford, 1965), pp. 1–21; F. Edward Cranz, "The Development of Augustine's Ideas on Society before the Donatist Controversy," *Harvard Theological Review* 47 (1954): 255–316.
7. R. A. Markus, *Saeculum: History and Society in the Theology of Augustine* (Cambridge, 1970), pp. 149–50.
8. *Tractatus In Ioannes Evangelium* vi.25–26. The translation is from *Works of Aurelius Augustine* [=WAA] (Edinburgh, 1871–76) 10: 90–91.

sonal relationships without taking the additional step of construct-
ing social abstractions. And the consistency with which Augustine
treated social issues in terms of persons instead of institutions suggests that we have instead not a feature of language but an aspect
of his cognitive structures. Because he did not cognitively organize
his experiences in terms of institutions, the concepts of the state or
of society as a whole thus had little meaning to him.

The best place to observe this tendency in action is Augustine's
writings about the Church. Viewed in the context of the late empire, the elusiveness of Augustine's conception of political organization is not hard to understand. As a practical matter he, like most
of his contemporaries, was bound to have experienced imperial
edicts as coming from afar, the product of political processes in
which he played little part and of which he had little knowledge.
Indeed, it is easy to hear in some of Augustine's remarks about
government an echo of imperial claims to divine establishment. But
in the Church, Augustine did have the experience of deciding policy
through deliberation with his equals. He also, throughout his career as bishop, had responsibility for defending the interests of the
institution, and in fact the great bulk of his writings was inspired
by this purpose as circumstances pressed Augustine to prepare answers first to the Manichees and the Donatists and later to the
Pelagians and educated pagans. Yet when Augustine wrote about
the Church he did so in the same kind of language he used referring
to the state. He wrote of individuals, not the community, and when
he thought of it in abstract terms it was as a divine and mystical
creation, not a human reality.

Augustine's conception of the Church developed primarily in response to the stimulus of the Donatist controversy.[9] The Donatists
had broken from the Catholic Church in the early fourth century
over accusations that certain Catholic bishops in Africa had sub-
mitted to pagan persecutions by handing Christian scriptures over
to be burned. The split between the two churches had hardened in
the course of the century, and by the time Augustine became bishop
two rival hierarchies faced each other in many dioceses, including
Hippo. The Donatists were, for Augustine, primarily schismatics,
and he denounced them in vivid, Biblical images: for separating
from the Church of which Christ is the sole head, for dividing the

9. For Augustine on Donatism, see F. van der Meer, *Augustine the Bishop*,
trans. Brian Battershaw and G. R. Lamb (New York, 1961), pp. 79–117;
Brown, *Augustine of Hippo*, pp. 203–43; and esp. G. G. Willis, *Saint
Augustine and the Donatist Controversy* (London, 1950).

body of Christ, for rending the garment of Christ. In less mystical formulations, however, Augustine portrayed the sin of schism as directed not against the church but against individual Christians: "both the origin and perseverance in schism consists in nothing else save hatred of the brethren."[10] In a striking passage he challenges the Donatists by recalling the rule of intentional ethics, "that no one can be involved in the guilt of unknown crimes committed by persons unknown to him." According to this rule, the Donatists do wrong both to contemporary African Catholics, who are generations removed from the alleged crimes, and from Catholics in other lands who know nothing about the rights or wrongs of Africa.[11]

Though here used for polemical purposes, this conception of the Church was not one adopted and discarded as a matter of convenience. Even when switching sides on an issue, Augustine consistently argued in terms of individuals and not institutions. His ideas about the use of force to convert one's opponents provide a particularly good case in point. Though in the twelfth century and later this would be justified by the need of the church to maintain its capacity for spiritually guiding its members,[12] Augustine consistently treated the matter purely as one between individuals. Thus, in his earliest writings Augustine treated the dispute with the Donatists as a matter of individual conscience. In a letter of 396 he respectfully addressed the Donatist bishop Proculeianus as "lord, seeing that we are both seeking to deliver each other from error . . . and therefore we are mutually serving one another."[13] His position at this time was that neither side should resort to violence to gain victory: "this feeling of mine is one tending toward peace, and . . . my desire is, not that any one should against his will be coerced into the Catholic communion, but that to all who are in error the truth may be openly declared."[14] After 405, however, when the Edict of Unity commanded the forcible reunion of Donatists and Catholics, the love and respect for one's opponent that earlier had led him to support coexistence now justified the use of coercion. While it is true, he wrote, that "no one can be good in spite of his own will," the fear of suffering can compel a person to renounce

10. *De baptismo* i.11,16; and in general, Willis, pp. 113–26.
11. Epistle 87 [Trans. WAA 6: 356].
12. See, for example, the discussion of Gratian's ideas on this issue in Stanley Chodorow, *Christian Political Theory and Church Politics in the Mid-Twelfth Century* (Berkeley and Los Angeles, 1972), p. 231.
13. Epistle 33 [Trans. from WAA 6: 101].
14. Epistle 34 [Trans. from WAA 6: 105].

"his hostile prejudices" or to examine truth "of which he had been contentedly ignorant."[15] Augustine argued, in effect, that Christians should persecute their neighbors out of love for them.

Because this is the first systematic analysis in the book, this is an appropriate place to make clear what I think is the value of assessing a person's cognitive processes. Intellectual history, as it is commonly practiced, is chiefly concerned with describing ideas: thus we learn what Augustine thought about the state, or the church, or nature. But those ideas are only the end product of his cognitive processes, and by understanding those processes we can better understand why thinkers arrived at the ideas they did. Augustine's cognitive processes, for example, account at least in part for the most distinctive and enduringly important characteristics of his theology—the concern with sin and grace. Doubtless Augustine's strongly emotional personality contributed some of his particular concerns about lust and disobedience. But it was his cognition that focused those emotions on the interior relationship between individual Christians and God. And because Augustine perceived society in terms of individuals instead of institutions, it did not occur to him to say much about the internal governance of either church or state. In fact, if this was an area where, in the twelfth century, scholars found themselves with little clear guidance from patristic authorities, that fact demonstrates that Augustine's cognitive processes were widely shared in his time and not just unique to him.

Augustine's cognition also helps explain the distance between his political ideas and those of classical antiquity. Classical philosophers had seen law as a social institution—an attitude closely related to their perception of society as an entity of which they themselves were members and toward which they had obligations. This was, for example, Cicero's point in *De Re Publica* when he defined *populus* as:

> not any collection of human beings brought together in any sort of way, but an assemblage of large numbers associated by an agreement with respect to justice and by a communion of interests *(iuris consensu et utilitatis communione)*. The first cause for such an association is not so much the weakness of the individual as a certain social spirit which nature has implanted in man.[16]

15. Epistle 93 [Trans. from WAA 6: 409].
16. *De Re Publica*, ed. Clinton Walker Keyes (Loeb Library), i.25. I have slightly modified Keyes's translation.

And because he saw the community as the course of political authority, it was possible for Cicero to conceive of illegitimate rulers—tyrants—who held their power unjustly.

The attitudes Cicero expressed were not inherently incompatible
with Christianity: medieval theorists of the twelfth and thirteenth
centuries arrived at a very similar position. And intimately familiar
with Cicero as he was, Augustine was not indifferent to this tradition of political thought. Indeed, he takes up Cicero's definition
twice in the *City of God* for the purpose of refuting the value the
ancients had vested in the commonwealth. But because Augustine
did not reason in terms of institutions himself, he saw no force in
Cicero's logic. His own definition of *populus*, "a gathering of a
multitude of human beings united in fellowship by their agreement
about the objects of love,"[17] omitted both law and consent. Instead
of law being the creation of the community, it became for him a
possession and creation of the emperor. Taking literally Paul's statement that there is no authority except from God, Augustine conceived of no reason that could justify subjects' rebelling. Quite the
contrary. He was sure that evil rulers themselves had their place in
God's plan. "Power and domination are not given even to such men
[as Nero] save by the providence of the most high God, when he
judges that the state of human affairs is worthy of such lords."[18]
Only when the ruler enjoined actions contrary to God's explicit
commandments was he to be disobeyed, and then submissively,
without violence or attempt at deposition.[19] Instead of being based
on mutual respect, the political order was thus regarded as something external to the will of the governed, a reality to which men
had to accommodate their existence. This conception, not greatly
different from that which the Germanic tribes would bring with
them, would become pervasive in the early Middle Ages.

In studying Augustine's moral reasoning we looked at his use of
intention as a measure of moral worth and his conception of the
relationship between individuals and their fellow humans. To study
the cognitive structures through which he understood everyday
events and the physical world the key concepts are chance, expressed in the systematic inquiry to distinguish meaningful events

17. Populus est coetus multitudinis rationalis rerum quas diligit concordi
communione sociatus. *City of God*, xix.24.
18. *City of God*, v.19.
19. Deane, *Political Ideas*, pp. 143–53.

from coincidences, and nature, expressed by a recognition that certain natural events happen through physical necessity. To describe chance and nature as concepts, however, is a slight misstatement. For as I shall be using them here, chance and nature refer to the cognitive processes that correct the egocentric expectation of order by looking for alternative explanations of events. Put another way, the question is not whether a person believed in miracles—all medieval Christians did—but what he or she took to be one, and what efforts were made to eliminate other explanations.

Cicero's *De Divinatione* can illustrate how this works. Cicero's theme throughout the book is the uselessness of prophecy. What is important, however, is that he upholds this idea not as an isolated principle but by illustrating how natural causes and coincidence can explain the successes claimed by diviners. Augury through reading entrails, for example, Cicero regarded with contempt. "If the entrails foretell an increase in my fortune and they do so in accordance with some law of nature then, in the first place, there is some relationship between them and the universe, and in the second place my financial gain is regulated by the laws of nature. Are not natural philosophers ashamed to utter such nonsense?"[20] Other prophecies he dismissed either as unbelievable myths or chance coincidences, for "if anything [predicted by soothsayers] comes true, then what reason can be advanced why the agreement of the event with the prophecy was not due to chance?" Even if a hundred casts of the dice yielded the same throw, "I do not see why" this could not be due to chance.[21]

One could write a history of Western thought by tracing the works of Cicero that were popular in different periods: *De Divinatione* was a favorite text of the *philosophes* who found there support for their own wide ranging skepticism. But there is nothing in Cicero's conceptions of chance or nature that is inherently incompatible with Christianity. Origen, writing in the East where scientific thought was better preserved, had no trouble reconciling divine omnipotence with the existence of natural law, and medieval thinkers after 1100 were to come to the same conclusion. Augustine himself cited Cicero's book against pagan opponents,[22] and borrowed Cicero's reasoning where it suited his purpose of denouncing the occasional successful predictions of astrologers as

20. *De Divinatione*, ed. and trans. William Armistead Falconer (Loeb Classical Library), ii.14(33).
21. *De divinatione* ii.24(52); ii.21(48).
22. *City of God*, iii.17.

chance.[23] Yet Augustine did not realize that Cicero's logic could apply equally to some Christian miracles. Thus Augustine readily took the dreams of his mother as inspired when they proved true. When they did not, he explained that she had been misled by her wishes.[24]

What one can see in Augustine's attitude toward his mother's dreams, and in his writings generally, is his expectation that particular events have meaning. Looking back on his life in the *Confessions*, for example, Augustine saw the hand of God in many of the events that had impelled him along the path that led to his conversion: the death of a friend, his meeting with the Manichee Faustus, the unruliness of his students that drove him to abandon Carthage for Rome, and—most dramatically—the book oracle in the garden through which he resolved his final doubts about becoming a Christian.[25] But though most clearly manifest in Christian contexts, Augustine's expectation of meaning was apparent well before his conversion. He wrote in the *Confessions* that what troubled him most as a Manichee was the regularity of the eclipses of the sun and moon that had been calculated by philosophers with such exactness that "one can foretell the year, the month, the day, and the hour when there will be an eclipse of the sun or moon and whether the eclipse will be total or partial."[26] Since Mani, in his books, had placed the sun and moon at the center of his fable of creation, Augustine the Manichee was certain these regularities were significant, and he expected the great teacher Faustus to be able to explain them. When Faustus could not, Augustine's Manichean faith was shattered.

Though Augustine's judgments of what was meaningful changed radically as he moved from being a Manichee to being a Catholic, his underlying cognitive processes—the expectation of meaning, the indifference to explanations based on chance and natural causation—remained the same. The contrast illustrates the interaction between cognition and doctrine. As Hallpike observed:

> When primitives say of some event that it 'just happened'
> what they frequently mean is that, in terms of the way they
> see the world, whatever may have caused such an event has
> no relevance to the factors they consider really important. An

23. *Conf.*, iv.3.
24. *Conf.*, v.7; v.8; v.14.
25. *Conf.*, iv.4; v.7; v.8; viii.6–12.
26. *Conf.*, v.3.

example will clarify this. The Konso regard God as the source of morality and justice, and believe that He punishes towns in which there is too much quarrelling or other sin, by withholding the rain from them and their fields. Again, certain cerebral disorders, such as encephalitis and meningitis, or states of possession, are regarded as the work of evil spirits, while witchcraft and magic can produce yet other fairly specific afflictions to people, beasts, food, crops, and land. . . . But when I asked Sagara Giya, one of my most intelligent informants, who was in the throes of dysentary, where the disease had come from, he replied that it just came and that there was no agency responsible for it. I would interpret this kind of response, which is in fact extremely common for a whole variety of events in primitive society, as signifying that there was not, for the Konso, anything about dysentary that made it appropriate to attribute it to any of the conventional agencies in their belief system. . . . There is, in other words, a notion of 'insignificant accident', but not of 'significant accident'.[27]

Similarly, the list of areas where Augustine expected significance changed when he adopted different religious beliefs: although as a Manichee he was intensely interested in astronomy, as a Catholic he was indifferent, even hostile, to the study of natural phenomena, finding significance instead in the events of his and his mother's lives, the course of history, and the miracles of the saints. The list of events where other individuals, even other Christians, would expect significance will naturally be different from Augustine's. Gregory of Tours, for example, regarded as significant virtually anything concerning St. Martin. But the type of reasoning would be nearly universal in the early Middle Ages.

Because in the *Confessions* one can observe Augustine imposing intellectual order on his experiences, they provide particularly clear evidence of the cognitive processes through which he experienced the world. In his later writings he articulated that experience into a theology of God's omnipotence that left no room at all for chance or nature. The concept of chance disappears even as an argument against astrologers: in the *City of God* Augustine preferred to explain their occasional successes by the action of demons.[28] The old bishop's grumpy denunciation of those who do not wish to acknowledge it is God who governs their lives is simply an extension

27. *Foundations of Primitive Thought*, pp. 457–58, 462.
28. *City of God*, v.7.

of this attitude. "It pains me," he wrote, in the *Retractions*, written near the end of his life, "to hear fortune named when I see men have the bad habit of saying 'Fortune wished this' when they ought to say 'God wished this'."[29]

Augustine's statements about nature show a similar hardening of positions implicit in his cognitive experience of the world. As a Manichee, he had seen in the predictability of eclipses not natural causes but hidden significance. As a Catholic he denied that the miracles supposed by Christian doctrine were more remarkable than the events of the everyday world. In a letter written around 412 to Volusianus, an educated pagan who had written to ask how the majesty of God could have been encased in a virgin's womb and then in a human body, Augustine denied that the incarnation is any more worthy of wonder than many everyday events. "Where," he asks, "in all the varied movements of creation is there any work of God which is not wonderful, were it not that through familiarity these wonders have become small in our esteem? . . . Take, for example, the properties of seeds: who can either comprehend or declare the variety of species, the vitality, vigor, and secret power by which they from within small compass evolve great things."[30] He took this contention still further in *De Trinitate*, a work written at about the same time. Beginning with the assertion that "nothing is done visibly or sensibly, unless by command or permission . . . of the supreme governor, according to the unspeakable justice of rewards and punishments,"[31] he distinguished miracles from other events not by the action of divine power, which is always present, but by the directness with which the divine power is manifest.[32] Augustine accordingly found little difference between the making of wine from grapes and Christ's turning water into wine except the "extraordinary quickness" of the miracle, and he elaborated by comparing the blossoming of Aaron's rod with the flowering of trees and the transformation of Moses' rod to a snake with the creation of life out of earthy matter common to both the rod and the snake. "When such things happen in a continuous kind of river

29. *Retract.* i.1(2): Hoc etiam ibi non tacui dicens . . . Dixi quidem hoc, verumtamen paenitet me sic ille nominasse fortunam, cum videam homines haber in pessima consuetudine, ubi dici debet: 'Hoc Deus voluit,' dicere 'Hoc voluit fortuna.'
30. Epistle 137.
31. *De Trinitate* iii.4(9). The translation is from *A Select Library of Nicene and Post Nicene Fathers* [=NPNF], 3: 59.
32. *De Trinitate* iii.5(11).

of ever-flowing succession, passing from the hidden to the visible, and from the visible to the hidden, by a regular and beaten track, then they are called natural; when, for the admonition of men, they are thrust in by an unusual changeableness, then they are called miracles."[33]

The elevated, rhetorical language of such passages should not deceive us into thinking Augustine is striking out a debating position. This theology is perfectly consistent with the way he himself perceived the world, and his interest in miracles as proof of the faith and as part of daily experience only grew as he aged.[34] Though he considered the miracles worked by pagan deities to be the work of demons, he accepted the authenticity of the events themselves and he took Christian visions and miracles still more seriously. He encouraged his congregation to publicize miracles which happened to them and took measures to assure that local miracles would be systematically recorded.[35] One difficult case between two of his clergy Augustine ordered settled by a kind of ordeal: the two parties were to go to Italy to swear to their stories before the tomb of St. Felix of Nola, who had the reputation of

33. De Trinitate iii.6(11). [Trans. from NPNF 3, 60]. See also City of God, xxi.4–8, where Augustine defends the belief that sinners will suffer an eternity of fiery torments without their bodies being destroyed by citing a long string of miracles, concluding "How is that contrary to nature which happens by the will of God, since the will of so mighty a Creator is certainly the nature of each created thing." (Translation by Marcus Dods [New York, 1950] unless otherwise noted.)

34. For Augustine's conceptions of nature and miracles, see van der Meer, Augustine the Bishop, pp. 527–57; D. P. de Vooght, "La notion philosophique du miracle chez saint Augustin," Recherches de théologie ancienne et médiévale [=RTAM] 10 (1938): 317–43; "Les miracles dans la vie de saint Augustin," RTAM 11 (1939): 5–16; "La théologie du miracle selon saint Augustin," RTAM 11 (1939): 197–222; Robert M. Grant, Miracle and Natural Law in Graeco-Roman and Early Christian Thought (Amsterdam, 1952), esp. pp. 215–20, 243–45; Brown, Augustine of Hippo, pp. 413–18. Some of the miracles Augustine cites in City of God, xxi.7, are also interesting as examples of psychological realism, defined by Piaget as the belief that reality ought to correspond to the categories of human thought and language: "the chaff so chilling it prevents snow from melting, so heating it forces apples to ripen; the glowing fire, which, in accordance with its glowing appearance, whitens the stones it bakes, while, contrary to its glowing appearance, it begrimes most things it burns; ... the charcoal, too, which by the action of fire is so completely changed from its original qualities that a finely marked piece of wood becomes hideous, the tough becomes brittle, the decaying incorruptible."

35. Van der Meer, Augustine the Bishop, pp. 544–49. For Augustine's role in founding the tradition of miracle collections, see Brown, pp. 414–15.

revealing perjurors, and Augustine hoped the guilty party would be forced by the saint to confess.[36] The conception of the natural world revealed by such activities explains why the science he knew led Augustine not to inquiry into natural causes but to a stress on the *mirabilia*—marvels. In that sense Robert Grant is correct in observing that Augustine's attitudes marked "the end of ancient science and indeed of ancient civilization."[37]

Instead of being typical, Augustine marks in a sense the limit of what could be attained by an intellectual of his time. We have already noticed that among Augustine's contemporaries there seem to have been many who judged morality by actions instead of intention. His prose too, as Erich Auerbach notes, sets him apart,[38] as does the coherence and intellectual power of his theology. And as we pass from Augustine to his contemporaries, the distance separating them from classical habits of thought becomes still more apparent, as does the closeness of their mentality to that which was to dominate the early Middle Ages.

A detailed discussion of the late empire would take me well beyond the borders of my subject, but there are three aspects of the cognition of this period that need to be mentioned because they continued to be important in the early Middle Ages. The first concerns the prevailing conception of society. We have already noticed how Augustine, departing from his usual practice of reasoning in terms of interpersonal relationships, saw the relationship between ruler and ruled as one of unilateral respect. Other evidence asserts the divine nature of kingship still more unequivocally, and with much less subtlety. In the third and fourth centuries, the size of the emperors' image grew to godlike proportions: Constantine was celebrated by a statue forty feet tall of which the remnants are still to be seen on the Capitoline hill today. Ramsay MacMullen notes that imperial documents claim that "Nature herself—good weather, calm seas, rich harvests—throughout the realm obeyed the emperor's *felicitas*, so that his fleets could navigate in safety and his people never suffer from want. . . . Plagues and defeats, undifferentiated, are equally ascribed to the fault of a bad ruler, just as good harvests and victories are equally to the credit of a good one."[39]

36. Epistle 78.
37. Grant, *Miracle*, p. 220.
38. *Mimesis*, trans. Willard R. Trask (Princeton, 1953), p. 70.
39. *Roman Government's Response to Crisis* A.D. 235–337 (New Haven, 1976), pp. 27, 30 and chapter 2 generally.

This exaltation of the emperor continued through the fourth and fifth centuries unaffected by the adoption of Christianity. Emperors were shielded from the public; visitors addressed them through a curtain or, if privileged, were permitted to kiss the hem of their robe. The imperial chancery prepared their written communications in purple ink with a florid handwriting that sacrificed legibility to impressiveness.[40] Jurists came to see the emperor as the source of all law and they altered the work of classical legists to conform to this preconception.[41] Such sentiments are not merely imperial propaganda. They are echoed in the imperial cults' practices in distant corners of the empire, and in the glorification of Christian emperors by Christian panegyrists. The underlying attitudes can scarcely be distinguished from those that the Germanic tribes would display in the fifth century.

The second point concerns the widespread belief in the supernatural and the miraculous among Christians and pagans alike. We have already seen how Augustine's cognition was nowhere more distant from classical thought than in his attitude toward the miraculous, and it is also the area where he is most typical of his time. Belief in the supernatural as a regular feature of everyday existence had resurfaced in the upper classes in the first century A.D.: Lucan's writings from midcentury reveal a thorough familiarity with magic, and Epictetus defended the use of animal entrails to foretell the future.[42] By the fourth century the question was less whether a person would believe in magic than what kind. Even the philosophy that survived was increasingly confused with theurgy, the invocation of spirits.[43]

My final observation concerns attitudes toward scholarship in general. The question is not, as it is sometimes put, one of sterility or creativity. In no generation is every scholar a creative one, and in some periods entire disciplines produce little that is new. Aristotle's disciples themselves produced chiefly handbooks—compendia of theories that had been enunciated by previous philosophers—and the genre remained an important one throughout antiquity. But

40. MacMullen, *Response to Crisis*, p. 33; and also his *Constantine* (New York, 1969), pp. 3–4, 11–14.
41. Fritz Schulz, *Roman Legal Science* (Cambridge, 1946), p. 285.
42. On the growth of belief in magic, see MacMullen, *Enemies of the Roman Order* (Cambridge, Mass., 1966), pp. 95–162; E. R. Dodds, *Pagan and Christian in an Age of Anxiety* (New York, 1970).
43. E. R. Dodds, *The Greeks and the Irrational* (Berkeley, 1951), pp. 283–311.

there is an important difference, familiar to every teacher, between approaching a theory with a critical attitude, aware that it must stand or fall by the test of evidence, and treating it as a fact itself to be memorized, an object to which the mind itself must be accommodated. The first is the attitude of Theophrastus, for example, or Varro, the second, roughly that of Pliny and the handbook writers of the later empire.[44] The intellectual life that resulted was not much different from those a scholar in the 1930's found in his students.

> Fashion dominated their interests: they valued ideas not for themselves but for the prestige they could wring from them. . . . Learning was something for which they had neither the taste nor the methods; yet they felt bound to include in their essays, no matter what their nominal subject might be, a survey of human evolution from the anthropoid apes to the present day. Quotations from Plato, Aristotle, and Auguste Comte would be followed by a peroration paraphrased from some egregious hack—the obscurer the better for their purpose—since their rivals would be the less likely to have happened upon him.[45]

Whether in the late empire or the twentieth century, when scholars approach works with the intention of reproducing the words of the masters instead of their thoughts, they miss the internal connections between ideas and the facts they were meant to explain. In the late empire what resulted were handbooks full of isolated comments, often torn out of context with crucial conclusions and steps of logic omitted. Philosophy, science, history, and law—indeed, all the key disciplines of classical culture—were subjected to this treatment at the hands of handbook authors who distorted meaning by being faithful to words, whose scissors clipped crucial distinctions away from the texts they carefully collected and pasted together.[46]

---

44. For Pliny's methods, see G. E. R. Lloyd, *Science, Folklore, and Ideology* (Cambridge, 1983), pp. 135–49.

45. Claude Lévi-Strauss, *Tristes Tropiques*, trans. John Russell (New York, 1971), p. 107.

46. In general, see Marrou, *Saint Augustine*. For law, cf. Fritz Schulz, *Roman Legal Science*, pp. 262–99, and especially 278–85. "Post-classical jurisprudence . . . is characterized by its lack of self-confidence, by its need for external support. Thus the jurists of the Principate became for them 'classics': their writings became the standard and measure, *norma et regula*" (p. 278). Along with the inclination to classicize old law, Schulz

Except for those few, such as Augustine, who found intellectual stimulation in the theological debates of the time, most educated men of the late empire conformed to this type. Students read Vergil, Cicero, and a few other authors so that they could appreciate fine literary style and by imitation learn to express themselves with fluency and grace, but memorization and classroom drill did little to develop analytical skills. Philosophy and history were little valued except as sources for rhetorical allusions, and erudition in these subjects, where it existed at all, tended to take the form of collecting facts and opinions. What we can see in this kind of culture, as in the heavily mannered Latin prose of the period,[47] is a dramatic change in the very conception of intellectual activity. Instead of classical learning being used to understand the world, and writing used to communicate understanding, both had become kinds of conspicuous consumption, ornaments and emblems of the leisured life. Ideas themselves had become, in Piaget's phrase, a thing external to the mind.

It was not just intellectuals who tried to mold the present to an imagined ideal. Faults in institutions were shored up by rigid prescriptions intended to preserve the revered past. Tax assessments, once established, were difficult to adjust, and many farmers had to flee their lands to avoid taxes they could not afford. If all did not work well the problem was blamed on evil men. To forestall any shortage of an essential good or service, peasants, soldiers, bakers, city councilors, and many others were bound with their descendants to their occupations. Imperial enactments took on a hortatory tone. "Let the greedy hands of the civil secretaries forbear, let them forbear, I say" began a law of Constantine against corruption. "If after due warning they do not cease they should be cut off by the sword."[48]

There is little reason to doubt that this substitution of imitative for conceptual intelligence also contributed to the success of the invasions by the Germans. The size of the invading forces was not large; perhaps 80,000 altogether for the Visigoths, Burgundians

---

notes as trends of late Roman jurisprudence a tendency to alter received law either by converting it to statute law—"under an absolute monarchy all law tends to be thought of as royal commands" (p. 285)—or by simplifying doctrine.

47. On this see Auerbach, *Mimesis*, chapter 3.

48. MacMullen, *Constantine*, p. 192. See also *Response to Crisis*, pp. 28–30, for a similar edict of Diocletian: "Government in its almost childish view appeals against inflation by excoriating greed."

and Vandals, or about 20,000 warriors after allowing for women, children, and other non-combatants. Roman forces in the west were much more numerous, but they were as bound by routine as everyone else in the empire. It was difficult for commanders to move units stationed in one region to meet a challenge elsewhere, and many troops were more adept at the routines of garrison life than the techniques of warfare. Only a small fraction of imperial forces ever saw action against the invaders, and when in Gaul in 406–407 and in Italy several tribes struck at once, defending forces were easily overwhelmed.[49] Throughout the west the structure of government was shattered, the movement of people and commerce disrupted. Urban communities, in whose schools and streets intellectuals down to Augustine's time had developed their abilities, were destroyed. By the middle of the fifth century northern Africa was controlled by the Vandals; Spain by the Visigoths. Gaul was divided among several tribes and Britain was under heavy attack by Anglo-Saxon raiders. Continuity with the classical past, more superficial than real even before the invasions, was now decisively broken.

Intellectuals of the Early Germanic Age

Since Romanized populations greatly outnumbered the invaders in every region, the successes of the Germans did not immediately transform the appearance of European society. Agricultural organization only gradually abandoned the forms it had taken in the late empire. Army units, their role as defenders forgotten, survived for generations as organized garrisons preying on the surrounding countryside. And people paid Roman taxes for centuries after the end of the empire, their fruits now turned to the use of the invaders. But all these survivals were essentially behavior patterns of the kind that can easily be learned by observation and imitation. They do not mean that early Germanic society was still, to any significant extent, culturally Roman. Thus while written documents remained in use for a variety of purposes, the lawyers and administrators who prepared them knew only how to repeat concrete tasks or draw up documents in a set form. They could train successors in

49. MacMullen, "How Big was the Roman Imperial Army?," *Klio* 62 (1980), pp. 451–60. I wish to express my appreciation to Prof. MacMullen for allowing me to see an advance copy of this article.

the mechanical skills of their professions; they could not transmit cognitive skills in manipulating legal rules that they no longer had themselves.

One of the behavior patterns that survived was the Roman model of education, because upper class families who could afford tutors had their sons taught the basics of grammar and rhetoric. Students composed exercises that had scarcely changed for centuries; among those done by Ennodius, who became bishop of Pavia around 500, were a lament of Dido abandoned by Aeneas and an argument against a man who placed a statue of Minerva in a brothel. The contorted and highly ornamented style thus mastered had its uses—Ennodius won the favor of Theodoric, king of the Ostrogoths, by his compositions in praise of Theodoric's philosophical character. But there is no mistaking the isolation of this learning either from real contemporary issues or from a genuine grasp of ancient intellectual traditions.[50] This isolation of learning from social context greatly increased its vulnerability to erosion over time: less was retained because there was less and less occasion to employ what was learned. The effects of that erosion can clearly be seen in the sixth- and seventh-century writers to whom the balance of this chapter is devoted.

In the eastern Mediterranean, conditions were not so serious: there a tradition of inquiry had been better maintained under the empire and there too more survived of traditional social structures. It was out of this context that came the only important Latin writer of the sixth century. Though Anicius Manlius Severinus Boethius was born into a Roman senatorial family about 480, his father may have been prefect of Alexandria, and he himself was probably educated at the Greek school of philosophy there.[51] He was not a thinker of great depth or originality: a modern philosopher has described his discussion of universals in the commmentary on Porphyry as "a confused, vague, and disorderly piece of philosophical writing."[52] Many of his original works were drawn more or less

50. Pierre Riché, *Education and Culture in the Barbarian West, Sixth through Eighth Centuries*, trans. John J. Contreni (Columbia, 1976), pp. 24–32, 48–49. Ennodius's works are published in MGH, *AA* 7. Erich Auerbach discusses the mannered style of this period in *Literary Language and Its Public in Late Latin Antiquity and in the Middle Ages*, trans. Ralph Manheim (Princeton, 1965), pp. 256–60.

51. Courcelle, *Late Latin Writers and Their Greek Sources*, pp. 273–330, 316 n.129; C. J. de Vogel, "Boethiana," *Vivarium* 9 (1974): 49–66, and 10 (1975): 1–40.

52. Martin M. Tweedale, *Abailard on Universals* (Amsterdam, 1976), p. 63.

directly from Greek sources, particularly works of Boethius's older
contemporary Ammonius of Alexandria. But the skill of Boethius' paraphrase leaves no doubt that he understood his sources completely, and if he solved no new questions he at least grasped which were the major problems and conveyed to his readers a sense of their importance.

The *Consolation of Philosophy*, the most popular of Boethius's books in the Middle Ages and the most accessible today, illustrates his skill at manipulating abstract concepts in a logically coherent framework. The scene is Boethius's prison cell, where Theodoric had placed him on suspicion of conspiring with the emperor around 524, a charge for which he was executed a few months later. Philosophy appears to him—in the form of a woman—to relieve his distress at finding himself ruined, removed from his library and companions, and stripped of reputation. Their dialogue ranges freely over a wide variety of topics. Philosophy's conclusion that God's omnipotence rules the world leads Boethius to ask whether there is such a thing as chance; her statement that God's providence knows the outcome of chance events prompts a discussion of whether man's free will can coexist with divine knowledge. The prisoner's argument that the two concepts are incompatible fills three tightly reasoned pages, Philosophy's reply another ten. Both discussants weigh hypotheses dispassionately and lucidly; they neither overwhelm them with a torrent of polemic, as Augustine does, nor submerge them in a cloud of rhetoric.

Until the establishment of the authenticity of the works of theology attributed to Boethius, many readers of the *Consolation of Philosophy*, medieval and modern, doubted that Boethius was a Christian. It is easy to see how the question arose. The whole premise of the *Consolation* contradicted a patristic tradition, of which Augustine's views are typical, that unequivocally asserted that God decided everything that happened.[53] Boethius knew this opinion. In the *Consolation* he despaired for his reputation because "the judgment of most people is based not on the merits of the case but on the fortunes of its outcome; . . . the final misery of adverse fortune is that when some poor man is accused of a crime, it is thought that he deserves whatever punishment he has to suffer."[54] But he did not shrink from explaining his fall from power as a whim of Fortune, discussing the role of chance, and he also seems

53. Pierre Courcelle, *La "Consolation de Philosophie" dans la tradition littéraire* (Paris, 1967), p. 135.
54. *Consolation* i, pr. 4. The translation is by Richard Green (Indianapolis, 1962).

to have believed that the natural world was governed by regular rules with which God did not interfere. His attitudes on these issues placed him outside what we have seen to be the mainstream of public opinion of his time, Christian or pagan, and it was not until the twelfth century that philosophers again resumed discussion of these problems.

For all his importance to education later in the Middle Ages, in his own time Boethius was an anomaly. Of his contemporaries, only his close friends took notice of his work. Ennodius acquired a house from Boethius but does not seem to have been interested in obtaining copies of his works. Cassiodorus recommended Boethius's translations to his monks, but he himself thought of philosophers as those who "say that one should venerate the sun, the moon and the stars."[55] Boethius's influence on subsequent generations was not felt for centuries; the *Consolation* did not find many readers until the ninth century (and its audience then did not understand much of what he had to say), and it was not until the eleventh that his logical treatises bore fruit in a serious resumption of philosophical studies. In these centuries, however, Boethius became, in Southern's phrase, the schoolmaster of medieval Europe; "no scholar . . . with so little original material, [has] made so deep and original an impression on the future."[56]

More typical of the intellectuals of the early Middle Ages are three writers who flourished around the end of the sixth century: Gregory, bishop of Tours; Pope Gregory I (the Great); and Isidore of Seville. Each of them was among the most educated and able men of their societies, and they all wrote copiously on a wide variety of topics. Their works were among the most widely read of the Middle Ages, and are today our best evidence of the culture that formed in the fifth and sixth centuries.

GREGORY OF TOURS

The dissolution of high culture under the impact of the Germanic invasions is perhaps most apparent in the works of Gregory of Tours (c. 538–94). Even by the meager standards of fifty years earlier, the list of books Gregory knew was not extensive: of pagan authors, he was familiar only with Vergil, and, though he knew the Bible well, out of the rest of Christian literature he was better

55. Riché, *Barbarian West*, pp. 45–47.
56. *Making of the Middle Ages* (New Haven, 1953), pp. 174.

acquainted with saints' lives than the writings of Augustine or Jerome.[57] His Latin, which must be close to the language he actually spoke, suffers from errors in gender and case, and his syntax is frequently imprecise or unclear. The excess ornamentation through which Ennodius or Sidonius Apollinaris had approximated an elevated style is also gone; Gregory admired their work, but he knew himself incapable of imitating it.[58] Yet in a Gaul in which some bishops scarcely knew how to read, Gregory was by no means an uneducated or undistinguished man. Of his lineage he could boast that "all the bishops but five who held the see of Tours were connected with my family,"[59] and he had attended the episcopal school where his uncle Avitus was bishop. Among his contemporaries Gregory admitted the superiority only of Fortunatus, a poet in the manneristic late Latin tradition.[60]

Despite the difficulties of his prose, Gregory's works are read today and Fortunatus's are not. The reason is simple: as the only major historian writing between Ammianus and Bede, he provides a unique picture of society in the centuries immediately following the fall of the empire. In the next chapter, when we try to reconstruct the mentality of his contemporaries, Gregory will indeed prove invaluable. Our purpose here is different. For Gregory's works—his *History of the Franks* and his collections of miracles— permit us to ask as we can of no one else, how he understood the events of his time.

What is immediately arresting about Gregory as a writer is the ease with which physical details overwhelm the frame of his narrative. To be sure, graphic recounting of events had been part of the classical historical tradition. Here is an example from Tacitus, the murder of Agrippina by Nero's agents:

> The assassins closed in around her couch, and the captain of the trireme first struck her violently with a club. Then, as the centurion bared his sword for the fatal deed she exclaimed, "Smite my womb," and with many wounds she was slain.[61]

57. Max Bonnet, *Le Latin de Grégoire de Tours* (Paris, 1890), pp. 48–76.
58. Auerbach discusses Gregory's language and his intentions in *Literary Language and Its Public*, pp. 103–10. See also his insightful essay on Gregory in *Mimesis*, pp. 77–95.
59. *Historia Francorum* [= *HF*] v.49.
60. Riché, *Barbarian West*, p. 271.
61. *Annals* xiv.8. The translation is that of Church and Brodribb (New York, 1942), p. 325.

The descriptions in this passage are meant to inspire horror, but they do more: they tell us of Agrippina's knowledge that her murderers had been sent by her son. In Gregory, however, description seems to have become an end in itself, as in this account of the murder of a Frankish king:

> Chilperic, the Nero and Herod of our time, went off to his manor of Chelles, which is about a dozen miles from Paris. There he spent his time hunting. One day when he returned from the chase just as twilight was falling, he was alighting from his horse with one hand on the shoulder of a servant, when a man stepped forward, struck him with a knife under the armpit, and then stabbed him a second time in the stomach. Blood immediately streamed both from his mouth and through the gaping wound, and that was the end of this wicked man.[62]

The time of day, the posture of the king as he dismounted from his horse, the placement of the wounds, the flowing of the blood—all these details Gregory gives us with such vividness it becomes nearly impossible not to visualize the scene. But where we would expect to learn the identity of the assassin and his motive, Gregory tells us nothing. It is not simply that he is ignorant, for he could have told us he did not know; and in fact he does mention much later one of the rumors then current about the murder. He either is not interested in these issues or, which is more likely, he does not see that his readers would be. His attention is riveted by the event; to its causes and consequences he is largely indifferent.[63]

This abundance of graphic detail is one sign of the concreteness of Gregory's reasoning. Another is his frequent inability to impose order on his subject matter. Take an example chosen at random: the story in book ten of count Eulalius. Gregory tells us that Eulalius neglected and beat his wife Tetradia; that his nephew Virus, who wished to marry her himself, encouraged her to seek refuge with duke Desiderius; that she fled with all Eulalius's property—"gold, silver, clothing, everything in fact which she could

---

62. *HF* vi.46. I used the Latin text edited by Rudolf Buchner (Darmstadt, 1974–77). Unless otherwise noted the translations are those of Lewis Thorpe (London, 1974).
63. An intermediate state between Tacitus' and Gregory's use of gesture may be seen in the fourth-century historian, Ammianus Marcellinus. Cf. Auerbach, *Mimesis*, pp. 50–76.

carry"—taking with her her elder son and leaving her younger; that Eulalius, discovering what had happened, nursed his resentment for a while, then ambushed and killed Virus; and that Desiderius, who meanwhile had lost his own wife, then married Tetradia. Gregory's purpose in telling this tale was to explain how, after the death of Desiderius, Eulalius sued his wife for a return of his property before a council of bishops. But Gregory does not summarize the issues of the case without telling the whole story, and he added to the confusion by including long digressions that were totally irrelevant to the court case. He began, not with Eulalius's marriage as I did above, but with a paragraph devoted to the murder of Eulalius's mother ("she was found garrotted, still wearing the hairshirt which she put on when she prayed," Gregory noted with typical thoroughness), and several sentences interrupt the account to describe the piety of Eulalius's son John. No principles of selection shaped this assortment of facts; Gregory seems simply to have written down everything he knew about Eulalius, more or less in chronological order.[64] Auerbach compared Gregory's narrative method to that "which is frequent in spoken conversation of careless speakers" who cannot syntactically organize complex facts into a single construction or foresee the difficulties and avoid them in an introductory sentence.[65] Similarly, Hallpike noted that "while one's informants may be able to answer questions on why a certain character in a story did a certain thing, there is little or no ability to ignore the chronological sequence of events and substitute for them an analysis of events in logical order."[66] A third parallel is the narrative style of children, which is both rich in concrete details and confused in organization. To relate an event that happened at school a child might have to tell how her schoolroom is arranged, who sits next to her, how her class is organized when walking as a group, or any of a number of details extraneous to her immediate purpose. (One can, of course, obtain a great deal of unintended information from such digressions, as one can from Gregory.) Her confusion, as Gregory's, comes from an inability to imagine what information her interlocutor needs to be told that she takes for granted, and from a lack of skill in imposing order on facts.[67]

64. *HF* x.8.
65. *Mimesis*, pp. 81–82.
66. *Primitive Thought*, p. 115.
67. For Piaget's observations, see *Language and Thought of the Child*, trans. Marjorie Gabain and Ruth Gabain, 3d ed. (London, 1959; orig. pub. 1926), p. 108.

The difficulty Gregory experienced selecting and organizing material plagues his *History* as a whole. Abstract concepts—society,
the state, the Church as a whole—have no place in Gregory's
thought and provide him with no criteria for including or excluding subject matter. The incoherence of Gregory's episodes is thus
echoed on a larger scale as struggles between kings are recounted
side by side with trivial quarrels among citizens of Tours. As historians we are grateful for the light these minor episodes shed on
everyday life, but their value depends more on Gregory's eye for the
colorful than his judgment of what is important.

The egocentricism of Gregory's reasoning—the source both of
the sensual power of his prose and its bewildering organization—
extended to all aspects of his intellectual life. Gregory has no doubt
that miracles occurred with great frequency. He seems to have recorded nearly any miracle story that came to his attention, and the
miracles he reports from his own experience show that he has little in the way of critical judgment. Extraordinary powers are attributed to consecrated objects; when recounting an assassination
worked by placing poison in an Arian communion cup, Gregory
remarks that "we Catholics, who believe in the Trinity co-equal
and all-powerful, if we were to drink poison in the name of the
Father, the Son and the Holy Spirit, the true and incorruptible God,
nothing would harm us."[68] Gregory's saints were primarily miracle
workers—he was little interested in the character of their lives—
and their miraculous powers survived them in their relics. The
sanctity of these relics was seen as an almost physical substance
that could spread from object to object. Gregory reports that a
cloth left on the tomb of St. Martin of Tours grew heavier over-
night, and that a rope used to move St. Martin's statue was afterward able to work cures.[69] Gregory asserted he himself had been
cured of dysentery by drinking a mixture of water and dust from
Martin's tomb, and he recommended touching one's body to the
tomb to find relief from minor aches and pains.[70] The line between

68. *HF* iii.31. The translation is mine.
69. *Miracles of Saint Martin (De virtibus beati Martini episcopi)*, i.11.27.
The entire first book of Martin's miracles has been translated by William
C. McDermott in *Gregory of Tours. Selections from the Minor Works*
(Philadelphia, 1949). See also Sofia Boesch Gajano, "Il santo nella visione
storiografica de Gregorio di Tours," *Atti del Convegno storico internazionale dell'Academia Tudertina sul tema: Gregorio di Tours, Todi, 10-13 oct.
1971* (Todi, 1973), pp. 29–91.
70. *Miracles of Saint Martin*, ii.1; iii.preface.

natural and supernatural was already starting to disintegrate in
Augustine; in Gregory the supernatural has become ordinary.

Because of their connection with Gregory's conception of right and wrong, the miracles in which he thought the judgment of God was revealed are of particular interest. Some of these incidents are actually ordeals: Eulalius, for example, was exonerated of suspicion for his mother's murder by successfully taking communion, and a bishop of Tours acquitted himself of having fathered a child by carrying burning coals in his cassock. But where Catholic heroes were involved, or villains, Gregory found divine judgment in practically any event. One of the few explicit moral judgments in the *History* comes at the end of a chapter about Clovis's annexation of the kingdom of Sigibert the Lame. Clovis's maneuvers included the instigation of Sigibert's son to murder his father and the murder of the son by agents bearing messages of Clovis's friendship, after which Clovis went to the kingdom, proclaimed publicly his ignorance of the whole affair, and accepted acclamation as king by the populace. Gregory let all these distasteful details pass without comment only to reach the surprising conclusion that Clovis's success was a sign of his virtue. "For," he observed, "God daily lay his enemies low under his hand and increased his kingdom, because he walked with an upright heart before him and did what was pleasing in his eyes."[71]

In this passage Gregory reasoned that those who were Catholic succeeded because they were pious. Elsewhere Gregory often concluded that those who invoked the saints and were not answered failed because they were insincere.[72] Both interpretations reflect the attitude that in certain areas everything is meaningful, that there are no accidents—the cognitive position already encountered with Augustine. Yet that is not the whole story. For just as different cognitive processes had ended up breaking classical culture into

---

71. *HF* ii.40. The translation is mine.

72. One example of this attitude is the story of Chararicus, a king of Galicia who tried to gain a cure for his son from St. Martin. The father's first effort was unsuccessful, leading Gregory to conclude that heresy then still clung to his heart; when the king built a church to receive relics the king's son recovered and the king "confessed the unity of the Father, Son and Holy Spirit." *Miracles of Saint Martin*, i.11. See also the episode of Eberulf, who was murdered while in sanctuary in St. Martin's church at Tours. Gregory concluded that "the wrongdoing of the man Eberulf, whom St. Martin had permitted to endure all this, was certainly very great." *HF* vii.29.

discrete, often poorly understood bits of information and forms of behavior, so too it had broken Christian morality up into individual rules whose relative importance became difficult to judge. When Gregory omits to condemn Clovis's murders, it was not because he approved of these or other crimes; he believed Christians should obey all the rules set down in the Bible, including those against killing. Murder is just one of many crimes, however, and Gregory could overlook it in someone who fulfilled a Christian's primary duties to profess Catholicism, as Clovis did so notably, and to be generous to churches and the poor. Gregory can praise Theudebert, of whose sexual involvements and plans to kill his brother he also informs us, as "a great king, distinguished by every virtue. He ruled his kingdom justly, respected his bishops, was liberal to the churches, relieved the wants of the poor and distributed many benefits with piety and friendly goodwill."[73] Thus, though Gregory was a Catholic apologist, his ideas of morality and piety were quite different from Augustine's and from what we today expect a Christian's to be.

GREGORY THE GREAT

Literate, educated, and intelligent, Gregory of Tours was by no means a common man, but he probably had few ideas greatly different from the great mass of his society. Pope Gregory I (the Great), in contrast, is of importance not as an approximation of an average man but as the best thinker his time produced. Despite the disruptions caused by Justinian's reconquest of Italy and then by the Lombard invasions, the Roman senatorial families to which he belonged still retained more of ancient learning than was available

---

73. *HF* iii.25. See also Gregory's description of Tiberius, *HF* iv.40. Of Clovis's widow he wrote that "Clotild showed herself such that she was honored by everyone; she always showed herself assiduous in almsgiving, unflagging in night services, and pure in chastity and in all that is respectable; she gave churches, monasteries and other holy places needed lands; she shared out with abundant and eager will, that in her own life she was thought of not as queen but the very handmaiden of the God she served with zeal, whom neither the kingdoms of her sons nor her worldly ambition and possessions brought to ruin, but humility led to grace." *HF* iii.18. (The translation is mine.) Gregory's conclusion suggests he was chiefly concerned to show that Clotild's riches would not bar her from heaven, although in the previous paragraphs of the same chapter he recorded how she preferred to have her grandsons killed by their uncles—her sons—than permit them to live shorn of their long hair.

in Gaul; and he had the additional experience of having lived in Constantinople for several years as a papal representative. The effects of such varied experience can be seen in the worldly confidence of Gregory's books and in the cogency with which he expressed his ideas, but even so we shall note important differences between his cognition and that of Augustine.[74]

In the opinion of one historian, Gregory's conception of nature marked "the low point of scientific knowledge" of the early Middle Ages.[75] Gregory of Tours, ever the eager observer of concrete phenomena, at least wrote a book on how to calculate liturgical hours from the stars. But Gregory I was indifferent to systematic observation and disregarded even what learning he had accumulated from his reading. In one place he even expressed doubt that the moon received its light from the sun.[76] Lacking as he did a clear sense of natural causes, it is not surprising that he took as miraculous virtually any event that confirmed Christian expectations. Miracles he witnessed himself were generally trivial. For example, Gregory hailed as miraculous the ability of a visiting priest to calm a lunatic so the other patients in the hospital could get some sleep, and he declared that the incident persuaded him to accept as true all the other stories told about the priest; these included a claim that the priest could cause snakes to burst by making the sign of the cross over them.[77] Much of his *Dialogues* is given over to miracle stories,

74. The best general treatment of Gregory is still F. Homes Dudden, *Gregory the Great. His Place in History and Thought*, 2 vols. (London, 1905). More recent studies of Gregory's spirituality include Jean Leclerc, *The Love of Learning and the Desire for God. A Study of Monastic Culture*, trans. Catherine Misrahi (New York, 1974), pp. 31–44; Leclerc et al., *The Spirituality of the Middle Ages* (New York, 1968); Robert Gillet, Introduction to *Morales sur Job*, 2d ed. (Sources chrétiennes, no. 32 bis) (Paris, 1975); Adalbert de Vogüé, Introduction to the *Dialogues* (Sources chrétiennes, no. 251) (Paris: 1978); and Claude Dagens, *Saint Grégoire le Grand. Culture et expérience chrétiennes* (Paris, 1977). Many of these authors, Leclerc in particular, must be used with caution, because in their enthusiasm for Gregory they sometimes overestimate the coherence of his thought and slight the evidence showing his limitations.

75. C. W. Jones, preface to his edition of *Bedae Opera de Temporibus* (Cambridge, Mass., 1943), p. 125.

76. *Moralia in Job* xxii.7.

77. *Dialogi libri iv* [= *Dial.*] iii.35. Dudden, who discussed this incident, concluded that "Gregory had no capacity either of weighing or testing evidence brought forward by others, or for drawing correct inferences from what fell within his personal observation." *Gregory the Great* 1: 343. For Gregory on miracles, see also John M. McCulloh, "The Cult of Relics

and, though Gregory tried to lend his stories authenticity by specifying his sources, he seems in practice to have believed nearly any tale he heard.

While Gregory I's attitudes toward the supernatural are not noticeably superior to those encountered in other sources from the period, his moral thought is distinctive and demands careful consideration. In his spiritual writings, such as his commentary on the book of *Job*, Gregory reveals an ability to write about the interior life of the believer that was unmatched in the early Middle Ages. Reading such works, one can easily gain the impression that Gregory at least judged morality by intentions as Augustine had. But that expectation is disappointed. For Gregory does not imbed his intentionality, as Augustine had, in relationships imposing obligations on both parties. He thought of relationships in strictly hierarchical terms, and emotional obedience was thus merely an amplification of literal, external obedience.

To see Gregory at his best, there is no better place to begin than the letters he wrote to the missionaries he had sent to England. The venture itself was a bold one, the beginning of the effort to convert Germanic Europe that was not to be finished for another 200 years, and Gregory's letters were to serve as sources of guidance for missionaries throughout this long period. But the letters themselves barely survived. Already in the eighth century the Anglo-Saxon missionary Boniface complained that no copies were to be found in Rome. He then wrote to England for the texts, which we possess today only because Bede included them in his history.

There are eight letters in all. The distance that separated the great pope from his contemporaries is amply illustrated by one in which Gregory answers the questions sent him by Augustine of Canterbury, the leader of the mission to England. Most of the questions are about details of church discipline: Could two brothers marry two sisters? Could a man marry his stepmother? Could a pregnant woman be baptized? How soon after childbirth may she enter a church? That a missionary would think these questions important enough to devote a rare letter home to them must strike the modern reader, and even Gregory seems surprised at some. ("Why should not an expectant mother be baptized?") Yet he replies to each question with care, sometimes reminding Augustine that Old Testament law is not to be taken literally, sometimes cau-

in Letters and 'Dialogues' of Pope Gregory the Great: A Lexicographical Study," *Traditio* 32 (1976): 145–84.

tioning him against applying the law so strictly to converts that
excessive severity causes them to fall away from the church, yet
always seeking the reasonable and moderate course.[78] Since Augustine had been educated in the east and was himself by no means an
uncultured man, the contrast between his questions and Gregory's
answers speaks volumes about the pope's unique place in his society. The intelligence of his advice is obvious, but it is not likely
there was another man of Gregory's time who could have offered
it.

Most of the letters are of little interest here because they are
concerned with such details or with maintaining the morale of the
missionaries, who understandably needed much encouragement.
But there is one letter in which Gregory turns his attention away
from specific problems to consider the general approach that ought
to be taken in winning the English to Christianity. Do not, he
wrote, try to stamp out heathen practices by destroying temples
and forbidding sacrifices. Let the temples instead be turned into
churches, so that the people, "flocking more readily to their accustomed resorts," may find something familiar in their new religion.
"And since they have a custom of sacrificing many oxen to demons
[Gregory means their pagan gods] let them have some other solem-
nity in its place" at which beasts may be killed and eaten in honor
of God. "If the people are allowed some worldly pleasures in this
way, they will more readily come to desire the joys of the spirit. For
it is certainly impossible to eradicate all errors from obstinate
minds at one stroke, and whoever wishes to climb to a mountain
top climbs gradually step by step."[79]

What enabled Gregory to transcend the fixation on rules that
dominated the mentality of his time was his interest in states of
mind. Yet while Gregory expected the subordinate to feel the wish
to be obedient in addition to performing the actions that are commanded, he does not expect the superior to reciprocate these good
intentions by, for example, accepting less than the rule requires if
the subordinate has done his best. The conception of God that
sprang from this attitude could only be fearsome and unforgiving,
and Gregory designed a penitential regime intended to appease him
by the acts of penance without which interior contrition was useless for winning salvation. He instructed Augustine of Canterbury

78. *Bede's Ecclesiastical History of the English People*, ed. Bertram Colgrave and R. A. B. Mynors (Oxford, 1969), i.27.
79. Bede, *Eccl. Hist.*, i.30.

that all those who steal from churches should be punished: if they stole from poverty, they cannot be expected to pay fines and should be beaten "for the purpose of such correction is to save the wicked from hellfire."[80] On hearing of pagan survivals in Sardinia, he exhorted Christian landlords to raise taxes on their peasants to force them to come to God, and he instructed the local bishop to have free men jailed and slaves whipped until they were "brought by bodily torments to the desired sanity of mind."[81]

Still more remarkable was Gregory's attitude when Justus, a monk of his monastery, admitted on his deathbed to having three hidden pieces of gold. Justus had often cared for Gregory during the pope's frequent illnesses, but Gregory was uncompromising in his response to Justus's sin: he ordered that he be left alone by the other monks to die without any consoling word, and after Justus' death had his body buried in a manure pile. Justus died, as Gregory wished, in terror and contrition, but Gregory did not assume that even this miserable end won him salvation. He still felt it necessary to order masses said on his behalf until, after a month of masses, a vision was received of Justus's release from torment.[82]

The results of Gregory's hierarchical reasoning can be seen most clearly in his penitential doctrines, but the absence of concepts of mutual respect can be seen in every aspect of his thought. In politics Gregory stressed the duty to show obedience to superiors, as when he warns subjects against criticizing their superiors, while warning the superiors against offending God.[83] Equally significant in a writer so deeply influenced by Augustine is the fact that Gregory rarely writes of relations between peers. I know of only one passage, a chapter in the Dialogues, where Gregory attempts to discuss love of neighbor, and his effort only shows how difficult such ideas were for him. The subject of the chapter is a saint who frees a prisoner from the Lombards, but he has nothing to say about the saint's personal feelings for the man he saved, nor does he think to tell what had been the prisoner's crime, although we would need that information before we could assess the morality of the action. The important thing for Gregory is that "because 'love of neighbor . . . fulfills all the demands of the law,' [the saint] kept the law in its

80. Bede, Eccl. Hist., i.27.
81. Dudden, Gregory the Great, 2: 149–50; Epistles iv.26; ix.65.
82. Dial. iv.57.
83. Reg. Past. iii.4. For Gregory's dealings with the emperor, in which he consistently sought to be obedient, see Dudden, Gregory the Great, 2: 238–67.

entirety."[84] The orientation is still to the divine rules obeyed by the saint, not to his actual attitudes displayed (or felt) toward fellow humans.

Gregory was undeniably the finest thinker of his age. Yet he did not achieve true intentionality in his moral judgment, or retain the sense, still evident in Augustine, that humans have duties to other humans. The conclusion is inescapable that these cognitive processes had, for a time, entirely disappeared from European society.

ISIDORE OF SEVILLE

Far less is known of Isidore of Seville than of either Gregory the Great or Gregory of Tours: although the best guess is that he was born twenty or thirty years later than Gregory the Great, the only reliable facts about his life are that he succeeded his brother Leander (who had supervised the formation of his character after their father's death) as bishop of Seville in 599, that he presided over councils held in 619 and 633, and that he was dead by 636.[85] This lack of information is not compensated for by any marked originality of thought, for Isidore's opinions, always well supported by authority, are cautious and unsurprising. Isidore himself would not have seen this lack of distinctive doctrines as a fault. He shared the aspiration of early medieval scholars not to discover what was new but to record what could be learned from others. The similarity to late imperial handbook writers is unmistakable, and it was a continuity as much of cognition as of genre.

Isidore's *Etymologies* may serve to illustrate his method. The name itself is significant. Isidore seems to have thought that words had a significance beyond transient meanings, and elsewhere he contrasted the usage of words with their true meaning.[86] This con-

---

84. *Dial.* iii.37.
85. Isidore's *Etymologicarum sive Originum* [= *Ety.*] was edited by W. M. Lindsay (Oxford, 1911); his *De Natura Rerum* by Jacques Fontaine (Bordeaux, 1960). Other works are in *PL* 81–84. Fontaine, *Isidore de Seville et la culture classique dans l'Espagne wisigothique* (Paris, 1959), is the basic study of Isidore. Ernest Brehaut, *An Encyclopedist of the Dark Ages, Isidore of Seville* (New York, 1912), provides an insightful if old-fashioned in tone introduction to a translation of selections from the *Etymologies*.
86. "Sicque ex his consuetudo [of poets' using words that fit their meter] obtinuit pleraque ab auctoribus indifferenter accipit, quae quidem quamvis similia videantur, quadam tamen propria inter se origine distingunter." *Differentiae, PL* 83: 9. Isidore thus distinguishes the true meaning of

fusion between external reality and the products of thought is typical of psychological realism, and, in fact, the belief that names have a real existence apart from human discourse was one Piaget found in children.[87] The idea of the *Etymologies*, therefore, as Brehaut noted, "was that the way to knowledge was by way of words, and further, that they were to be elucidated by reference to their origin rather than to the things they stood for."[88]

Following the manner of the handbook writers of Augustine's time, Isidore composed the *Etymologies* chiefly by quoting or paraphasing bits of Christian and pagan authors. At times it seems that nearly every passage in Isidore has its origin somewhere else. Even on short acquaintance, I discovered that his comments on chance had been borrowed from Lactantius.[89] What is significant about this method, however, both for Isidore and the other authors who employed it, is not just that their only originality came when they misunderstood the sources they were trying to paraphrase. For Isidore can be compared to a mosaicist in his attitude to his materials as well as in his manner of arranging fragments to form a new whole. Ideas to him were not suggestions of ways to view the world or analyze a problem. They had an existence apart from thought, and he treated them as objects to be cut and trimmed to fit his plan.

Assessing the reasoning of a writer as derivative as Isidore can be a tricky business, because it is difficult to know whether he understood the implications of all the texts he copied. Brief quotations or definitions especially can be deceptive. For example, in the *Etymologies* Isidore gives a definition of *populus* close to that of Augustine: "Populus refers to a human multitude associated by a juridical consensus and a community of agreement."[90] This definition implies that law derives from the community, and in another place (where it is plain he was copying from a law book) Isidore does define *lex* as an enactment of the people (*constitutio pop-*

---

words from human usage. For children's ideas about words, which are clearly congruent with Isidore's, see appendix.

87. See appendix. Cf. also Hallpike, *Primitive Thought*, pp. 409–15.

88. *Encyclopedist*, p. 33.

89. Radding, "Superstition to Science," *American Historical Review* 84 (1979): 962–63.

90. *Ety.* ix.4, 5. For Isidore's use of this term, see Jeremy Adams, "The Political Grammar of Isidore of Seville," *Arts Libéraux et Philosophie au Moyen Age* (Montreal/Paris, 1969) (Actes du quatrième Congrès international de philosophie médiévale, 27 August–2 September 1967), pp. 763–75.

uli).[91] But in his most extended discussion of law and politics he employs the term *populus* far more loosely than his own definition, either to contrast a ruler with the people, or simply to designate a plurality of persons.[92] Isidore's contact with classical political theory is thus far more tenuous than his vocabulary would indicate.

Although Isidore had something to say about practically every subject, he is of particular interest for his scientific writings because his *Etymologies* and *De Rerum Natura* for several centuries provided the most readily available access to a number of classical theories. Isidore's own grasp of theory, however, was far from secure, because he tended to give primacy to his sensory impressions with which he then reconciled doctrines obtained through reading. The universe seemed very small to him; he thought that the heavens were close enough to the earth for meteors to be pieces of celestial fire dislodged by strong winds, and for Ethiopians to be burned by the proximity of the sun.[93] And though he described the earth as spherical in *De Rerum Natura*, he had trouble using this concept in thinking about climatic zones, which he described as if they were circles laid out on a flat surface: the torrid zone "is uninhabitable because the sun speeding through the midst of the heaven, creates an excessive heat in these places, so that on account of the parched earth crops do not grow there, nor are men permitted to dwell there, because of the great heat;" the arctic and antarctic circles, "adjacent to each other" on the other side of the surface, were too far from the sun; the remaining zones, situated on the east and west, "are temperate for the reason that they derive cold from one circle, heat from the other."[94] (See diagram.) The passage well illustrates the difference between knowing an idea and being able to apply it to phenomena.

Part of Isidore's confusion comes from his sources, of which he used an amazing variety: his science was drawn from commentaries on Vergil, Plato's *Timaeus*, and the Bible as well as scientific handbooks. The passage just quoted appears to be a paraphrase of a gloss on Vergil's *Georgics*; in another place, where Isidore follows an astronomist in describing the zones of the sky, his account is

91. *Ety.* iv.10.
92. *Sententiarum* iii.47–57 (PL 83: 717–730).
93. *Ety.* iii.71,3; *De Rerum Natura* x.4.
94. *De Natura Rerum* x; the translation is by Brehaut, *Encyclopedist*, pp. 51–52. For Isidore's science, see also W. Brandt, *The Shape of Medieval History: Studies in the Modes of Perception* (New Haven, 1966), pp. 2–11.

Primus circulus articos frigore inhabitabilis—
    First circle (articos)
    cold, not habitable

Secundus circulus therinos temperatus habitabilis—
    Second circle (therinos)
    temperate, habitable

Medius circulus isemerinos torridus inhabitabilis—
    Third circle (isemerinos)
    torrid, not habitable

Quartus circulus xeimerinos temperatus habitabilis—
    Fourth circle (xeimerinos)
    temperate, habitable

Quintus circulus antarcticos frigidus inhabitabilis—
    Fifth circle (antarcticos)
    cold, not habitable

much more accurate.[95] But the contradiction between the sources was compounded by Isidore's uncritical acceptance of what he read. He seems to have believed that all his sources were equally authoritative—he does not, for example, feel it necessary to inform us of when or whom he is copying so we can assess for ourselves the value of the information. And he appears to have transcribed any relevant passage that came to hand without inquiring whether the text made sense on its own or contradicted another authority.

Scholars such as Isidore, who make up in diligence and memory what they lack in originality or understanding, are to be found in every age including our own. What is important about Isidore is that he was the best read and most diligent scholar of his time, and that nearly every man of learning of the early Middle Ages belonged to his type. Their deference to antiquity (and not necessarily an old antiquity—Isidore took Gregory the Great to be an authority, as later generations took Isidore) deterred them not only from venturing new ideas but from inquiring too closely into the ideas they encountered in their reading. A ninth-century writer expressed the common opinion when he disclaimed his own words as "of little value" because in patristic texts one can "behold perpetually as if in a looking glass what one ought to be, to do, and to avoid."[96] Most books before 1000 were compiled rather than written, often, as with Isidore, without any mention being made of the sources that were being quoted.

Of the many factors that shaped the culture of the early Middle Ages the role of cognition is the most easily overlooked. It is possibly also the most important, for its effects were felt by the early centuries of the Roman Empire, and by the fourth century had created a mental world that was already very different from that of classical times. Even occasional geniuses, such as Augustine, no longer fully understood classical authors. The long-term results, as seen in the Byzantine empire, could be a thousand years of cultural sterility. The Germanic invasions prevented this dismal outcome in the West by making impossible the rote transmission of socially acceptable behaviors. But the mentality that emerged in the sixth and seventh centuries was prone to every kind of superstition and lacked the capacity to manipulate abstractions in a logical and consistent way. Short of the mass destruction of libraries, a more complete collapse of a classical civilization is hard to imagine.

95. Fontaine, Isidore, 2: 486–89.
96. Jonas of Orleans, De Institutione Regis, ed. J. Reviron (Paris, 1930), p. 113.

THREE

Visions of Order

Law and Monasticism in the Early Middle Ages

Among the gentiles . . . monarchs . . . commanded what they believed to be the will of the gods as shown in the auspices, and consequently were subject to no one but God.

—*The New Science, 25.*

Heroic jurisprudence [was] all verbal scrupulosity. . . . With their limited ideas, the heroes thought they had a natural right to precisely what, how much, and of what sort has been set forth in words; as even now we may observe in peasants and other crude men, who in conflicts say that their right stands for them in the words. . . . And if, as a consequence of this [civil] equity, the laws turned out in a given case to be not only harsh but actually cruel, they naturally bore it because they thought their law was naturally such.

—*The New Science, 38.*

The books left by early medieval intellectuals provide the most
accessible evidence of changing cognitive processes, but the historian of mentalities naturally wishes to know how those who were not intellectuals thought about themselves and their world. What responsibilities did they feel toward their neighbors? How did they define their community? What expectations did they have of God and what did they believe he expected of them? Our sources for the early Middle Ages are simply too scanty to answer such questions for any except lay elites, but this restriction is not as serious as it seems. For while the material interests of elites certainly differed from, for example, those of peasants, they had no more education than anyone else, and until Charlemagne's time there existed no court culture to alter their manners or ideas from those commonly accepted. Thus there is little reason to believe that their cognitive processes were particularly distinctive, and their values were probably not much different from those of other classes.

To examine the reasoning of these elites, we shall look at two kinds of evidence. The first are the Germanic law codes that preserve the largely customary rules which regulated people's dealings with each other and their rulers; the second are the monastic constitutions set down to establish ideal societies. We shall see that despite their diverse subject matter these texts reveal essentially congruent visions of how human society is and ought to be organized. But these texts do more than record conceptions of order. The role of the king, the role of the abbot, the structure of the monastery, the practice of the feud—all the other evidence we have confirms the accuracy of the picture that emerges from the legal and monastic codes. The cognitive processes that formed these sources were active forces in society, shaping institutions and behavior by shaping expectations and perceptions.

Law

Upwards of twenty codes survive from the Visigothic and Burgundian codes of the fifth century to the Anglo-Saxon codes of the eleventh (and, if one counts the *Leges Henrici Primi*, the twelfth) century. The law contained in these codes seems to have been largely or entirely based on custom.[1] This does not of course mean

1. On the motives of the kings who issued the early codes, see J. M. Wallace-Hadrill, *Early Germanic Kingship in England and on the Continent*

that the laws as they have come down to us are the same as the Germans lived under before the conquests.[2] Some innovations were introduced by royal decree, though the kings were usually careful to call attention to their alterations of custom. Other innovations, such as the transfer of property by written instruments, appear to have been adopted directly from the practices of the Roman populations among whom the Germans lived. Yet such novelties need not disturb us as long as we remember that it is not archaic Germanic law but the law as actually practiced in the early Middle Ages that is our concern.

The actual writing down of custom appears to have been inspired by Roman examples—*iuxta exempla Romanorum*, as Bede wrote of the earliest English laws—and it was probably lawyers from the indigenous, Romanized populations who prepared the written versions. It is not surprising therefore that some Roman terminology filters into the codes as when the royal treasury is referred to as the *fiscus*. But the distortions of reasoning caused by Roman influences should not be exaggerated. The decay of legal skill began by the third century, and by the fall of the empire had caused a simplification of many classical concepts to the point where their merger with Germanic custom need have caused no major innovations.[3] The very structure of the codes, moreover,

---

(Oxford, 1971), pp. 33–43, who observes "Early Germanic written law records a selection of customs: it does not consequently alter them" (p. 39).

2. We know so little about pre-fifth-century German law that historians often must go on little but their intuition in discussing it. Katharine Fischer Drew, for example, in the introduction to her translation of *The Burgundian Code* (Philadelphia, 1949) considers the use of compensatory payments to be a comparatively recent substitution "for the Germanic idea of the blood feud where the killing of a man obligated the members of his family to avenge his death upon the killer or upon his family" (p. 8). Though such a reading is certainly not out of the question I myself doubt that the feud was ever that rigid.

3. The law of property, for example, in classical times had carefully distinguished between ownership (*dominium*) and other rights in property, such as usufruct, that fell short of ownership. By the fourth century, however, lawyers treated all rights in property indiscriminately as possession (*possessio*), often with the result, which classical law had avoided, of recognizing several coexisting possessors. The parallels between this vulgar Roman law and Germanic law are so close that it would be hard to calculate the share of each in the formulation of the medieval notions of *seisin* or *Gewere*. Ernst Levy, *West Roman Vulgar Law* (Philadelphia, 1951), pp. 96–99.

testifies to the limited capacity of the lawyers who drew them up.
Principles of law are rarely stated, definitions are never given, and the laws themselves are brief and often eliptical. Determining the rules governing a specific case was further complicated by the chaotic organization of the codes. Even in the Burgundian code, whose compilers had a contemporary compilation of Roman law to follow, the ordering of subject matter frequently breaks down. Thus titles 14 and 42 deal with inheritance, titles 1 and 43 with gifts, while laws concerning crimes of violence are scattered throughout the text. In the Frankish and Anglo-Saxon codes, which are still more distant from Roman models, the confusion is still greater, for laws are arranged in a thoroughly helter-skelter fashion, held together by the barest association of ideas.

Because the codes are essentially enumerations of rules covering specific circumstances, it would be fruitless to look for clear statements about political power, social structure, or moral values. But by paying attention to what acts were regarded as deserving of punishment, to the kind of punishments inflicted, and to the procedures for reaching judgments, one can obtain a clear picture of cognitive processes that gave shape to Germanic laws: the conceptions of the sources of the law, the community, and the relation of human to divine justice. Though these conceptions were not necessarily conscious in the sense of being the object of reflection and debate, by structuring thinking about law and society they determined what factors went into assessing the severity of an offense, and indeed what constituted an offense.

In what follows I shall focus primarily on the *lex salica* of the Franks as it was drawn up at Clovis's command and amended by his successors, because these are among the earliest of surviving codes.[4] But those conceptions are found equally, and with remarkably little variation, in the other Germanic codes. Thus while there are differences in terminology—what the Franks called *fredus*, the Anglo-Saxons called *wite* and the Burgundians *mulcta* (this last a borrowing of Roman terminology)—all codes recognize compensa-

---

4. The most recent editions of the *lex salica* are those by K. A. Eckhardt in the MGH and the series of *Germanenrecht*. Both series provide editions of most other major codes. Anglo-Saxon laws are available in F. Liebermann, *Die Gesetze der Angelsachsen* (Halle, 1903); and with English translation in F. L. Attenborough, *The Laws of the Earliest English Kings* (Cambridge, 1922), and A. J. Robertson, *The Laws of the Kings of England from Edmund to Henry I* (Cambridge, 1925). Drew translated both *Burgundian Code* and *The Lombard Laws* (Philadelphia, 1973).

tions owed a superior for violations of his commands. And while later codes, particularly those of the Anglo-Saxons, develop the underlying conceptions of the law with a detail that did not occur to Clovis, the development took place within the framework to be described here. It was not until the twelfth century that different ways of thinking about law and justice forced an abandonment of the Germanic pattern.

KING AND LAW

The law codes themselves invariably take the form of royal enactments. This is not so by chance or the particular perspective of the kings who had them drafted. All our evidence points to the conclusion that people in the early Middle Ages conceived of law as coming from the king, and that they believed the king himself received his authority from God. Belief in divinely inspired kingship is not, of course, unique to the early Middle Ages; the same idea was commonly expressed in the sixteenth and seventeenth centuries. But whereas Bodin, for example, or Bossuet saw obedience to the king as part of obedience to law, and law as a property of the whole community,[5] in the early Middle Ages both the king's authority and the law were conceived of as external to the community. Fredegar, for example, attributed the origin of law to the first Merovingian: "and they chose Faramund . . . and raised him in long-haired kingship over them: then they began to have laws".[6]

There is no inherent contradiction between such beliefs and the undoubted fact that the laws were customs practiced within a given tribe. Whether customary laws are experienced as a possession of the community or as rules stemming from an external authority depends less on social reality than on the cognitive processes through which those laws are perceived. As we saw in Piaget's study of the game of marbles, customs are not always perceived as an expression of community opinion even when, to an outside observer, it is clear that they vary over time as people interpret rules to fit different cases. Thus while it was certainly common in the early Middle Ages for men to consult with each other to determine what customs governed an issue at hand, the consultations were

5. Quentin Skinner, *The Foundations of Modern Political Thought: The Age of Reformation* (Cambridge, 1978).
6. "Et elegerunt Faramundum . . . et levaverunt in regem super se crinitum: tunc habere et leges coeperunt." MGH *SRM* 2: 244.

regarded by participants less as deciding on customs than as establishing what customs already existed.

Yet because Germanic law was customary, many historians have
concluded it was also in some manner the expression of the community will, that the king was obliged to consult with the community, and even that the king was a representative of the community.
This position has been upheld in two ways. Some historians have
argued that the community created law in the early Middle Ages by
supposing that the written royal law stood in opposition to a traditional folk-law. This school of interpretation holds that in their
early history the Germanic tribes were self-governing communities that enforced a folk-peace by expelling from the community
all malefactors. Later, so the theory goes, under the influence of
Christian and Roman thought the orientation of Germanic society
changed so that the king became legislator and took over the
guardianship of the folk-peace. King's law and king's peace thus
supplanted folk-law and folk-peace, but even then the king did not
escape restraint and remained under the law. " 'Law'," asserted
Fritz Kern in a classic study, "was the living conviction of the community . . . which the king could not disregard . . . without falling
into lawless 'tyranny.' " Kings who acted unjustly, Kern believed,
could be lawfully resisted and, if necessary, deposed and killed.[7]

The difficulty with this interpretation is that it owes more to
Romantic idealization of preindustrial societies than it does to any
medieval sources. The right to resistance depends, at best, on elev-
enth- and twelfth-century materials, while no sources at all speak
of either folk-peace or folk-law.[8] When early medieval writers do

7. *Kingship and Law in the Middle Ages*, trans. S. B. Chrimes (New York,
1970), p. 73. A more recent proponent of this view has been Walter Ullmann, who writes casually of how "*Volksrecht* gave way to *Königsrecht*."
Principles of Government and Politics in the Middle Ages (New York,
1966), p. 127. On Ullman see Francis Oakley, "Celestial Hierarchies Revisited: Walter Ullmann's Vision of Medieval Politics," *Past and Present*, no.
60 (1973): 3–48.
8. The distinction between king's law and folk-law was severely criticized
by Ekkehard Kaufmann, *Aequitatis Iudicium. Königsgericht und Billigkeit
in der Rechtsordnung des frühen Mittelalters* (Frankfurt, 1959), pp. 60–
92, while Julius Goebel, Jr. effectively destroyed the basis of the peace
theory in his under-appreciated *Felony and Misdemeanor. A Study in the
History of Criminal Law* (New York, 1937. Reprint Philadelphia, 1976).
More generally, J. M. Wallace-Hadrill has questioned whether one can
speak, as Ullmann does, of the Carolingian "emancipation" of kingship
from the *populus*: "I cannot easily picture the pre-Carolingian kings as

speak of the king's relationship to his subjects, they are unequivocal in describing it as one of command. We have seen that Augustine and Gregory the Great stressed the duty of subjects to obey and held that to rebel against the king was to defy God who had established him on his throne. Gregory of Tours portrayed a bishop preaching to convert Gundobad as telling him that "it is better that the people should accept your belief, rather than that you, a king, should pander to their every whim. You are the leader of your people, your people is not there to lord it over you." Gregory himself took a similar approach when he wished to lecture Chilperic on his behavior. "If one of our number has attempted to overstep the path of justice it is for you to correct him. If, on the other hand, it is you who act unjustly, who can correct you? We can say what we think to you. If you wish to do so, you listen to us. If you refuse to listen, who can condemn you for it, except him who had promised eternal justice." One could disregard this evidence as relevant to clerical and not popular attitudes (though I think it would be wrong to do so) except that the same ideas appear, for example, in the scene where Clovis's followers tell him "Everything in front of us is yours, noble king, for our very persons are yours to command. Do exactly as you wish, for there is none among us who has the power to say you nay."[9]

The other approach to this problem is better based in the sources, because it begins from the statement made in some of the codes that the king legislated with the advice and consent of various notables. But to conclude from these statements, as is often done, that the approval of the community was necessary if the laws were to be changed pushes such evidence too far, for it is by no means clear that in the sixth and seventh centuries consultations were binding in any way. The virtually contemporary Benedictine Rule admonished the abbot both to take the advice of seniors and

---

conscious of being answerable to any *populus* for their authority or sovereignty; so that, if I am right, we have with the Carolingians not so much the substitution of a theory of descending delegation of authority for an ascending one, as the happy acceptance of what was already implicit had become explicit through looking harder at the Old Testament: it made sense to everyone—clergy, king and people—but nobody said, so far as I know, that a substitute had been found for a clearly-understood Germanic theory of popularly-derived sovereignty." "The *Via Regia* of the Carolingian Age," *Trends in Medieval Political Thought*, ed. Beryl Smalley (Oxford, 1965), p. 32. On the right to resistance see pp. 38–39.

9. *HF* ii.34; v.18; ii.27.

ignore it if he wished, and Gregory of Tours, in the address to Chilperic I just quoted, allowed for the possiblity that Chilperic would do the same thing. There is, further, the fact that even within the laws of one people there is no consistent requirement that counsel or consent be obtained. Thus although Clovis cited the presence of advisers in enacting the Salic law, Childebert did not when enacting the ambitious reforms of the *Pactum pro tenore pacis*.[10] The only possible conclusion is that of Ekkehard Kaufmann, that while the concurrence of the king was necessary and sufficient to give a law legal force, the concurrence of the people was not.[11]

The real problem of both these approaches is that they disregard what the sources of the period invariably say and what I see no reason not to take seriously, that the kings received their authority from God and that they were accountable only to God if they ruled wrongly. Nearly all royal legislation is enacted "with God's aid" *(Deo auxilante)* as the Salic law says, and with God's commands in mind, but the most elaborate expression of this idea belongs to the prologue of the Lombard king Liutprand. "This Catholic prince," he wrote, "has been influenced to promulgate these laws and to judge wisely not by his own foresight but through the wisdom and inspiration of God. He has conceived [these laws] in his heart, studied them in his mind, and happily fulfilled them in his word. For the heart of the king is in the hand of God. . . ." Liutprand is proclaiming something more than the pious wishes common in all Christian centuries; he has real confidence in the actual identity of royal and divine wills. An earlier Lombard king used the same language in exempting from punishment all who commit homicide at the king's command, "for since we believe that the heart of the king is in the hand of God it is inconceivable that anyone whose death the king has ordered could be entirely free of guilt."[12] The

10. The *Pactum pro tenore pacis* is discussed in considerable detail by Goebel, *Felony and Misdemeanor*, pp. 65–81. For similar efforts of the Visigothic king to limit feud, see P. D. King, *Law and Society in the Visigothic Kingdom* (Cambridge, 1972), pp. 85–87.

11. "Die Mitwirkung des Volkes und des Adels bei der Gesetzgebung hatte aber keine konstitutive Bedeutung, der Gesetzescharakter eine Bestimmung war von der Zustimmung des Volkes nicht abhändig. In frühen Mittelalter kann ein Gesetz zwar ohne die Zustimmung des Volkes Rechtskraft gewinnen, niemals aber ohne die Zustimmung des Königs." *Aequitatis Iudicium*, p. 131.

12. Rothar, c. 2. The prologue of Liutprand's laws are from the collection of the first year. Both translations are by Katharine Fischer Drew.

thought is close to that of Piaget's subjects, who believed that punishment itself was evidence of guilt.

This conception had deep roots in both Christian and Germanic traditions. Germanic kings of the period before the invasions were expected to be on good terms with the gods, and the king's "luck" was the proof of this good relationship. Disasters suffered by a people meant the king's luck had run out in more ways than one: Ammianus tells us that the Burgundians deposed their kings if the tribe suffered military defeat or serious crop failures rather than risk further misfortune by retaining a king who had lost the gods' favor.[13]

Conversion to Christianity meant the adoption of a new vocabulary—kings came to be described in ecclesiastical terms as minister or vicar of God, or as Christ's deputy[14]—but because Christian doctrine agreed with Germanic custom in holding that the king received his power from God, the two traditions blended easily. The tract "De duodecim abusivis saeculi" (the twelve afflictions of the world), a seventh-century Irish work important to us because the missionary activities of the Irish extended throughout Europe, described the misfortunes accompanying the rule of a king who is unjust or unchristian in terms that would have been easily intelligible to the ancient Germans:

> often the peace of the peoples is broken and disturbances take
> their rise from within the realm; the fruits also of the earth
> are diminished and the enslavement of peoples is hastened on;
> the deaths of relatives and children bring sadness; the inva-
> sions of enemies bring desolation on provinces far and wide;
> wild beasts rend the herds of cattle and flocks of sheep; hurri-
> canes and stormy winters forbid the earth's fertility and the
> sea's good gift, and at times the strokes of lightning burn up
> crops and the flowers of fruit trees and the vines.[15]

13. For sacral kinship, see Wallace-Hadrill, *Early Germanic Kinship*, pp. 1–16; William A. Chaney, *The Cult of Kingship in Anglo-Saxon England* (Berkeley, 1970); O. Höfler, "Der Sakralcharakter des germanischen Königtums," in *The Sacral Kingship. Contributions to the Central Theme of the VIIIth International Congress for the History of Religions (Rome, April 1955)* (Leiden, 1959), pp. 664–701.

14. On the language applied to kings, see King, *Law and Society*, pp. 26–28; Chaney, *Cult of Kingship*, pp. 197–200.

15. Text edited by S. Hellmann, *Texte und Untersuchungen zur Geschichte der altchristlichen Literatur*, ser. III, 4 (Leipzig, 1909) pp. 1–62. The translation is from Laistner, *Thought and Letters*, p. 145.

In the eighth century the book of Samuel inspired Bede to similar
observations: bad weather and poor harvests can be caused by kings who do not fear God, and the king himself can often end up like Saul, losing his kingdom.[16]

The clearest expressions of this belief in the divine origins of kingship naturally came from the educated classes. The belief was not theirs alone, however: indeed it had profound consequences for behavior at every level of society. Toward God, kings acted with respect bordering on fear, often making and unmaking policies out of a desire to obtain divine favor. Considering violations of God's churches or law as offenses to themselves, for example, the Merovingians required church-breakers to pay a fine *(fredus)* to the royal fisc in addition to the composition owed the church.[17] Because they also rescinded actions which they came to believe met with God's disapproval, the attitude that assumed that innovations in the law were repugnant to God was a powerful force for preserving tradition in the early Middle Ages. Gregory of Tours left a memorable picture of how Chilperic and his queen Fredegunda, when their sons fell ill, burned the lists of taxes they had recently tried to impose,[18] and other examples could easily be cited. Further, just as toward God the king felt no autonomy, toward his subjects he felt no obligations. Frankish documents convey this idea through references to the king's *gratia* or grace, a grace that the scribes linked to that of God. On their favorites, the kings casually bestowed "God's and our grace" *(dei et nostra gratia)*; those who displeased them they threatened with "God's anger and our enmity" *(Dei iram . . . et nostram offensam)*. What was important in either case, as F. L. Ganshof observed, is the fact that royal actions were perceived as subject neither to rule nor outside restraints. "There was the idea that agents and subjects had no right to receive the goods, rights,

---

16. Wallace-Hadrill, *Early Germanic Kingship*, pp. 56, 76–77.

17. Lex Alamannorum 3.3. This practice is considerably developed by the Carolingians, as we shall see, and independently by the Anglo-Saxons. In seventh-century England the fine for breaking the protection of the church *(mundbyrd)* was 50 shillings "like the king's" and the king collected a fine *(wite)* from those who worked on Sunday. Wihtred 2.9; Ine 3. Later Anglo-Saxon codes developed an elaborate system of equivalences between the fines owed the king and the church. On this, see Chaney, *Cult of Kingship*, chapter 7.

18. HF v.34. The sons died anyway, but the lesson was apparently lasting, because Gregory commented that "from this time onwards Chilperic was lavish in giving alms to cathedrals and churches, and to the poor, too."

privileges, and diverse advantages [that came with a grant of grace]."[19]

If the Germanic king expected from his subjects the unilateral respect he himself owed to God, he received it because his subjects thought the same way. I have already quoted the view of Gregory of Tours on this subject, but the truth of this picture, and the accuracy with which it reflects popular as well as royal ideas, is attested equally, and unexpectedly, by the caution with which the last Merovingian king was removed from office in the middle of the eighth century. Real power had passed decades before to the family of palace mayors, the Carolingians. These mayors were not self-effacing or ineffectual men—they included Charles Martel, who in his nearly thirty years of rule greatly extended Frankish territory by conquering the Bavarians and Alamans, held off the Arabs at Poitiers, and promoted the Anglo-Saxon mission to other parts of Germany. But they did not dare take the name king until a way was found to certify the legitimacy of their title. This was finally accomplished in 751 when the pope was prevailed upon to approve a change in dynasty, the magnates of the kingdom ratified the rule of mayor Pepin, and—in a ceremony previously unknown among the Franks—the new king received priestly anointment from the missionary Boniface. Power alone evidently could not make a man king; he had also to establish he was the recipient of divine grace. In a real sense, doctrine structured reality.

PENALTIES

Belief in the divine origin of kingship does not necessarily preclude a conception of a community under the king; such indeed was the case with divine-right kingship of the sixteenth and seventeenth centuries. But if we look in the Germanic codes for evidence that people thought in terms of society as a whole, we will be disappointed. The greater part of the codes is given over instead to detailing the sums of money to be paid by those who inflict various kinds of injuries on others, and these payments fall into two broad categories: fines to lords, most often the king, and compositions paid to the individuals one harmed. The first protects the interests of the king and others high in the social hierarchy. The second

19. "La 'Gratia' des monarques francs," *Anuario de Estudios Medievales* 3 (1966): 22. Ganshof notes, moreover, that Frankish kings often would restore their grace to a subject who had lost favor if he passed a judgment of God.

protects the interests of individuals and kin groups. Neither, however, as Julius Goebel observed, points to "any conception of public order . . . in the sense of a state guaranteed" or aspired to by law.[20]

The most important fines collected by kings were those from persons who committed crimes of violence. The Burgundian king, for example, collected fines—generally of twelve shillings though occasionally of a fraction or multiple of twelve shillings—for acts ranging from assault to theft. Though the term used for fines (*mulctae*) shows the influence of Roman law, as perhaps the wide range of offenses covered does also, the basic idea was German. Tacitus knew of similar exactions by Germanic rulers in the first century,[21] and similar rules are found in codes relatively free of Roman influence. Aethelberht, for example, imposed a flat fifty shilling *wite* on those who committed acts of theft or homicide against freemen.[22]

The Frankish fine of this sort was the *fredus*, valued at a third the composition owed the injured party or kin, and it well illustrates the difficulty of grasping the purpose of these fines. Brunner, the great nineteenth-century legal historian, was encouraged by the similarity between the name of the fine and *Friede*, the German word for peace, to believe that the *fredus* was a payment made by a malefactor for readmission into the peace of the community. Later philology cast doubt on this etymology, and when in the 1930's Julius Goebel launched a devastating attack on the peace theory, he suggested that the *fredus* was merely a payment for the state's intervention to arrange a settlement between two private parties. Goebel was certainly correct in questioning whether there existed sufficient

---

20. *Felony and Misdemeanor*, p. 19.
21. *Germania*, chapter 12, explains that fines are divided between king and kin: "pars multae regi vel civitati, pars ipsi qui vindicetur, vel propinquis exsolvitur."
22. Aethelberht cc. 6, 9. These laws have occasioned some discussion. H. G. Richardson and G. O. Sayles simply treat these chapters as referring to crimes in the king's presence. *Law and Legislation from Aethelberht to Magna Carta* (Edinburgh, 1966), pp. 4 n. 3, 10 n. 2. F. Lieberman, the editor of the Anglo-Saxon laws, took c. 6 on homicide as a fine for infraction of sovereignty, expressing doubt that the king was personal lord of every freeman. The term used, however, is *drihtinbeage*, which Attenborough in *Earliest English Kings* points out means "personal lord," and the equivalence between this fine and that for breaking the king's *mundbyrd* suggests that all freemen may have been regarded as being in the king's personal protection.

sense of public order to require the community be mollified for the commission of crimes, but he went too far when he denied the *fredus* had any penal character. A comparison with other codes suggests that Germanic kings could collect fines regardless of whether other composition was paid, and a seventh-century Frankish compilation commanded a church-breaker to pay forty *solidi* to the king as *fredus* because "he acted contrary to the law *(contra legem)*, did not respect the honor of the church, and had no reverence for God."[23]

But if these fines are penal, what crime is being punished? Some indication of the reasoning behind these fines can be gained by looking at other cases in which *fredus* was imposed. *Fredus* is mentioned five times in the *lex salica* and twice more in the early capitularies of the Frankish kings usually preserved with it.[24] Only one of these references, c. 24.7, which exempts children under 12 from the *fredus* if they commit homicide, appears to concern fines for lawbreaking of the kind we have just discussed, and only one other case concerns *fredus* paid to the king: c. 13.6, which sets the fine for rape of a girl under royal protection *(in verbum regis)*. The remaining five cases concern offenses to lords of lower rank than the king. Three involve rights of jurisdiction: c. 50.3 requires *fredus* be paid to a count if his intervention is required to enforce promises made in his court; c. 53 deals with the redemption of a man's hand from the cauldron used for the ordeal of boiling water; and c. 92 of the *Pactum pro tenore pacis* deals with cases where pursuit of a robber has crossed borders, which reserves *fredus* to the judge in whose jurisdiction the malefactor was apprehended. The last two chapters (35.9; 88) use the phrase *inter fredo et faido* to describe the compensation due a lord for harm which had come to his servant. In these cases there is no public or official dimension at all. The intent was simply to punish an offense to a social superior.

The same picture is found in Anglo-Saxon law. Aethelberht's *wites* for homicide and theft belong to a group of fines primarily concerned with violations of the king's protection or *mundbyrd*. Among the offenses specifically mentioned were fighting in the

23. Lex Alamannorum 3.3. For Goebel, see *Felony and Misdemeanor*, pp. 9 n. 14, 23. Goebel's position has received the support of J. M. Wallace-Hadrill, *The Long-Haired Kings and Other Studies in Frankish History* (London, 1962), p. 188.
24. The chapter numbers are taken from Eckhardt's edition of the *Pactus legis salicae*.

king's presence, harming his servants, or molesting the king's nobles as they came to answer his summons; the fine in each case was
50 s., the value of the king's *mundbyrd* and the sum exacted from
thieves and manslayers.[25] Again, too, it was possible to incur a fine
for offending a lord other than the king, although the price naturally rose with the status of the offended party. Perhaps worst of all,
from an offender's standpoint, was that the claims of the lords were
not mutually exclusive. The abundant evidence of the later Anglo-
Saxon codes reveals that an offender could owe *wites* to the lord of
the man he injured and to the lord of the place where the injury
occurred as well as to the king, with the *bot* or compensation to the
victim and his kin still to be paid. This elaborate system is simply
an extension of tendencies explicit in the earliest codes.[26]

The use of *fredus* and *wite* to uphold authority is consistent with
much else that we know of early medieval culture. Treason against
one's lord was a heinous crime, whether known by the borrowed
Roman term *laesa majestas* found in some early texts, or an offense
against the *ban* or power of command, or by the somewhat later
term *felonia*.[27] Yet what was offended was the lord as an individual, not as a representative of the public order—at least if we
take that term to mean a possession or interest of the whole community. This conclusion does not explain why theft or homicide
was thought deserving of *fredus*, but it opens up many possibilities.
Perhaps all subjects were simply regarded as the king's dependents
and therefore at least nominally under his protection. Whatever the
reason—and nothing in the codes obliges us to believe the matter
was thought through very clearly—the essential point is that fines
like *fredus* and *wite* reveal again the tendency of early medieval
people to reason in terms of hierarchy and authority when thinking
about their society.

The second category of compensations, those to individuals
whom one has harmed, takes us to the consideration of how people
thought about their peers. The bulk of the *lex salica*, as of any
Germanic code, is made up of such compositions—for thefts of
different kinds, for personal injuries, for homicides. Some of the

25. Aethelberht cc. 2–12.
26. See for example Hlothhere & Eadric, c. 12.
27. Wallace-Hadrill, *Early Germanic Kingship*, pp. 55; and Goebel, pp.
45–49, 91, especially pp. 46–49 where he notes the tendency of *ban* to
grow from a particular offense to a general category of insubordination.
For Anglo-Saxon denunciations of those who betrayed their lord, see
Chaney, *Cult of Kingship*, pp. 206–12.

later codes, Alfred's for example, are almost obsessively concerned with spelling out such details, specifying the sums to be paid for loss of teeth (8 shillings for a front tooth, 4 shillings for a molar, 15 shillings for an eyetooth) as well as the sums for loss of an arm, an eye, thumbs or fingers, and the nails of different fingers. In reading such catalogs one is reminded of modern insurance policies that list with grisly precision the payments the company will make for various degrees of maiming or disfigurement.

Behind this system lay the *faida* or bloodfeud of the injured party and his or her kin against the person, property, and kin of the injurer. Some historians explain the feud by placing it in a social context where public powers of coercion were too weak to restrain those who would break the peace; in these circumstances, they argue, "the vendetta . . . was not the law of the jungle but a duty regulated by custom that one owed to the community for maintenance of law and order."[28] Such a view would doubtless have surprised the barbarian invaders of Europe, who felt feud needed no such justification. Not all, perhaps, would have shared Attila's opinion that there was nothing more to the taste of a strong man than seeking vengeance with his own hands.[29] But everyone thought it was right to seek to do to others what they had done to you, and understood that failure to avenge oneself invited possible enemies to attack. The Beowulf poet can describe, as something obvious to all of his readers, the despair of a father unable to avenge the death of one son because another son, inadvertently, was the slayer.

> . . . He can raise
> His voice in sorrow, but revenge is impossible.
> . . . No son to come
> Matters, no future heir, to a father
> Forced to live through such misery.[30]

Even the clergy, whose doctrine set them firmly against the bloodshed of the feud, expected God to act as the avenger of their own injuries and other infringements of his law like "any head of a family or a warband."[31] Hot blood, justice, and prudence all de-

---

28. Wallace-Hadrill paraphrasing Whitelock, *Long-Haired Kings*, p. 3. For an excellent discussion of the feud see ibid., pp. 121–46.
29. Wallace-Hadrill, *Long-Haired Kings*, p. 114.
30. *Beowulf* (trans. by Burton Randall), ll. 2448–53.
31. Wallace-Hadrill, *Long-Haired Kings*, p. 127.

manded the feud, and when the first had cooled the last two motives could be satisfied by the provision of money compositions.

The relationship between composition and feud can be illustrated by a celebrated episode from Gregory of Tours's *History of
the Franks*.[32] Gregory had reason to be well-informed about this
feud, because it took place in the neighborhood of Tours, and he
himself had a role in re-establishing peace. The quarrel began at a
Christmas party given by Sichar and his friends, when one of the
guests killed a servant of the village priest. Gregory typically does
not explain the reasons for the killing—he tells us only that the
servant had been sent by the priest to invite the partygoers to his
house, which scarcely seems provocation for a killing—nor does he
name the killer. Presumably it was Austregisil or a connection of
his since it was he that Sichar, a friend of the priest, waited for,
armed, at the church. This probably was not an ambush, for
Austregisil had heard of Sichar's intentions and came to find him.
A "pitched battle" ensued, and Sichar fled, leaving four wounded
servants, money, and clothes in the priest's house. Austregisil then
broke into the priest's house, seized Sichar's property, and killed the
four servants.

Sometime afterwards the first effort was made to compose the
differences. The parties appeared before a tribunal (*iudicium civ-
ium*) which ruled that Austregisil, who had committed homicide
and taken goods without witnesses, should pay the legal penalties.
A preliminary agreement to pay the compensation was reached, but
a few days later Sichar heard his property was still in the hands of
Austregisil's kinsman Auno and others. Disregarding the agreement
that was to have ended the feud, Sichar then broke into Auno's
house with armed men at night, killed those he found there, and
stole their property and cattle. Gregory himself intervened at this
point, joining with the judge to summon the feuding parties before
him, exhorting them to establish a composition that would end the
violence, and offering to pay the sum with the church's money if
the party who owed compensation was unable to pay it. Auno's son
Chramnesind refused to compose his differences with Sichar and,
when he heard erroneously that Sichar had been killed by a slave,
he gathered his family and friends to raid Sichar's house. The parties were summoned again by the judge to the city, where the composition owed Chramnesind was reduced by half on account of the

32. *HF* vii.47; ix.19. See Wallace-Hadrill's comments, *Long-Haired Kings*,
pp. 139–42, as well as Auerbach's essay on Gregory in *Mimesis* which
focuses on these chapters.

damage he inflicted on the house of Sichar and others in the raid. (Gregory comments that this action, though against the law, was intended to restore peace.) The church then paid the money as it had promised, and the parties swore solemn oaths not to rise in arms against each other. "And so," Gregory concluded, "the fighting came to an end."

Composition, as this episode instructs us, was not so much a consequence of public policy as a bargain between the warring kins. External authorities had no ability to impose a settlement. The bishop, judge, and townsmen were at best arbitrators whose proposals either side could reject, and others of Gregory's stories show that the king was equally powerless to command the end to a feud. Occasionally, even after a final concord, there could be a return to feud, as there was in this particular case when Sichar had the poor judgment to tell Chramnesind, now his friend, that he should be thankful since his prosperity was due to the compensation he had received for his relatives' deaths. Saying to himself, "If I do not avenge the death of my kinsmen I ought to forfeit the name of man and be called a weak woman," Chramnesind doused the lamps, split Sichar's head, and—to indicate the killing was in pursuit of feud—stripped the body and hung it on a fencepost. And when he afterward told his story to the king (as he had to do for Sichar was under the queen's protection) he escaped despite the queen's anger because the killing was held to be *super se*: for his honor or of necessity.

The relentless demand for vengeance reminds us that Germanic law was preeminently a law governing the relations of autonomous individuals. The system of compositions helped limit the destructiveness of the feud, a purpose aided in some places by kings who decreed that the feud could be visited only on the person of the offender, that his kin should not be molested as long as they offered him no aid. This kind of intervention could take interesting shapes: in Spain, Visigothic law instructed judges to order floggings, administered by the victim, as composition for certain minor beatings. But as long as it remained the task of the victim to bring malefactors to justice, these expedients did little to create a conception of public order, and society as a whole continued to feel no injury in crimes against its members.

VALUES

A society such as we have been considering, in which there is no consciousness of obligation to the whole community, is bound to

have conceptions of right and wrong very different from our own:
instead of the focus being on whether a person has shown himself a good member of society, the concern is with how one autonomous individual deals with another. In Germanic law, this difference is perhaps brought home most forcibly in the attitude toward clandestine crimes, which the codes are unanimous in regarding with special horror. In general, the thought appears to have been that while violence was acceptable, underhandedness that deprived the other fellow of an even chance was not. Theft, for example, was invariably subjected to much higher rates of composition than robbery—commonly ninefold instead of fourfold restitution—although robbery necessarily entailed a risk of physical violence absent in theft. Similarly, murder [Anglo-Saxon = *morth*, Latin = *murdrum*], or homicides committed in secret, and killings accomplished through ambush and poisoning were punished more severely than other homicides. Often secret homicides were treated as unemendable, requiring the death of the slayer without possibility of composition. In these provisions one catches an echo of the Old West of myth and movie, where men of integrity may defend their interests and their honor in a fair fight but only backshooters, the lowest of the low, would attack their enemies from hiding.[33]

A second area of interest is Germanic conceptions of human worth. In modern law, and this idea can be traced back at least to the thirteenth century, status is regarded as an incidental characteristic that modifies but does not alter one's essential humanity. The codes, however, attribute greater value to higher-ranking persons by assigning them a higher *wergild* (literally, man-price) than ordinary freemen or unfree persons. Frankish law, for example, valued the life of a Frank at twice the price of a Roman and that of a close associate of the king at three times the price of an ordinary freeman. Similar scales could be cited for any of the Germanic tribes.

Since modern tort law now makes it more expensive to run over a prosperous businessman than a waiter in a late-night restaurant, these provisions seem perhaps less strange today than they did to historians of a hundred years ago. But the values described by wergilds went beyond earning ability to a statement of a person's worth that was "real" both in Piaget's sense and in its applicability to a wide variety of situations. In legal systems where compurgation was practiced, the size of the oath was specified not as a

33. On theft, see *Law and Society in the Visigothic Kingdom*, pp. 251–58; Pollock and Maitland, *Hist. Eng. Law.*, 2: 485–61; Liebermann, *Gesetze Angelsachsen*, 2: 587 Mord 2. See 2 Aethelstan 6 for an example of legislation against homicide by sorcery.

number of persons who had to swear but the sum their wergilds had to total; thus the oath of a high-ranking individual was worth more than one of ordinary rank.[34] All Germanic systems, moreover, used the wergild to determine the price for which a condemned person might repurchase his or her life. A nice illustration of this latter practice is provided by the Burgundian king Sigismund's judgment in a case dealing with fornication by a woman who had betrothed herself by accepting part of her marriage price from a suitor. (She was a widow; had it been her first marriage, the money would have gone to her kin.) Though custom, declared Sigismund, would require the death of both the woman and her lover, "in consideration of the holy days [Easter?]" the king ruled that the two could redeem themselves by payment to the wronged fiancé of their respective wergilds, 300 solidi in her case, 150 solidi in his. This rule, which was universal in Germanic Europe, resulted in a situation perhaps unique in legal history in which higher-ranking individuals paid stiffer punishments for the same act than those of less privileged classes.[35]

The same case also opens a window on the question of unintentional harms, an issue to whose importance in moral reasoning Piaget forcefully drew attention, for as part of his judgment Sigismund held that the man might be quit of all payment if he could prove by his own oath and that of eleven others that he was unaware of the woman's betrothal. Though Sigismund was clearly trying to take intention into account, he was by no means confident that he was right to do so: he commanded that in the future "whoever incurs that guilt of such a deed not only may sustain the loss of his property, but also be punished by the loss of his life. For it is preferable that the multitude be corrected by the condemnation of a few than that the appearance of unsuitable moderation introduce a pretext which may contribute to the license of delinquency." Sigismund's uncertainty is understandable once we realize that Germanic law rarely tried to take into account the intention of an actor when assessing punishment. There is nothing unusual in this. Greek legend, for example, tells us that Oedipus was punished for

34. For Anglo-Saxon law, see Ine 14, 46, 52, etc. where the value of oaths is expressed as a sum of the value of compurgators. Lombard practices are discussed by Drew in the preface to her translation to the Lombard codes and in *Notes on Lombard Institutions*, Rice Institute Pamphlet, vol. 48.2 (Houston, 1956).

35. *Lex Burgundionum*, 52. The translation here and below is by Drew. See also *Pactum pro tenore pacis*, 3.3; Ine 15.

parricide and incest though he committed neither crime knowingly. (It was only with *Oedipus at Colonus*, one of Sophocles's last plays, that Oedipus finally makes the plea we expect all along: that he was innocent because he intended no harm.) The same reasoning commonly appears in Germanic literature, most notably in the vengeance taken on Hodur for accidentally slaying Baldur.[36] One need not assume such tragedies were often or ever acted out to see that the poignancy of such stories depended on the idea that unintentional harms ought to be paid for.

Quite different demands are placed on law-givers than on poets, but, though the rules stated in the codes are often more complex than the simple vengeance exacted in myth, exceptions to the principle of objective responsibility are few in number and restricted in application. Salic law has little at all to say about intention. Some of the other codes are more complex in their attitude, as when Lombard law appears to take into account the state of mind of the offender by referring to acts committed maliciously, knowingly, lustfully, or with premeditation *(ex priori disposito)*. But only rarely did the question of intention have any legal significance. Often a word or phrase seems merely to have added emphasis, as when Rothar's code addresses the cases of a person who "intentionally" *(iniquo animo)* throws a freeman from his horse (c. 30), who "maliciously" *(doloso animo)* accuses his nephew of being born in adultery (c. 164), or "deliberately and with evil intent" *(asto animo, quod est voluntarie)* burns another's house. In none of these cases, as in the vast majority of laws that refer in this way to mental states, was provison made for determining what the perpetrator's intention actually was or were different penalties prescribed for unintentional wrongs.[37] The most confusing situation existed in Visigothic Spain, where a law of Euric's—from the fifth century when Roman influence may still have been strong—tried to distin-

36. For a discussion of Germanic legends' handling of unintentional acts, see E. Kaufmann, *Die Erfolgshaftung*, Frankfurter Wissenschaftliche Beitrage no. 16 (Frankfurt, 1958), pp. 23–24; Heinrich Brunner, "Ueber absichtlose Missetat in altdeutsch Strafrecht," in *Forshungen* (Stuttgart, 1894), p. 488 ff.

37. Rothar's code has been analyzed in detail by Kaufmann, *Erfolgshaftung*, who cites a number of laws where the language of the code appears to point toward an interest in intention. In only three cases, however, are different punishments imposed for those who can prove innocent intention: that of a boatsman who conveys a criminal to safety (c. 265), that of a herdsman whose animals destroy crops (c. 344), and that of a man who sells another's property (c. 229). For proof of intention by oath, see below.

guish between willful and accidental killings. What this law meant in actual practice is hard to say, however, for other of Euric's enactments provided for payment of wergild in cases of accidental homicides, and a late seventh-century law specifically stated that "whoever should have killed a man, whether intending to or not intending to *(volens aut nolens)*, . . . let him be handed over into the *potestas* of the parents or the next of kin of the deceased."[38] Evidently, the belief that retribution was just had triumphed over the subtleties of Roman law.

Whether the lack of interest in intention derives from a belief that a person ought to be responsible for the consequences of his or her actions or from a tendency to regard all consequences as intentional is impossible to say. The evidence is very contradictory, and in all likelihood there was no coherent theory.[39] But the failure of the codes to take intention into account does not, as some legal historians have suggested, result from the difficulty of making judicial inquiries into the internal workings of the mind. Judgments of God were, at least in theory, entirely suitable for determining questions of intention, and in the few cases where intention was thought crucial, as in Sigismund's judgment on the adulterer, no one seems to have doubted that oaths or ordeals could reveal the truth.[40] It was not the availability of proof but a belief that guilty deeds ought to be paid for that seems to be the main concern.

38. King, *Law and Society*, pp. 259–63. The text quoted was cited by F. B. Sayre, "Mens Rea," *Harvard Law Review* 45 (1932): 977, who concluded (p. 981) that "up to the twelfth century the conception of *mens rea* in anything like its modern sense was non-existent." Anglo-Saxon law, particularly Alfred's code and some eleventh-century materials, offers a few mitigations of this pattern, as does the chapter of the Burgundian code on chance occurrences (c. 15), where, however, it is also clear that the idea of exempting accidental harms was a new one, probably borrowed from Roman law. But these exceptions are too rare and applied with too much uncertainty substantially to affect my case. See, on this, my comments in "The Evolution of Medieval Mentalities: A Cognitive-Structural Approach," *American Historical Review* 83 (1978): 578–79, and the references there.

39. But see C. R. Hallpike, *Foundations of Primitive Thought* (Oxford, 1979), who notes (pp. 467–70) that the Azande believe all witchcraft is deliberate even though those accused of witchcraft, aware that they have done nothing intentionally, often claim that their witchcraft operated unconsciously.

40. Alfred permitted a man whose weapon was used by another in a slaying to clear himself by oath, and similar provisions can be found in other codes. Alfred c. 15.2a; cf. also Alfred c. 36.

Since the amount of compensation had to meet the outraged party's sense of injury, we can assume with some confidence that the severity of the compositions set by the codes corresponds to the degree of harm different acts were felt to have inflicted. If these evaluations of harm often differ significantly from our own, that is only to be expected for people whose conception of society imposed on them no positive obligations to their peers. Reparations and fairness were their chief concern, and in calculating a punishment they rarely tried to penetrate the facts on the surface of events. "The rank of the slayer, the rank of the slain, the rank of their respective lords, the sacredness of the day on which the deed was done, the ownership of the place at which the deed was done—these [Maitland remarked] are the facts which our earliest ancestors weigh when they have to mete out punishment."[41] In this choice of facts we can observe the working of a mentality very different from our own.

TRIAL AND JUDGMENT

Although of procedure and proof (important issues in any sophisticated system of law) the codes have little specific to say, enough can be gathered from other sources for us to be fairly certain how trials were conducted. Pleading apparently had to be conducted according to strictly prescribed forms, and any deviation from the proper ritual exposed a party to penalties and possibly entailed the loss of his or her case. The emphasis on formal exactness was often at the expense of any effort by the court to determine the facts of the case; questions of evidence in general loomed less large than they do today, in part because it tended to be assumed that the only certain facts were those known to all. In many, perhaps most, cases the key issue for the court to decide was not the truth of the matter but which proof—and this usually meant some kind of judgment of God—was to be employed to resolve the dispute.

Trial might be avoided altogether if the criminal could be caught redhanded at the scene of the crime, and every effort was bent to bring about this result. To aid the capture and prevent the wrongdoer from later denying his deed, the hue and cry was raised immediately upon the discovery of a crime. Failure to raise the hue, or to respond when it was raised, opened a person to suspicion and

41. "The Early History of Malice Aforethought," *Collected Papers* (Cambridge, 1911), p. 328.

possibly to a fine.[42] If the hue and cry did succeed in catching the malefactor in the act or with the evidence on him, he was guilty of a "hand-having" crime and—his deed having been publicized by the hue—he was dealt with by a summary process. A thief might have the goods bound to his back. He was tried directly without being permitted to say one word in his defense and then hanged, beheaded, or thrown over a cliff with the wronged party perhaps acting as executioner. One curious feature of this procedure was the heavier penalties paid by hand-having criminals than by those who escaped and were later brought to trial; a thief caught in the act might be killed while one who escaped might need only to pay compensation. Such rules betray cognitive processes that recognize rules not as deriving from general moral principles but as tied to concrete circumstances.

In cases where the offender escaped immediate apprehension, accusations took the form of an oath stating the facts of the case, though the oath might be omitted if there was material evidence pointing toward the accused. The material evidence might be slight —a trail leading into his land that he could not show led out again, or a bramble scratch incurred in flight—but its existence was important because it excused the accuser from the risks of fine to which he or she ordinarily would be vulnerable if the defendant proved his innocence.[43] After the accusation was made, the accused was obliged to deny the charge word for word. Failure to make the denial in the proper form resulted in immediate conviction.

When both accusation and denial had been made in the correct form, it was up to the court to decide which would be the method of proof. In most cases the choices came down to judgments of God: compurgation, battle, and ordeals. Though all these tests were held to be equally valid, they were not—paradoxically to our way of thinking—considered equally difficult to make and in time a complicated body of jurisprudence grew up to decide which test ought to be used. Widely regarded to be the easiest was compurgation, in which the swearing party was obliged to bring to court

42. Goebel, *Felony and Misdemeanor*, pp. 66–68, on the *Pactum pro tenore pacis* and, for Anglo-Saxon law, Pollock and Maitland, *Hist. Eng. Law*, 2: 578–79.

43. Goebel, *Felony and Misdemeanor*, pp. 41–43; an example from Anglo-Saxon law is given in Dorothy Whitelock, *The Beginning of English Society* (London, 1952), p. 148; Pollock and Maitland, *Hist. Eng. Law*, 1: 40; 2: 157. On liability for false accusations: Lex salica cc. 18, 48, 49; P. D. King, *Law and Society*, pp. 91–92.

compurgators or oath-helpers ready to swear to his or her innocence. Courts could make the oath more difficult by requiring the
accused to bring more compurgators or, depending on the severity
of the case, by demanding an oath of triple difficulty. (By the
twelfth century oaths had been devised that made some litigants
prefer the hot iron.) Courts could also bar a man who had been
accused before of purging himself by oath and send him directly to
ordeal, or they could permit his accuser to prove his charge by
bringing to court his own compurgators to support his accusation.[44] Finally, because oath helpers could sometimes be recruited
by promises of payment, some kings (the Burgundians among others) permitted an accuser to refuse the offered oath and insist that
one of the oath-helpers settle the case by judicial duel. If the accuser
won the duel all the oath-helpers were fined though they had not
sworn at all.[45]

Though the court, through its assignment of proof, could affect
the outcome of a case, the real appeal was to God, and one could
be certain of obtaining divine judgment only if rituals were followed exactly. The litigants fought not to persuade human judges
but to win divine favor while the court and the community stood
by as spectators—their judgment was confined to points of procedure. I have said enough about ordeals already for no detailed
description to be needed here; it is enough to observe that the fact
that all judgments of God had clearly defined rituals could only
have enhanced the formal, almost liturgical quality of the rest of
the proceedings in which formal statement met formal denial.

Monasticism

If the value of law as evidence for mentalities stems from its roots
in everyday life, the interest in monasticism is due to its freedom
from practical restrictions. Founders of monasteries began anew in
ways secular leaders never could, for they could select or write a
rule that embodied their idea of Christian life, without being bound
by a community already set in its ways. Further, since monastic

44. Whitelock, *English Society*, pp. 139–47. Rebecca Colman points out
that these rules mitigated the reliance on ordeal, though I think she overstates the discretion the doomsmen enjoyed in applying them. "Reason and
Unreason in Early Medieval Law," *Journal of Interdiciplinary History* 4
(1974): 571–92.
45. *Lex Burgundionum*, 45.

authority was spiritual, not temporal, the availability of coercive force was not a problem to abbots as it might be to kings, while the absence of large numbers of people or great distances made feasible arrangements of government that were impractical for kingdoms.

Another reason for studying monasticism is the opportunity it provides for tracing the development of traditions going back to the ancient church. Cenobitism, the gathering of monks into communities around spiritual leaders, originated in Egypt as an ascetic alternative to the solitary life of hermits. By the mid-fifth century a small but important literature existed in Latin: the rule of St. Basil, translated from the Greek; a brief informal rule of Augustine; and the *Conferences* and *Institutes* of Cassian, a younger contemporary of Augustine. Because monastic writers of the early Middle Ages knew these works and usually tried to be faithful to them, the departures from ancient models provide important evidence of the difference in outlook between the late classical and early medieval worlds.

For a study of early medieval monasticism the choice of the Rule of St. Benedict is an obvious one.[46] It was written sometime in the middle of the sixth century and possibly not even by Benedict, but little is known of the Rule in its first half century, and it does not seem to have spread far from its origins in central Italy. At the end of the sixth century, however, Gregory the Great devoted an entire book of his *Dialogues* to the life and miracles of St. Benedict, and the fortunes of the Rule rose steadily from that time on. By the end of the seventh century most of the major houses in Gaul used some form of the Benedictine Rule, and in the eighth century missionaries—notably Sts. Boniface and Willibrord—carried the rule with them into Germany. Though it was often in conjunction with another rule (particularly that of the Irish missionary Colomba) that monasteries of this period adopted the Rule, there can be no doubt about its popularity before 800, and it was soon to drive all others from the field.[47]

46. The Rule of Saint Benedict [= RB] is available in a number of good editions. I have used that of Adalbert de Vogüé in the series *Sources Chrétiennes* (vols. 181–86). De Vogüé edited the *Regula Magistri* [= RM] in the same series (vols. 105–7) and the commentary included in the edition of the Benedictine Rule does an excellent job of placing the Rule in its textual and historical context. On the length of the Benedictine Rule see 181: 29–30. *La communauté et l'abbé dans la Règle de Saint Benoît* (Paris, 1961), also by de Vogüé, develops certain key issues in greater detail.

47. F. Prinz, *Frühes Mönchtum in Frankreich* (Munich, Vienna, 1965), especially pp. 263–92.

Though short by some standards—the faculty handbook of my university is longer—its brevity is not, as has sometimes been suggested, the source of its popularity. Quite the contrary. Only one postclassical rule, the *Regula Magistri*, is longer; the next longest to the Benedictine Rule is a third shorter, and many are concise enough to fill only a few pages in a modern edition that requires twenty-two for the Benedictine Rule. This extra length came about because the Rule made provision for many aspects of monastic life that other rules left unspecified, and it was certainly this thoroughness, which relieved individual monks of the doubts that might come from consciously deciding their own customs, that accounts for much of the Rule's popularity. These details, moreover, have the additional value of enabling us to grasp with exceptional clarity the intention of the Rule's author.

If one reason for beginning with the Benedictine Rule is its popularity, another is its kinship to the rest of Latin monasticism.[48] The authors of rules in the barbarian west did not feel obliged to rely on their own inventiveness in drafting their prescriptions, and it is unlikely their efforts would have met much approval if they had. Their method, instead, was to mine sources they knew for passages and ideas they could incorporate into their own text. Sources did not have to be of any great antiquity to be eligible for this kind of veneration; founders of monasteries freely used rules only a generation or two old or the customs of monasteries they admired to supplement what they could glean from the Bible or patristic writers.

For a long time the Benedictine Rule was thought to stand apart from this pattern of imitation as an original masterpiece, but since World War II this view has been drastically altered.[49] A careful study of the *Regula Magistri*, the Rule of the Master, has revealed that it was a text older than the Rule itself, and not, as used to be supposed, a later imitation. The passages shared by the two rules— and these include nearly all the famous passages of the Benedictine Rule—were therefore written by the unknown Master rather than

48. On the place of the Rule in monastic tradition see A. de Vogüé, "Sub Regula vel sub Abbate: the Theological Significance of the Ancient Monastic Rules," in *Rule and Life: An Interdisciplinary Symposium*, ed. M. Basil Pennington (Cistercian Studies Series no. 12) (Spencer, Mass., 1971), pp. 21–64.

49. On the Rule of the Master see, in addition to de Vogüé's works, R. W. Southern, *Western Society and the Church in the Middle Ages* (Baltimore, 1970), pp. 218–23; David Knowles, *Great Historical Enterprises* (London, 1963), pp. 135–66.

by Benedict. Benedict's contribution was still considerable, for in paring the Rule of the Master down by two-thirds he removed many wordy passages and contradictions, and he devised arrangements for the daily functioning of the monastery far more workable than those the Master had envisioned, but it is no longer possible to view his work as a "revolution in monasticism." It was as a summation of monastic tradition more than as innovation that the Benedictine Rule found such wide acceptance.

In what follows we shall be concerned with the Rule's treatment of three of the issues that arose in our consideration of early medieval law: the sources of authority, the conception of community, and the value placed on intention.

ABBOT AND MONK

If one omits the sections of the Rule setting down the liturgical routine of the monastery, most of what remains describes either the abbot's duties toward the monks or the monks' duties toward him. The concentration on this relationship is necessary not because it is complicated, for it is not, but because it is the only relationship Benedict conceived to be of any importance. The abbot's salvation depended on the skill of his stewardship; the monk's on the completeness of his submission.

The success of the Rule has made this conception of monastic organization so familiar that it is with some surprise that one turns to early monastic literature such as the rule of St. Basil.[50] Writing in the fourth century, Basil took up the responsibilities of the "superintendent" only infrequently in his more than 200 chapters, some of which were not even translated into Latin by Rufinus. It is clear, however, that the superintendent's authority is primarily moral

50. There exists no Greek text precisely equivalent to the Latin version of Basil's rules. The traditional opinion has been that Rufinus abridged two Greek works, the long and short rules, in making his translation, but the existence of a Syriac version equivalent to the Latin text led J. Gribomont to argue that both the Latin and Syriac translations were made from an early draft that Basil later revised into the long and short rules. *Histoire du texte des ascétiques de S. Basile* (Louvain, 1953). I find Gribomont's hypothesis excessively complicated since his evidence for a Greek original—a sixth-century scholia describing a rule by Basil—is not conclusive. It appears more probable that the Syriac translation was made from Rufinus's Latin text than that a Greek text common in the fourth and fifth centuries was lost while other works of Basil, apparently less well-known then, survived.

rather than disciplinary. In one of the sections omitted from the
Latin version, Basil made the suggestion, inconceivable for Bene- dictine monasticism, that it was possible for a community to have two or more superiors. (An example of the same arrangement is given in Cassian, who in a similar spirit rated the value of submis- sion to a superior only last in the list of advantages of cenobitic life.)[51] In a further recognition of the essentially spiritual role of the superintendent, moreover, Basil also recommended that heads of communities regularly meet together for mutual criticism.

The author of the Benedictine Rule was not ignorant of the older models; he knew and recommended the works of Basil and Cas- sian. But his efforts to remain faithful to them only serve to em- phasize how radically different his own cognitive processes were from those of his models. For when he thought about a monastery, the important relationships were not the horizontal ones between individual monks, but the vertical, unilateral relationship between abbot and monk. The direction of monastic spirituality shifted ac- cordingly, from charity and love to obedience. Attention was now focused on the relationship between abbot and monk, and with the abbot elevated over the rest of the monks by his authority and relationship to God the patristic conception of community disap- peared without a trace, to be revived only in the eleventh and twelfth centuries. The patristic monastery had been recast in the image of the Germanic kingdoms.

The orientation toward hierarchy of early medieval cognition in- evitably transformed this conception of the role of authority within the community. The Benedictine abbot's position in the monastery is captured by the words the Rule uses to describe him: *abba* (fa- ther), *doctor* (teacher), *maior* (superior), *pastor* (shepherd).[52] To the abbot's judgment are left the vital issues of discipline and gov- ernment; he had full discretion in imposing or lifting punishments, in determining the food and clothing of the monks, in caring for

51. Basil, *Regula fusius tractatae*, cc. 35, 42. This rule is available in an English translation as "The Long Rules" in *Saint Basil's Ascetical Works*, trans. M. Monica Wagner (New York, 1950), pp. 223–337 [volume 9 of the series *Fathers of the Church*]. For Cassian on multiple abbots, see *Conferences*, xix.1, where Abbot John is introduced as a member of the cenobium of Abbot Paul. In his discussion of the advantages of cenobitic life over the existence of a hermit Cassian listed freedom from the tempta- tion to take pride in one's asceticism and the reduced burden of preparing food and welcoming guests ahead of the spiritual advantages of submission to a superior.
52. De Vogüé, *La communauté et l'abbé*, p. 141.

the sick, in welcoming pilgrims and guests. He is to consult with the brothers on important business—the Rule is not specific about what this might include—but he is in no way bound to follow their advice. If these provisions remind us of the Germanic king, the vicar of Christ who might consult others but made law by his word alone, they struck one ninth-century writer the same way for he adapted sections of his treatise on the king to describe the abbot in his work on monasticism.[53]

Because the abbot was the center of monastic life, his selection was a problem of considerable importance. The Rule of the Master provided that a dying abbot might appoint his own successor or, if his death came unexpectedly, that the successor be chosen by the local bishop. The Master placed some emphasis on this arrangement; indeed, in a chapter quite at variance with the rule's usual stress on humility, he described in some detail how the monks were to be encouraged to compete for the designation. They were, he wrote, "to pant with thirst for this honor, each one eager to display holy works in what is good according to the precepts of God."[54] All this the author of the Benedictine Rule omitted, however, establishing instead that the community make the choice. Only if the community chose as abbot an unworthy person who consented to its vices was the local bishop to intervene and name an abbot.

In providing for an elected abbot, Benedict was returning to earlier monastic custom, and perhaps expressing some doubt about the unconditional trust the Master put in the abbot's judgment.[55] But we must not suppose the Rule meant to suggest the abbot's power in any way derived from the community. It was hardly possible that it could, for the monks have no corporate existence in the rule: apart from electing the abbot, the monks are mentioned as gathered together only to give advice to the abbot—advice he is free to ignore. In any case, Benedict's conception of the monastery was too hierarchical to recognize that the abbot might have obligations to those he ruled, and it is God's punishment rather than breach of faith with the monks that the abbot is cautioned against. The majority of the admonitions to remember the last judgment— and there are many, because the God of the Rule is more vengeful than loving—are directed against the abbot. "Let the abbot remember that there will be discussion of his teaching and the obedience

53. Wallace-Hadrill, *Early Germanic Kingship*, pp. 73–74, referring to Abbot Smaragdus.
54. *RM*, c. 92.71.
55. *La communauté et l'abbé*, pp. 348–67.

of his disciples at the dread judgment of God." "Yet in all his judgments let the abbot think upon the retribution of God." "Yet let the abbot keep in mind that he will render account to God for all his judgments."[56] These warnings come throughout the Rule and at unexpected points. The last two quotations, for example, end the chapters on the clothing of the monks and on the prior.

The obedience the abbot owed God, the monks owed the abbot. Twice the Rule describes the abbot as "acting in the place of Christ"; the name *abba* itself was one commonly applied to Christ, and a term the Bible had used to refer to God the father.[57] The abbot, accordingly, is to be obeyed as if he were God: instantly. "The first degree of humility is obedience without delay" begins the fifth chapter. "As soon as anything has been ordered by the abbot *(maior)* let [the monks] not know how to endure delay in doing it, as if it were divinely ordered." Complaining about the abbot's commands is forbidden in the strongest language. "Above all," the rule says in two places, "there is to be no murmuring." The admonition against murmuring—the best colloquial translation would be griping—is repeated seven times in all. The seriousness with which complaints about the quantity of drink, kitchen work, or waiting on guests is regarded leaves no doubt about the Rule's desire that the abbot find the monks totally compliant to his will.

MONK AND COMMUNITY

Instead of subordination to an abbot, both Basil and Cassian saw the opportunity for a communal existence as the essential feature of cenobitic asceticism and the reason for its superiority to a hermitic existence. Man, Basil wrote, was a social being. "Who does not know that man is a humane and gregarious animal, and not wild or unsocial. For what is more characteristic of our nature than to long for one another, and to need each other, and to love what is needed."[58] In addition to providing an arena for men to express their social impulses—and to obey God's injunction to love one's neighbor—communal living had the further advantage of helping monks achieve their primary objective of renouncing mundane concerns. Chores could be divided among the brothers so that none

56. *RB*, cc. 2.6; 55.22; 65.22.
57. *La communauté et l'abbé*, p. 453.
58. *PL* 103: 491C.

would be overburdened, vainglory avoided more easily since all would share the same fare, and the brothers could assist their fellows' striving for humility by serving as examples and correcting each other's faults.[59]

Just as the shift in reasoning between the fourth and sixth centuries had elevated the abbot, it drastically reduced the role of fraternity and community. The author of the Rule does not speak of fraternity or mutual affection between the monks; indeed, he rarely refers at all to the relations between monks. This omission does not reflect reality. Monastic histories and other documents in which monks wrote about their communities make it plain that the distinctive character of individual monks was recognized, and that the members of the community felt affection for one another. But early medieval cognition, with its attention rigorously focused on obedience and authority, had no way of thinking about such relationships as important. While they existed as social facts, because they had no intellectual value the authors of monastic constitutions omitted them from their scheme.

Thus when the author of the Rule reflected on the community, what he described was a hierarchy within the body of monks. In chapter 3, for example, where he writes of the abbot's hearing the advice of the monks, he feels the need to justify inviting the younger monks at all by explaining that God may speak through the youngest. In chapter 63, he established that the order of the brothers should follow the dates of their entrance into the monastery and sets down as a general principle that "juniors should honor their seniors and seniors love their juniors." This rule, rephrased in chapter 71—"let all the juniors obey their seniors with love and diligence"—contrasts instructively with Romans 12:10, which is quoted in the same passage: "Be joined in a brotherhood of mutual love, trying to outdo one another in showing respect."[60] Where Paul had urged mutual love, therefore, the Benedictine Rule substituted obedience and hierarchy.

SPIRITUALITY INTERIOR AND EXTERIOR

A final area where one can observe the effect of changing cognition upon monastic organization is in the conception of asceticism. Withdrawal from the world and its pleasures is, of course, essen-

59. *PL* 103: 494–96.
60. De Vogüé, *La communauté et l'abbé*, pp. 348–67.

tial to monasticism in any period, but early monastic writers had stressed the point that asceticism was not an end in itself. Their focus, instead, was on the psychology of monastic life. One can open Cassian's *Conferences*, for example, to almost any page and find discussions that carefully point out the difference between externally correct behavior and true, internal piety. The very first conference treats peace of mind as the goal of the monk: "fastings, vigils, meditation on the Scriptures, self-denial, and the abnegation of all possessions are not perfection but aids to perfection. . . . He will practice these exercises to no purpose who is contented with these as if they were the highest good."[61] Other conferences discuss topics such as renunciations ("A renunciation in body alone . . . will not do us any good if we do not succeed in achieving that renunciation in heart which is far higher and more valuable"),[62] prayer (ix), friendship (xvi), and penitence (xx). Cassian's discourses could be quite detailed and were vivid enough that the nineteenth-century translator of them into English discreetly omitted those on chastity and nocturnal illusions.

By the time of the Benedictine Rule, however, this concern to distinguish thought from behavior had disappeared. The Rule itself opposes thought to behavior in three places. In one, as we would expect, the necessity to be pure in intention is given a higher place than the desired outward behavior. But in the other two the implication seems to be that living up to an ideal in action is more important than living up to it in thought.[63] This confusion extends to the famous ladder of humility, which is the Rule's most detailed account of the objectives of monastic life. The steps of the ladder, borrowed by the author of the Rule from the Rule of the Master, themselves derive from a passage in Cassian's *Institutes*.[64] Cassian had seen two steps—fear of God to be transcended by love of God—and had described ten "signs" of the first kind of humility. The Master altered the plan by making fear of God the first step, developing the ten signs into eleven steps leading to love of God,

61. *Conferences*, i.7; trans. *Nicene and Post Nicene Fathers*, 11: 298.
62. *Conferences*, iii.7; trans. *Nicene and Post Nicene Fathers*, 11: 328.
63. The first of these instances is RB 7.51, a paraphrase of Cassian, *Institutes* iv.39: Septimus humilitatis gradus est si omnibus se inferiorem et viliorem non solum sua lingua pronuntiet, sed etiam intimo cordis creat affectu. . . . Contrary cases are RB 5.17: Nam, cum malo animo si oboedit discipulus et non solum ore sed etiam in corde si murmuraverit; and RB 7.62: Duodecimus humilitatis gradus est si non solum corde monachus sed etiam ipso corpore humilitatem videntibus se semper indicet.
64. *Insti.* iv.39.

and adding appropriate passages of scripture to what had been a bare list. The result is an impressive statement, yet by converting the signs to steps the Master (and after him the author of the Rule) also destroyed the logic of the original passage. Not only is the order of the steps by no means progressive: in what sense, for example, is it better to be silent (step 9) than to be content with mean provisions (step 6), or to look downward (step 12) than to remain silent? But what had been to Cassian exterior signs of interior states became acts of value in themselves, a serious distortion of the meaning of Cassian's list. The Master and Benedict in fact speak of ascending the ladder "by our acts."

The confusion between behavior and intention is not limited to verbal formulas that, it might be thought, the author of the Rule expected to be supplemented by other sources. It went to the heart of monastic society, the recruitment of the monks themselves, for instead of voluntarily joining the monastery as adults, many Benedictine monks entered as children, oblates given by their parents and preferably accompanied by gifts of property as well. The presence of children in monasteries was not itself an innovation. Basil had regarded it as an act of charity for monks to receive children— both boys and girls—and he gave detailed directions for their upbringing. But Basil had not assumed the children raised in the monastery would inevitably go on to be monks themselves. No ritual marked their entry into the community, though Basil advised the reception of children from their parents (as opposed to the taking in of orphans, which was a Christian duty) should be accomplished "before many witnesses" to avoid any imputation of wrongdoing. Only when the children were old enough to understand what they were doing were they permitted to make a vow of chastity, and then in the presence of ecclesiatical officials called in as witnesses to the decision. "One who does not wish to submit to the life of virginity . . . should be dismissed in the presence of the same witnesses. He who makes a vow, however, after a great amount of careful deliberation which he should be allowed to engage in for several days, so that we may not appear to be kidnapping him, should be received forthwith and made a member of the community."[65]

Though Basil's concern for witnesses suggests it was not unheard of even in his time for parents to make vows for their children—a conclusion supported by other evidence—the practice was still rare

65. *Regula fusius tractatae*, trans. Wagner, pp. 267–68. Only part of this chapter was translated by Rufinus (*PL* 103: 498C ff.), perhaps itself evidence for a stronger tendency toward oblation in the West than the East already by the fourth century.

and not altogether approved.[66] The Rule, however, countenances
oblation—which even the Master had not recognized—by setting down the procedure by which boys were to be received, describing the punishments they were to be given for their faults, and taking their presence in the monastery entirely for granted. It is impossible to be certain what percentage of the sixth- or seventh-century monastic population left the secular world through no decision of their own, but the number was certainly large and by the tenth century probably came to half or more of the total number of monks. The Rule reveals, moveover, how interest had shifted from the profession of the child to the oblation of the parents. The ceremony for admission of children, described in chapter 59 of the Rule, is based on the ritual for profession by adults. Mature postulants, following a trial period as novices, were read the Rule and required to draw up a petition promising stability, conversion of life, and obedience; their profession was accomplished by their laying the petition on the altar and joining the congregation in a psalm. For a boy, the petition was drawn up by his parents who then offered him by wrapping him and the petition in the altar cloth. Parents were further obliged to promise never to provide the child with property of any kind "and in this way let every opening be stopped, so that no expectations remain to the boy through which he might be ruined" (by leaving the monastery). The parents' offering apparently stood as a final vow for the child, for no mention is made of a profession or ceremony to be performed when the child was older.[67]

Leaving the monastery could be difficult in practice. When Gottschalk, a ninth-century writer, tried to obtain release from his vows because they had been made on his behalf by others, his request was refused after his abbot complained; he was permitted to change monasteries, but eventually he was detained for insubordination and incarcerated for more than twenty years.[68] There is

66. On the early history of oblation, see de Vogüé's Commentary to his edition of the RB, 6: 1358–60. Actual practice is described in Mayke de Jong, "Growing up in a Carolingian monastery: Magister Hildemar and his oblates," *Journal of Medieval History* 9 (1983): 99–128. A crosscultural perspective is provided by John Eastburn Boswell, *"Expositio* and *Oblatio*: The Abandonment of Children and the Ancient and Medieval Family," *American Historical Review* 89 (1984): 10–33.
67. Somewhat later Gregory II expressed the opinion that "it is impious for children offered to God by their parents to abandon themselves to pleasure." MGH *Epist.* 3: 276.
68. M. L. W. Laistner, *Thought and Letters in Western Europe A.D. 500 to 900*, 2d ed. (Ithaca, 1966), pp. 295–96.

no reason to believe that most or even many oblates were as un-happy as Gottschalk; Southern is right that if "the monasteries were filled with a conscript army [it] was not an unwilling or inef-fective army."[69] But the passing of the idea that monks had to make a voluntary profession is highly instructive about the character and objectives of early medieval society. Monks were no longer distinct from other men because of the holiness of their character or their desire to seek God, but simply because they followed a different routine of daily existence. It was purity of deed more than purity of thought that monasteries offered secular society, and the flood of gifts to monasteries in the early Middle Ages stands as eloquent testimony to the fact that most people found this standard of piety entirely satisfactory.

69. *Making of the Middle Ages* (New Haven, 1953), p. 162.

FOUR

The Search for a Rule, 700–1000

To this conceit of nations is added that of scholars, who will have it that what they know is as old as the world.

—*The New Science*, 127.

The heroic fathers must have been . . . the wise men in the wisdom of the auspices of vulgar wisdom . . . and finally they must also have been the kings who had the duty of carrying the laws from the gods to their own families.

—*The New Science*, 521.

The mentality we have discussed in the previous two chapters can easily result in intellectual complacency: what need is there to undertake the labor of inquiry if one knows that God ordained the rules by which one lives? In early medieval Europe, the circumstance that gnawed away most strongly at this certainty was the existence of a variety of Christian traditions that each claimed for itself divine inspiration. The anxiety that awareness of this variety could cause is perhaps earliest revealed by the correspondence of Augustine of Canterbury with Gregory the Great. Himself a Greek, Augustine was also familiar with Roman and Gallic customs, and he wrote from England asking which customs he should instruct his converts in. Why, he asked, "if there is one faith, are there varying customs in the churches, so that one form of the mass is held in the holy Roman church and another in the churches of Gaul?"

Gregory's reply was not really very helpful: he advised Augustine   *109* to "choose from every individual church what is pious, religious, and right," without telling him how to differentiate customs that pleased God from those that did not.[1] But later generations found they could not treat this issue so carelessly. By 700 the belief that there had to be one true tradition brought an intellectual tension to the early medieval world that distinguished it not only from what had gone before but from comparable societies where differences in custom were taken for granted.[2]

The search for rules unites the intellectual history of the eighth to tenth centuries, but for the convenience of discussion it is possible to distinguish three shorter periods within the longer span. The first, beginning around 700, is dominated by the work of the great monk Bede, who led the effort of English scholars to assimilate the body of knowledge they were introduced to by their conversion to Catholicism. The second, lasting from the late eighth to the end of the ninth, is dominated by the Carolingian empire, which by uniting nearly all of Latin Christendom under one ruler made apparent the internal contradictions of Europe's cultural heritage and prompted efforts to standardize customs according to a true rule. Finally, the tenth century saw a return to regional diversity as the collapse of the Carolingian empire deprived Europeans of the guidance of central authority and forced them to make independent judgments on which rules were good. While none of these periods produced major revolutions in Western consciousness, they are of interest as illustrations of the possibilities for change within a still traditional mental outlook.

Bede and the Anglo-Saxon Revival of Learning

The light of Western culture was probably never closer to extinction than it was in the seventh century. Saints' lives make up the great bulk of what survives of seventh-century literature, and the few nonhagiographic works suggest no high level of intellectual

1. *Bede's Ecclesiastical History of the English People*, ed. Bertram Colgrave and R. A. B. Mynors (Oxford, 1969), i.27.
2. Hallpike writes, in a personal communication, that "in a primitive society [the assumption that there is a single true law] is usually absent, and local differences are simply accepted as normal—'we have our fashion, they have theirs.' The growth of the idea that there is one right or true way of doing things in society and religion is an important change in social evolution."

accomplishment. One of the few works that made any effort to transmit ancient learning was the *Liber Scintillarum* (book of sparks). Of the author, a monk of Ligugé, we know only that his name was Defensor, and this because he tells us so "not out of vainglory but that whoever reads this book will remember me." The book itself is a collection of spiritual sayings—the "sparks" from the "glowing books" of the Fathers—arranged according to topics; Defensor himself, as he admits in his preface, added "nothing but good will and work." Though in another age a book such as this would scarcely merit a glance, the *Liber Scintillarum* was virtually the only book written in later seventh-century Gaul that made even a rudimentary attempt to transmit ancient learning, and the situation in Italy and Spain was not much better.[3]

What stirred European society from this torpor? Pierre Riché, to whom we are indebted for much that we know about education in this period, suggested three reasons: the establishment of political stability; the growing wealth of monasteries; and the increasing frequency of travel between regions, "which could only favor intellectual and artistic renewal [a]s the treasures of each country found whatever was needed to fructify them in foreign lands."[4] The similarity between these causes and the ones usually given for the revival in the twelfth century need no comment here; and they are, unfortunately, no more relevant to the eighth than the twelfth century. The region where Riché's interpretation would lead us to expect the greatest activity is Italy, for it is there that manuscripts were abundant, that grammarians and poets were still occasionally to be found, and that Greek scholars, displaced in sizable numbers from regions conquered by the Arabs, fled in the greatest numbers. Yet no revival of learning is to be found in Italy, as Riché admits with some disappointment, nor can he claim that Northumbria, where lived Bede whose work does mark the beginning of the return to ancient learning, either enjoyed political stability or experienced the mixture of Roman and Celtic culture found elsewhere in England. Bede's education was almost purely Roman in inspiration, a fact that leaves us with the puzzle of why the copy should show vitality when the original had none.

Riché's mistake, and it is a common one, lay in looking only

3. *Liber Scintillarum* (ed. H. Rochais), *CCSL* vol. 117. Cf. Laistner's comments, *Thought and Letters in Western Europe A.D. 500 to 900*, 2d ed. (Ithaca, 1966), p. 176.
4. *Education and Culture in the Barbarian West*, trans. John Contreni (Columbia, 1976), pp. 361–68.

for the conditions that made scholarship possible. But if one asks instead what motives would lead a person to undertake a life of study, the reasons for Northumbria's sudden preeminence are easier to find. One factor certainly was the rivalry with the Irish church, for the slight but important differences between Roman and Irish customs meant that Catholics of northern England were under unusual pressure to defend and explain their beliefs. Arguments between Catholic and Irish Christians were frequent and fierce and Bede's monastery of Jarrow was often an active participant in these debates: Andoman, abbot of the great Irish monastery of Iona, was converted to Roman practices during a visit to Jarrow around 686 when Bede was about 17, and in 710 Bede's abbot prepared a lengthy defense of Roman customs at the request of the king of the Picts. Bede therefore grew up in an atmosphere of discussion that must have been unusual in seventh-century Europe.[5]

The arguments reported by Bede in his account of the synod held at Whitby in 664 to settle the date of Easter must be typical of these debates. Oswiu, the king of Northumbria who had called the meeting, saw the problem as one of finding the true rule, because "it was fitting that those who serve one God should hold one rule of life and not differ in the celebration of the heavenly sacraments"; and all involved agreed that the decision should be made on the basis of which side could cite superior authority. The issue was eventually settled in favor of the Catholics when Oswiu decided that Peter, as doorkeeper of heaven, was better connected with God than the saints the Irish claimed in support of their customs. But the arguments made along the way show that Catholics had been forced to investigate the history of both their own customs and those of the Irish. When, for example, the spokesman for the Irish claimed that their customs were valid because they were established by the apostle John, "who was worthy to lie on Christ's breast," the Catholic representative replied that the Irish did not follow John's example accurately, because they always celebrated Easter on Sunday whereas John always celebrated Easter on whichever day followed the full moon. The details of this argument, which Bede reports at length, need not concern us here; what is important is the evidence it provides of how the Easter controversy stimulated

5. On Irish learning, cf. Laistner, *Thought and Letters*, pp. 138–49; Ludwig Bieler, *Ireland, Harbinger of the Middle Ages* (Oxford, 1963). England in the age of Bede is discussed in detail by Peter Blair, *World of Bede* (London, 1970).

efforts to assemble information that must have been considerable by the standards of the time.[6]

The influence of the Easter dispute is readily apparent in Bede's works. *De Temporibus*, one of his earliest works, carefully explains the proper method for calculating Easter, and some of his mature works deal with questions of celestial phenomena and the measurement of time. These are important writings, for they are virtually the only works on scientific subjects written between Isidore and the eleventh century, and they correct many of Isidore's errors.[7] But Bede's real accomplishment came from applying the habit of returning to patristic sources that the English had learned in the course of the Easter debate to the problem of instructing the English in Catholic doctrine. This necessity of teaching Christianity to a people whose allegiance to the church was recent and superficial was the second major influence on Bede, for it gave his work an urgency that was lacking in regions that had been Catholic for centuries. In learning to condense and explain orthodox beliefs he acquired a mastery of Catholic tradition that was without equal in his generation.[8]

One area where Bede's work marked a path for subsequent generations was the study of Latin. More than in Romance-speaking parts of Europe, Latin stood between the Anglo-Saxons and the Bible, and Bede never entirely forgot the problems that might face the reader who came to Latin as a foreign language. One of Bede's duties was running the school at Jarrow, and he knew firsthand the difficulty of teaching Latin: three of his early works—guides to grammar, poetry, and rhetoric—were apparently prepared for his own students. His own Latin is a model of correctness and simplicity, with few complicated sentences that might trouble a beginner; and his *Liber Retractionis*, a late work revising his commen-

6. *Eccles. Hist.*, iii.25.
7. For an instance in which Bede avoids the errors of Isidore see his discussions of the zones of climate in *De Natura Rerum*, c. 9 *(CCSL* 123A: 199–200) where he goes back to Pliny instead of perpetuating the errors of Isidore in *De Natura Rerum* c. 10. For Bede's distrust of Isidore, see also C. W. Jones's introduction to his edition of *Bedae Opera de Temporibus* (Cambridge, Mass., 1943), pp. 128, 131. Bede is also celebrated for having been the first to observe that the hour of tides varied according to the port, though, as Jones points out (p. 126), not all of his direct observations were so accurate.
8. See on this Bede's letter to Egbert, esp. sections 5–7, 10–15. The text of this letter is available in Bede, *Opera Historica*, volume 2, trans. J. E. King (London and New York, 1930).

tary on Acts, reveals him writing to a Roman friend to determine the meaning of an unfamiliar word.[9] Bede was also—exceptionally for his time—interested in the advantages that might be obtained by making the basic Christian texts available in the vernacular. Translations could, he observed to Egbert, in the letter that may be his last work, be a solution to the problem of unlettered priests. "I myself have often given to these unlearned priests the Creed and the Lord's Prayer translated into the English tongue."[10] Whether he made the translation himself he does not say, though he had experience with translations: when he quotes Caedmon's poem in the *Ecclesiastical History* he remarks how difficult it is to translate verses from one language to another;[11] in the *Liber Retractionis* he carefully provides advice on how a passage of Acts might be translated into English;[12] and according to Cuthbert who left an account of Bede's death, the great scholar's last days were spent on a translation of the Gospel of John.[13]

A second area where Bede was clearly motivated by the needs of a nation of recent converts was his concern with teaching correct Catholic doctrine. His preferred tool for inculcating correct beliefs was the Biblical commentary; he wrote twenty-three in all, including several longer than one book in length, which he listed at the end of the *Ecclesiastical History*. Bede's purpose in these works, as he explains in one of his prefaces, was to present the teachings of the Fathers in a form that could easily be grasped by the uneducated reader *(rudis lector)* who could not obtain or master the volumes of patristic exegesis.[14]

The commentaries do indeed consist primarily of excerpts from the Fathers woven together by Bede with some of his own comments to form a continuous gloss, and the didactic, conservative nature of the works was accentuated by the emphasis he placed on allegorical interpretations. This method of interpretation, which was typical of the early Middle Ages, made it impossible for the commentator to find anything in the Bible he did not know before he began. The account in Genesis of Noah's ark being borne on the

---

9. *Retractio in Actus Apostolorum* at xix.12 in *Expositio Actuum Apostolorum et Retractio*, ed. M. L. W. Laistner (Cambridge, Mass., 1939), p. 139.
10. Letter to Egbert, section 5.
11. *Eccles. Hist.*, iv.24.
12. At verse ii.20; p. 100.
13. This letter is printed pp. 580–87 in the Colgrave and Mynors edition of the *Ecclesiastical History*.
14. *In Genesim* [CCSL 118A: 1].

waters, for example, prompts Bede to compare the ark with Peter who came to Christ on the sea, an image itself of the Church's escape from the fluctuations of the world to heavenly peace; and Bede continues by observing that the water which lifted the ark over the mountains represented the sacrament of baptism by which the church was made sublime.[15] In effect, the Bible itself was subjected to the authority of the church.

The most original feature of Bede's Biblical studies is the interest he shows in textual criticism. The existence of two Latin translations of the Bible—the Old Latin version, which was perhaps the more common, and the Vulgate of Jerome—had to be unsettling to those who saw in the Bible the exact words of God, and Bede was perhaps in a better position than most to recognize the problem because his own monastery possessed both translations: the Codex Amantianus, the oldest complete manuscript of the Vulgate, was in fact copied at Wearmouth and Jarrow during Bede's lifetime. As a translator himself, Bede could understand how the differences arose, and as he acquired some knowledge of Greek he increasingly preferred to settle doubts by referring to such Greek versions of the New Testament as he could obtain. The *Liber Retractionis* of his old age in particular shows the pride he felt in his hard-won skill in Greek, which he manages to bring to bear on explaining the derivations of certain words and suggesting possible translations of the Bible into English.[16]

Bede's respect for authority often made him draw back from the more serious implications of his own learning; his comments, he says, are for erudition only, and the reader "should not insert them in his own volume unless perchance he had found them interpreted of old in the Latin codex of his own edition."[17] But the practice of returning to original sources, learned in the debates with the Irish and perfected over years of scholarship, found its perfect expression late in Bede's life with the writing of the *Ecclesiastical History*. This work, though not greatly different in inspiration from Gregory of Tours's *History*, is throughout marked by the care which Bede brought to everything he did. The same qualities that make Bede's other works unreadable today make the *Ecclesiastical History* essential reading for all students of the early Middle Ages.

15. *In Gen.* vii.18 [CCSL 118A: 119].
16. *Liber Retractionis* (Laistner) 160–62.
17. Preface to *Retractio in Actus*, p. 93–94; see also the discussion by Claude Jenkins, "Bede as an Exegete and Theologian," in *Bede, His Life, Times, and Writings*, ed. A. Hamilton Thompson, (London, 1932), pp. 152–200.

Perhaps because Bede worked within the mentality of his time, his impact on his own society was enormous. His work—in Latin, in textual criticism, and in the preservation of ancient learning— defined the direction of the next three centuries of intellectual life. Few would equal his accomplishments; fewer still surpass them. And Bede's significance lies not exclusively in the written works he left to posterity. Essentially self-taught, Bede managed to found educational facilities in England that were for the first three-quarters of the eighth century the best in Europe. When, forty years after Bede's death, Charlemagne decided to establish a palace school, it was eventually to England, to a student of a student of Bede, that he had to turn.

The Carolingian Ordering of Society

The dominant fact of the eighth century was the unification of Europe under the Franks. The importance of the Franks was nothing new—at the beginning of the sixth century Clovis had annexed the Burgundian kingdom and posed a threat to the Visigoths in Spain—but the rise of the Carolingian dynasty gave new vigor to their expansionist tendencies. By 800, when Charlemagne took the title of emperor, he controlled the territories that are now modern France and Italy and most of modern Germany; not until Napoleon was one man to rule so much of Europe. Charlemagne himself deserves much of the credit for this achievement, for fear of his reprisals was the main force that held his empire together. He had the determination he needed to gather his army, spring after spring as the season approached when military campaigns were possible, to move against rebels or to conquer new territories; and he had the ferocity to make those who rebelled regret their defiance. Saxony, for example, required attention nearly every summer for thirty years after Charlemagne first conquered it; afterwards, however, it was submissive not only to him but to his heirs.

The effect of this unification of Christendom was similar to that of the Easter controversy. It laid bare for all to see the diversity of regional customs that had resulted from centuries of independent development. And it confronted thoughtful men with evidence that some, at least, of Europe was not conforming to God's laws. The Carolingians themselves responded by trying to impose uniform social and religious institutions on all their empire. In the field of learning, the desire to determine which of the many rules were the right ones inspired scholars to a systematic effort to recover much

of classical learning. These efforts resulted in both a reordering of
the institutions of society and the giving of new impetus to the revival of intellectual activity that had begun with Bede.

THE INSTITUTIONS OF DAILY LIFE

Though the empire was very much Charlemagne's creation, in reading the commands that issued from his court it is impossible not to be struck by the absence of vanity from most of what he did. He seems to have had no desire to preserve the unity of his empire, for his wills provided that his territories be divided among his sons; that the empire survived him was due to the chance that left only one son alive at his death. Most of his projects appear to have been motivated less by ambition for self-aggrandizement or temporal gain than by the earnest desire to do what God commanded. This concern to enforce God's law was not wholly idealistic. In common with the other Carolingians, Charlemagne knew that what God had given he could also withdraw, and he seems to have taken every setback he experienced as a sign of God's anger. This attitude helped make him in most respects the ideal incarnation of early medieval kingship. Despite our sometimes spotty information about the events of his reign, only the General Admonition of 789 of all his major legislation was not clearly provoked by external events: his first major reforms in 779 followed his defeat in Spain and a revolt in Saxony; the capitulary of 794 followed another Saxon rising, a year of bad harvests, and the discovery of a conspiracy led by Charlemagne's bastard son Pepin the Hunchback; in 807 and again in 810 Charlemagne interpreted a famine as a sign that "inwardly we are not finding favor with God" and ordered his subjects to keep a three day fast and do penance for their sins.

I stress Charlemagne's attitudes toward government because one must understand his mentality to comprehend why he chose to govern as he did. The easiest course would have been to permit each district to retain its own customs; this policy, which minimizes conflict between central authority and subject peoples, enabled the Roman emperors and the old regime kings of France to control diverse polities for centuries. To minds accustomed to the idea that human society should be governed by God's law, however, the diversity of the Carolingian empire could only mean that some customs were illicit and sinful. The Carolingians, and especially Charlemagne, therefore moved to impose reforms, and their efforts affected virtually every area of human endeavor.

Charlemagne's approach to government was to set out rules and order his agents, usually the counts, to enforce them. He does not seem to have been especially interested in building institutions. No effort was made to create bureaucracies that could function without the king's constant supervision: instead of having his agents specialize at manageable tasks Charlemagne constantly moved them from one chore to another as suited his convenience. And though use of written documents became more common in his reign, both for issuing commands and collecting information, the royal archives were kept haphazardly. Whether he could have done more given the abilities of the men available to him is not certain, but Charlemagne unquestionably added to the confusion by issuing instructions that could not possibly be carried out. Here, for example, is part of a capitulary of instructions from the early 800's:

> Receive strangers in your home, visit the sick . . . ransom captives, help the unjustly oppressed. . . . Let wives be subject to their husbands in all goodness and modesty. . . . let them raise their children in the fear of God . . . let men love their wives and not say unsuitable things to them . . . let children love their parents and honor them.[18]

Whatever Charlemagne expected to accomplish in issuing these commands, they reveal a conception of government that is far more heavily weighted toward enactment than enforcement.[19]

Charlemagne followed the advice of contemporary political theory by attempting to impose order on religious as well as secular institutions. The capitulary of 802 that, as the first major legislation following Charlemagne's imperial coronation, seems to have been drawn up with special care is a good illustration of the extent of royal power. The opening paragraph gives the emperor's agents the following instructions:

> All shall live justly and by just judgments in everything according to God's precept and reason, and each one admonished to remain harmoniously in his profession or course of life: canonical clergy should live the canonical life fully without the business of filthy money; nuns should keep their life under diligent guard; laymen and secular clergy ought to live rightly according to their laws without malicious fraud; and all should live in mutual charity and perfect peace.

18. MGH *Cap.* 1: 239–40.
19. For parallels in the late empire, see Ramsay MacMullen, *Roman Government's Response to Crisis A.D. 235–337* (New Haven, 1976), chapter 4.

Subsequent chapters amplify this admonition; in them the *missi* are told to see

That bishops and priests live according to the canons and teach others the same. (cap. 10)

That abbots live where the monks are and wholly with the monks according to the rule . . . ; and abbesses do similarly. (cap. 12)

Let monks live firmly and strictly in accordance with the rule, since we know it is displeasing to God that anyone is lukewarm in his will. (cap. 17)

That counts and hundred-men (*centenarii*) compel all to do justice. (cap. 25)

That judges judge justly according to written law, not according to their own will. (cap. 26)[20]

Carolingian clergy evidently accepted this kind of tutelage willingly; only late in the ninth century, when the empire was already in disarray, did bishops begin tentatively to assert the existence of a clerical sphere separate from lay society.

In the context of a heterogeneous empire, the desire for order often meant that Charlemagne had to determine which customs had the best claim to being authoritative and then to require all his subjects to obey them. Monastic policy is a particularly revealing illustration of this process, since it took the exertions of three generations of Carolingians to complete the reforms. When Charlemagne's father Pepin became king most of the monasteries were governed, as we have seen, by customs which combined two or more rules. Pepin's main concern was that monks "live regularly according to the rule" (*secundum ordinem regulariter vivant*) or "under the holy order" (*sub ordine sancto vivant*), but too little evidence survives from his reign for us to judge whether he had any particular rule in mind.[21] About Charlemagne's intentions, however, there can be no doubt: in 787 or 788 he had a copy made of the manuscript of the monastery of Monte Cassino believed to be Benedict's original autograph and had the copy brought to Aachen to serve as an exemplar for subsequent copies; in 802 he had the Rule read to an assembly of abbots and monks so that "whatever was done in monasteries or among monks contrary to the rule of St. Benedict they should have corrected in accordance with the

20. MGH *Cap.* 1: 91–99 (capitulary 14).
21. MGH *Cap.* 1: 34 (capitulary 14 c. 5); 1: 43 (capitulary 18 c. 2). Capitulary 14 c. 10 legislates against travel by monks, a precept established by the Benedictine Rule and later reaffirmed by Charlemagne.

same rule"; and in 813 he ordered synods of five regions to enact observance of the Benedictine Rule into canon law.[22] Adherence to the Rule was also enforced under Charlemagne by his commissioners *missi* who frequently found chapters on monastic discipline included in their instructions.[23] The process of reform was completed in 817 when Louis the Pious published the customs prepared by Benedict of Aniane for the interpretation of the Rule.

Similar methods were employed to standardize church liturgy. Here, too, the process of reform began with Pepin, who discovered the existence of discrepancies between Roman and Gallic rituals in the course of his dealings with the pope. Again diverse customs were taken as proof that there had been a falling away from a true rule, and reforms were conceived of as returns to an inspired prototype. Pepin's efforts seem to have centered on the circulation of a sacramentary that brought together a number of different Roman customs. Charlemagne improved on his father's policy by obtaining from Pope Hadrian a sacramentary thought to contain in an "unmixed" form the customs of Gregory the Great, though in fact it dated from the 730s or 740s; this "authentic" copy was kept at Aachen to serve as a model from which other manuscripts could be copied. Employment of Roman liturgical forms was also repeatedly mandated by royal decrees and church councils held under royal auspices, and an edition of Hadrian's sacramentary, supplemented and commented upon by one of Charlemagne's court scholars, became the model for the missal, one of the basic works for the unification of Latin church usages.[24]

This zeal for order extended across every field of social activity. Canon law was published in an official compilation, again based on a text obtained from Rome. A collection of homilies was pre-

22. *Annales Laureshamenses*, MGH *Scriptores* 1, at the year 802. Charlemagne's monastic policy is discussed in detail by Josef Semmler, "Karl der Grosse und das frankische Mönchtum," in *Karl der Grosse*, ed. B. Bischoff (Düsseldorf, 1967), 2: 255–89.

23. In the capitulary of 802, for example, Charlemagne cautioned monks against leaving their monasteries, desiring worldly things, being argumentative; participating in drunkenness and feasting, and—especially—engaging in fornication "which extremely saddens and disturbs us because since some monks are said to be sodomites damage has come from that which is believed to be the source of the greatest hope for the salvation of all christians, that is the life and chastity of monks." MGH *Cap.* 1: 94 (capitulary 33 c. 17).

24. Cyrille Vogel, "La réforme liturgique sous Charlemagne," in *Karl der Grosse*, 2: 217–32.

pared at Charlemagne's direction by Paul the Deacon, a Lombard monk who was attached for a while to the royal court. Weights and measures were standardized, and the coinage apparently redefined in terms of the new units. The chief area where unification of the rules was incomplete was secular law, and even here the Carolingians made great efforts. Before 800, Charlemagne had published laws for the newly conquered Saxons and initiated preparation of revised texts of the Salic law and the codes of the Bavarians, Alamans, and Ripuarian Franks. Charlemagne moved more actively to supplement existing laws in 802, at the assembly where he required monks and abbots to accept the Benedictine Rule, and through the general capitulary from earlier that year enacted laws against homicide, incest, and other crimes that might incite God's vengeance.[25] Despite later urgings by Agobard of Lyon to abolish all but the Salic law,[26] the establishment of one code faced an insuperable obstacle in the principle of early medieval law that held an individual ought to be governed by the law he inherited from his ancestors. This "personality" of law (modern law is "territorial") meant that law tended to be thought of as a personal possession—something one "had," not rules to which one was subject. The Carolingians apparently felt justice was best served by guaranteeing each of their subjects the right to his or her law.

In making these reforms, the Carolingians appear to have believed they were enforcing God's law. This intention is most obvious in areas where authoritative texts existed and in matters of ecclesiastical discipline: Charlemagne did not think of the imposition of the Benedictine Rule as an innovation of his own, for late in life he queried his advisors whether religious men who lived according to other rules—he was thinking of Martin of Tours, who lived before Benedict—could correctly be called monks.[27] But he also justified the standardization of weights and measures by citing Leviticus and Proverbs,[28] and Agobard of Lyon's chief argument in favor of unifying law codes was that the diversity of laws constituted an obstacle to the unity of mankind under Christ. Even in areas that to us are secular, it was God's rules the Carolingians believed they were enforcing.

25. F. L. Ganshof, *Frankish Institutions under Charlemagne* (Providence, 1958), pp. 71–73; H. R. Loyn and John Percival, *The Reign of Charlemagne* (New York, 1976), p. 43.
26. *Liber Adversus legem Gundobadi*, PL 133: 113 ff.
27. MGH *Cap.* 1: 161, 164 (capitularies 71 c. 17; 72 c. 12).
28. MGH *Cap.* 1: 60 (capitulary 22 c. 74).

The religious and economic unity of the later Middle Ages owed much to the efforts of the Carolingians, but the debt is perhaps nowhere greater than in the field of education and learning. The chief force behind the revival of interest in learning was Charlemagne himself, who took alarm (as he explains in his letter on the subject) that the "uncouth language" *(lingua inerudita)* of correspondence received at the court might mean that "as skill in writing was less, wisdom to understand sacred scripture might be far less than it ought rightly to be."[29] Charlemagne's solution to this problem is found in chapter 72 of the *Admonitio Generalis*: each bishopric and monastery was required to operate a school for the teaching of reading, chant, and computation and was to have available "catholic books, well emended."[30] We know from other capitularies that Charlemagne made some effort to enforce this standard; in 805 the missi's instructions began simply

> of reading
> of chant
> of scribes, that they not write badly
> of notaries
> of the other disciplines
> of computation
> of the medical arts.[31]

These commands were probably not obeyed everywhere, but some progress was certainly made for, in the last year or two of Charlemagne's life, Leitrade archbishop of Lyon wrote the emperor proudly describing a school devoted to chant, reading, and (for advanced students) Biblical interpretation.[32]

This improvement in educational facilities would have been less significant without the contributions of the scholars Charlemagne gathered around him. Charles himself seems to have had a taste for learning: soon after his conquest of the Lombard kingdom, he enlisted Peter of Pisa to write a grammar for his use, and later descriptions of his court tell of his participation in the discussions of the school. But Charles also had practical motives for employing scholars: he needed expert assistance in carrying out his reforms. The

29. MGH *Cap.* 1: 79 (capitulary 29).
30. MGH *Cap.* 1: 59–60.
31. MGH *Cap.* 1: 121 (capitulary 43 cc. 1–7).
32. MGH *Ep.* 4: IV, no. 114.

preparation of an authentic text, for example, demanded considerable learning, especially when (as in the case of liturgy) there were
many rival versions of a work to contend with. Charles recruited
men from all over Europe to help in these labors and rewarded
them with appointments to the most important bishoprics and
monasteries in the empire. In those offices, as in their work in the
palace school, these scholars took charge of rebuilding Europe's
educational institutions.

The activities of this first generation of Carolingian intellectuals
may be illustrated by the career of Alcuin. An Englishman educated
in Bede's own diocese of York, Alcuin became the undisputed
leader of the palace school after joining Charlemagne's service in
782; in 796 he was named abbot of the prestigious St. Martin's of
Tours. As a thinker Alcuin was unoriginal, nor did he wish to be
otherwise. "There is nothing better for us," he wrote, "than to
follow the teaching of the Apostles and the Gospels. We must follow these precepts instead of inventing new ones or propounding
new doctrine or vainly seeking to increase our own fame by the
discovery of new-fangled ideas."[33] And Alcuin's works live up to
this ideal: his letters on kingship, though the most extensive writings of his time on politics, largely repeat the lessons of Pseudo-
Cyprian on the unjust king; his *Disputatio de Rhetorica* derived
directly from Cicero; and his Biblical commentaries were a patch-
work of patristic quotations without the redeeming quality Bede's
commentaries had had of avoiding contradictions between the excerpts given. A man who sought in wide reading authoritative judgments on which he could rely, Alcuin was the prototype of several
generations of scholars.[34]

Alcuin's main endeavors were in the field of educational reforms.
It was a good matching of the man to the job, because Alcuin's
rigorous attention to rules was exactly what was needed to reestab-
lish minimum standards of learning. In Gaul, for example, where
correct Latin usage had been eroded by the closeness of the Ro-
mance vernacular, Alcuin worked hard on spelling and pronuncia-
tion. Following Cassiodorus, he cautioned his students against con-

33. Heinrich Fichtenau, *The Carolingian Empire*, trans. Peter Munz (New
York, 1964), p. 98, quoting MGH *Ep.* 4: 61 (no. 23).
34. On Alcuin in general see Arthur Kleinclausz, *Alcuin* (Paris, 1948); C. J.
Gaskoin, *Alcuin* (London, 1904); Eleanor Duckett, *Alcuin, Friend of
Charlemagne* (New York, 1951). Wallace-Hadrill discusses Alcuin, Lupus,
Hraban Maur, and other scholars of the period in *The Frankish Church*
(Oxford, 1983), pp. 205–25, 304–89.

fusing *b* and *v* by pointing out that *beneficus* (benefactor) was
sometimes written *veneficus* (poisoner), or *vivere* (to live) written
bibere (to drink).[35] The textbooks Alcuin wrote to correct such
errors are very elementary—all except the treatise on orthography
are in dialogue form with a master answering a student's questions—but he seems to have gauged his audience well for the works
proved immensely popular throughout the ninth century.

A second area of Alcuin's enterprise was the establishment of
libraries. When Alcuin took office as abbot of St. Martin's of
Tours, he evidently found the stock of books quite small; building
up the collection became one of the preoccupations of his last
years. The first step in acquiring books was locating an existing
copy that could be copied. Alcuin's intimate familiarity with some
of Europe's best libraries greatly simplified this process, for he
knew who could loan certain manuscripts for copying at Tours,
and he obtained other books by sending monks to York to copy
books he had used as a master there.

Yet building up libraries was not exclusively a matter of finding
and copying manuscripts. Before the invention of printing, inaccurate texts were an endemic problem—not all scribes were educated
or attentive to their work, and even skilled copyists could introduce errors by misreading unfamiliar handwriting or guessing in-
correctly at the meaning of an already garbled text. Charlemagne's
attempts to gather "authentic" versions of important works such as
the Rule of St. Benedict was one solution, but where no authoritative manuscript existed an editor had to undertake the emendation.
To satisfy Charlemagne's desire for a correct Latin text of sacred
scripture, Alcuin prepared an edition of the Bible, just one of the
works he is known to have edited. This was time-consuming and
difficult work: several libraries had to be persuaded to lend manuscripts, and librarians were perhaps even more reluctant then than
now to let books out of their personal care; variant readings had to
be collated and a decision made on which was the best; and a
corrected text had to be prepared to serve as an exemplar for future
copies.[36] Finally, when the exemplar was ready, the work of the
scriptorium had to be supervised. At Tours, Alcuin forbade idle

35. Gaskoin, *Alcuin*, p. 193.
36. F. L. Ganshof, "Alcuin's revision of the Bible," in *The Carolingians and
the Frankish Monarchy*, trans. Janet Sondheimer (Ithaca, 1971), pp. 28–
40; B. Fischer, "Bibeltext und Bibelreform," in *Karl der Grosse*, 2: 156–
216, shows that Alcuin was but one of many who worked on the text of
the Bible at this time.

chatter as detrimental to the accuracy of the copies and exhorted his scribes to insert punctuation so the work could be read aloud without distortion of meaning.[37]

The final area of endeavor that concerns us was the broadening of the school curriculum to include the liberal arts. Here, perhaps, one can see the influence of Alcuin's own taste, for while Bede had frowned upon the study of profane subjects, Alcuin wrote openly of his pleasure in Vergil and he knew works of Cicero and Boethius that had lain unread for centuries. Yet what he felt justified the study of the classics was not the pleasure they could give but the aid they could provide toward interpreting sacred scripture. In letters drafted by Alcuin, Charlemagne invited his subjects to "the thoroughgoing study of the liberal arts" and urged schools to teach literature as an aid to understanding "the figures and tropes and other forms of speech" in the Bible, and Alcuin in another place remarks "how necessary arithmetic is for understanding the Bible."[38] The effect of this relaxation of prohibitions on what was actually taught is hard to judge, for, except in one letter where he mentions teaching his monks at Tours about the movements of the stars, Alcuin's descriptions of his classes generally emphasize the traditional skills of reading, writing and chant.[39] Probably only advanced students could expect to be initiated into the reading of pagan authors, though on these the impression made by Alcuin's love of the classics could be great. Alcuin's student Einhard modeled his biography of Charlemagne on Suetonius, and in his preface to the work included a quotation from Cicero.

The founding of schools and libraries by Alcuin and others of the palace school marked an epoch in the history of European education. In the place accorded Latin as the language of scholarship and in the study of the liberal arts, schools retained for centuries the impress of Carolingian reforms. The legacy of ninth-century scriptoria was equally important, for many ancient works survived in Carolingian manuscripts that otherwise would have been lost altogether. Despite a decline in the level of intellectual activity in the tenth century, the continuity of learning was never again broken as it had been in the seventh and eighth centuries; and in the eleventh century the monastic and cathedral schools established at Charlemagne's order provided the first home for the new generations of students.

37. Duckett, *Alcuin*, p. 259; Laistner, *Thought and Letters*, pp. 204–5.
38. MGH *Cap.* 1: 60 (capitulary 30); MGH *Ep.* 4: 285.
39. MGH *Ep.* 4: no. 128; cf. also no. 114, 128.

All this was far in the future when Alcuin died in 804. The more immediate fruits of the Carolingian educational reforms are to be found in the broadened interests and heightened productivity of ninth-century scholars whose activities are sometimes referred to as the "Carolingian renaissance." But while the ninth century saw a reorganization of the educational curriculum, cognitive processes were less affected by the redirection of intellectual inquiry to the liberal arts and classical antiquity. Most scholars continued to conceive their purpose chiefly as mastering what was already known, with the result that collecting quotations and facts remained the characteristic type of intellectual activity.

The nature of the intellectual community of the ninth century can be illustrated by the collection that has survived of the correspondence of Lupus Servatus.[40] Born in the first decade of the ninth century of a Frankish mother and a Bavarian father, Lupus received his early education from Adalbert and Aldric, two students of Alcuin who were successively abbots of Ferrières, the monastery to which Lupus was sent as an oblate. Around the year 830 Aldric sent him to Fulda to study with Hraban Maur, another student of Alcuin, and after returning to Ferrières in 836 Lupus became abbot himself in 842. Lupus's correspondents include some of the most illustrious scholars of his time—Einhard, Hraban Maur, Gottschalk, Hincmar of Reims, and Paschasius Radbertus—as well as Emperor Charles the Bald and the English king Aethelwulf. But the most impressive feature of the collection is the extent of the circle who seem to have shared Lupus's interests. The letters are addressed not only to famous scholars but more than forty different individuals, many of them otherwise obscure. Lupus appears to have felt confident that nearly all his correspondents were familiar with and interested in learned questions. Most of the topics Lupus treated—the correct determination of Latin meter, for example, or the nature of comets (elucidated by quotations from Vergil, Justin Martyr, and Josephus)—would have been beyond the ken of scholars a century earlier; by the mid-ninth century they were becoming commonplace.

It is as a collector and editor of classical texts that Lupus is best remembered today, and his letters vividly document his activities in

40. For the Latin text of Lupus's letters, together with a French translation see the edition of Léon Levillain (Paris, 1927, repr. 1964). An English translation has been made by Graydon W. Regenos (The Hague, 1966).

this important field. The first letter in the collection is to Einhard, Charlemagne's biographer, whom Lupus had met at Fulda. Lupus writes to borrow Cicero's *De Rhetorica* and a few other books he had seen mentioned in a catalog of Einhard's library—the very existence of a catalog to facilitate borrowing marks an important advance from Alcuin's time—because the manuscripts of *De Rhetorica* Lupus had read previously were corrupt. Another letter tries to use an intermediary to borrow Boethius's commentary on Cicero's *Topica*; evidently Lupus was in disfavor with the owner of the manuscript because he advises his correspondent not to mention his name.[41] A third letter to Archbishop Hincmar of Reims explains his reluctance to send Hincmar Bede's *Collectanea* on Paul's letters "because the book is so large that it cannot be concealed on one's person nor very easily contained in a bag, and even if one or the other were possible one would have to fear an attack of robbers who would certainly be attracted by the beauty of the book."[42]

Lupus's editorial methods, which can be reconstructed from manuscripts that survive in his hand, illustrate how cognition continued to shape Carolingian scholars' conception of intellectual activity. In the mechanical aspects of collating manuscripts, Lupus showed great thoroughness: he preserved archaic forms, left vacant spaces where there were gaps in his archetypes, and recorded variant readings with great care.[43] Yet if it happened that none of the available manuscripts contained certain passages in uncorrupted form, Lupus did not offer conjectures about the correct reading. Unquestionably this is difficult work; poet and classicist A. E. Housman's comments on a satire of Juvenal may serve as an example of the kind of reasoning involved. One editor, he observed, by following the best manuscripts too closely, gave the following reading of two lines from satire eleven:

> *non Phryx aut Lycius, non a mangone petitus*
> *quisquam erit: in magno cum posces, posce Latine.*
> 'in magno' is supposed to mean 'in magno poculo': when you call for a drink in a *large* cup, call in Latin; 'in paruo, Graece' I presume, and possibly 'in modico, Osce': such things is Ju-

41. Letter 53.
42. Letter 108, trans. Regenos, p. 126.
43. Charles Henry Beeson, *Lupus of Ferrières as Scribe and Text Critic* (Cambridge, Mass., 1930), reproduces in facsimile Lupus's copy of Cicero's *De Oratore* (British Museum *Harleian* 2736). See also R. J. Gariepy, Jr., "Lupus of Ferrières: Carolingian Scribe and Text Critic," *Medieval Studies* 30 (1965): 90–105.

venal made to write in order that Juvenal's editors may not be forced to throw their crutch away. The other class [of editors] gives *et* for *in*, [and it] must be full twelve years ago that by considering this reading and the scholiast's comment 'quales uendunt care maniparii' I was led to the correction

> non a mangone petitus
>> qui steterit magno: cum posces, posce Latine.

quisteterit was mistaken for *quis et erit* and then altered to *quis erit et*, . . . then quis was expanded for metres sake to quisquam. Last year I found in cod. Burn 192 of the British Museum an earlier stage of the corruption: it had *quis erit et magno.*[44]

Such work requires a combination of talents rare in any age: a sense of style; an understanding of the author's intention; an understanding of the errors a scribe can make; and above all, as Housman noted acerbicly with an eye to some of his contemporaries, a brain and the willingness to use it. It was precisely this willingness to approach a text critically that Lupus lacked, and the same can be said of his eighth-century predecessors such as Alcuin. They looked to the authority of one manuscript or another and chose the best reading. But because they regarded the words of their authorities as realities existing apart from consciousness instead of as a logical development of ideas, they did not see that it would be possible to correct corrupt manuscripts by reconstructing the thoughts of the authors and scribes.

A still more striking testimony to Carolingian reliance on authority is the group of works produced in the course of a theological controversy that roiled Lupus's circle.[45] The controversy began in 848 when Hraban Maur, now archbishop of Mainz, took alarm at the monk Gottschalk's teaching that God had predestined some to salvation and others to eternal death. What Gottschalk was doing, as Wallace-Hadrill observed, was looking at creation from God's point of view. But not only was this perspective an uncommon one in the Carolingian age, suggestive of cognition different from the ordinary; it threatened the Carolingian emphasis on works and sacraments as a path to salvation. Not surprisingly it

44. Preface to his edition of *M. Manilii Astronomicon* (Cambridge, 1937), I: xxxvi–xxxvii.

45. For the controversy as a whole, see Laistner, *Thought and Letters*, pp. 296–98; Jean Devisse, *Hincmar Archevêque de Reims* (Geneva, 1975), I: 118–280; and especially Wallace-Hadrill, *The Frankish Church*, pp. 362–71.

was Augustine's writings against the Pelagians, where the issue of
works was also central, that gave Gottschalk his greatest inspiration.

Hraban and Gottschalk had crossed swords before, for it had been Hraban who as abbot of Fulda had insisted that Gottschalk be bound by the monastic vows made on his behalf at the time of his oblation. This time Hraban obtained Gottschalk's condemnation by a synod at Mainz and had him sent to Archbishop Hincmar of Reims, who had him imprisoned and whipped in accord with the punishments laid down in the Benedictine Rule. The controversy did not end there, however, because Gottschalk's writings had inspired others to reread Augustine—on whose writings he had based his position—and had aroused the interest of Charles the Bald. When Hincmar consulted his friends on the issue, he found that Prudentius of Lyon agreed with Gottschalk and that Lupus held to a doctrine of dual predestination only slightly different.

All the works that came out of the early phase of this controversy relied heavily on quotations from scripture and the Fathers. Of course, writers in every period cite quotations, either to establish key facts or to lend resonance or fine phrasing to their own conclusions, but the works in question use quotations not so much to support arguments as to render them unnecessary. Gottschalk simply took the quotations that favored his position without troubling to deal with those—often from the same authors—that did not. Lupus's letter to Charles the Bald on the same subject was similar: he quoted passages from the Bible, Ambrose, Augustine, and Jerome in favor of his own position, interpreted the passages to suit his purposes, and concluded by posing the question "who except those who are unashamed to appear without sight would dare contradict such brilliant scholars as these?"[46] The arguments of those who opposed Gottschalk were, if possible, still more rudimentary. Hraban did not understand why predestination, which is not mentioned by name in scripture, should arouse so much interest, while Hincmar kept insisting that Gottschalk should not have contradicted Hraban, "a student of the great Alcuin"; he prepared a collection of quotations of his own, including several from a heretical work of Pelagius that had mistakenly been attributed to Jerome.[47]

The controversy might well have ended there, with both sides deadlocked and Gottschalk in confinement, had not Hincmar tried

46. Letter 78, trans. Regenos, p. 90; for Gottschalk, see M. Gibson, "The Continuity of Learning circa 850–circa 1050," *Viator* 6 (1975): 2–4.
47. Devisse, *Hincmar*, pp. 120 n. 23, 132–44.

to strengthen his position by inviting John the Scot (Erigena) to write in opposition to Gottschalk. John had the advantage over his contemporaries of knowing Greek, but it was his cognitive processes that really distinguished him from his contemporaries: he conceived his role not as the mastering of what authorities said but using concepts he had learned to impose intellectual order on a problem. This method is apparent in John's treatise against Gottschalk, for to Gottschalk's assertion that God had saved some souls by grace and damned others by justice, John replied that such a dual predestination was inconsistent with God's unity. This answer had the advantage of bringing the discussion back to central questions of theology, but John's reasoning was far too daring for his contemporaries. He was roundly denounced for presenting his own argument instead of relying on patristic authority: Prudentius wrote of John's "vain and puffed-up learning"; Florus of Lyon, who may not have read all of John's book, referred to it as the "writings of a boastful and garrulous man" and denounced John for "glorifying himself by citing neither Scripture nor the Fathers but using philosophical arguments."[48] John's doctrine was condemned by a synod which described it as "old wives tales and Scots' porridge,"[49] and his later, more sophisticated writing had no discernible influence. "It would not be easy," commented Laistner, "to find another thinker of equal stature whose contribution to human thought aroused so few echoes either amongst his contemporaries or with posterity."[50] The controversy itself dragged on several more years, though in the end no one suffered greatly when the doctrine of dual predestination was condemned at a council in 860. John the Scot, who had aroused the ire of nearly everyone, continued to receive commissions from Charles the Bald to do translations from the Greek. Evidently it required more sophistication than was to be found in the Carolingian age to discover the advantages of burning one's theological opponents.

The debate on predestination was probably the longest and most absorbing of any learned dispute of the ninth century, and the participants in this controversy were not marginal figures in the history of the ninth century. Hraban was the greatest scholar of his

---

48. Prudentius *PL* 115: 1015; Florus *PL* 119: 101–3; see also Devisse, *Hincmar*, pp. 150–53, 187–91, who remarks (p. 190 n. 14) that "l'univers intellectuel carolingien a besoin de noir et de blancs; Jean Scot y introduit les nuances."
49. Quoted by Laistner, *Thought and Letters*, p. 297.
50. Ibid., p. 329.

generation, and his works cover nearly every subject and fill seven volumes—nearly four thousand pages—in the *Patrologia Latina*. Hincmar dominated politics throughout the reign of Charles the Bald, and his opinions often proved decisive in both ecclesiastical and political affairs. Yet when one considers the energy expended and the stature of the participants, the results of the controversy are remarkably small. The works produced, excepting those of John the Scot's that everyone else condemned, consist chiefly or entirely of excerpts from the Fathers. Instead of reasoning independently, the debaters quoted authority as a substitute for argument. One sees in these methods of composition not a revival of classical thought but the survival of the egocentricism we found in Bede and before him in Isidore and Gregory the Great.

Since the reasoning Carolingian scholars use in their own works bears little resemblance to the classical books they loved, the ninth century will always disappoint those who expect revolutions in education to have a profound effect on thought. Yet the Carolingian period provides much of interest to the student of cognition in the number of cases that can be found of reasoning unconsciously transformed from one logical structure to another. Probably the best examples concern Boethius's *Consolation of Philosophy*, for this was a book that challenged early medieval ideas on a number of issues: the undeserved punishment of the prisoner raised the question of God's justice; the physical world is described as under the control of Nature; and fortune or chance is portrayed as governing human affairs. Several ninth-century commentaries and one translation illustrate a variety of solutions to the problem of assimilating Boethius's concepts to the mentality of the early Middle Ages.

The earliest commentary on the *Consolation* was written in midcentury by an anonymous monk of St. Gall. This commentary has the appearance of being written for beginners, for the overwhelming majority of the glosses suggest synonyms for unfamiliar words and paraphrases of difficult constructions. When the anonymous author does attempt to discuss doctrine, his primary objective is to develop an interpretation of the *Consolation* that is compatible with Catholic dogma. Some of Boethius's ideas are dismissed out of hand as "gentile" or "philosophical rather than Catholic." At other places, however, the anonymous author was able to discover orthodox doctrine though often at the expense of surface meaning. Philosophy, for example, becomes the Wisdom of God (*Sapientia Dei*) or, in an alternate reading, Christ himself because he, too, was reduced to human form though he touched heaven with his lofty doctrine; the world-soul (a concept Boethius took from platonic writers) becomes the sun; and the neoplatonic spirits that populate Boethius's universe are explained as the angels and men. By thus dismembering the *Consolation* into isolated phrases and concepts that can be interpreted without regard to their place in the whole work, the anonymous monk rendered innocuous whatever challenge Boethius might have posed to Carolingian readers.[51]

One finds in the anonymous monk of St. Gall the curious results of applying the techniques of allegorical interpretation to a secular work; the commentary of Remi of Auxerre reveals the methods of a typical Carolingian man of letters.[52] Writing around 900, Remi could draw upon a century of scholarship as well as his own experience as a commentator on a variety of classical works, and all this learning is displayed in the course of his work on the *Consolation*: a brief essay by Lupus on poetic meters is reproduced in Remi's preface, and the meter of each poem is carefully noted in its proper place; pagan mythology is explicated in great detail (Remi had previously written a book on this subject); and other classical allusions are explained by references to Cicero, Suetonius, and other ancient authors. The information provided on Remi's reading alone makes the commentary worthy of notice. Our own chief interest in Remi is in the glosses where he gives summaries of entire sections or poems, because slight changes in emphasis often betray Remi's tenuous grasp of Boethius's train of thought. A case in point is the sixth poem of book 1, where Philosophy speaks of the impossibility of violating the natural order; Remi's gloss, by introducing the verb "ought" (*debere*), shifts the meaning subtly from physical necessity to moral duty.[53] Similarly handled is the second poem of book 3, where Boethius's purpose is to evoke the immutability of Nature's law: "Now I will show you . . . how mighty Nature . . . providently

51. For the doctrines of this commentary, see Courcelle, *La "Consolation de Philosophie" dans la tradition littéraire* (Paris, 1967), pp. 275–78. Courcelle's concentration on the rare passages where the commentary discusses ideas does however give a somewhat misleading impression of the whole work; the manuscript I consulted was Bibliothèque Nationale [=B. N.], Lat. 13953.

52. Courcelle, *La "Consolation de Philosophie,"* pp. 278–90.

53. "Tenor huius metri totus comparatonibus constat quibus ostenditur quia nihil extra ordinem debere fieri, quod si fiat non habebit laetum exitum. Pertinent autem ad hoc quot ordinabiliter prius levioribus, deinde acrioribus sanandum esse." B. N., Lat. 17814, 22 recto, N. A. Lat. 1478, 10 recto.

governs the immense world by her laws, how she controls all things, binds them with unbreakable bonds." The concept of nature as a system, though central to the meaning of the poem, had no impact on Remi, who concentrated instead on the nature of individual things ("He shows that all things retain their nature") and then headed off on the tangent of arguing that everything is created good in essence even if it is not just in action.[54] In this, as in many other passages, Remi shows himself no less adept than the monk of St. Gall in finding Christian meaning in the most unlikely places.

The last work we have to consider is perhaps the most interesting. King Alfred's rendition of the *Consolation* into Anglo-Saxon was ostensibly a translation—"sometimes word for word, sometimes sense for sense," Alfred says in his preface—but the Anglo-Saxon text in fact reveals a radically different conception of the world from that of Boethius. The question of God's justice does not arise in the Anglo-Saxon *Consolation* with the same force as in the Latin original, because instead of the prisoner being innocent he is guilty of the charges against him. Nature as a symbol of physical necessity disappears altogether, for in the second poem of book 3 Alfred substitutes God for Nature as the force that controls all and omits the phrases "the force of nature," "imitation of nature," and "nature of things."[55] Wyrd, the word that translates Fortune, is not chance but uncertainty; Wisdom defines Wyrd as "God's work that he does every day."[56] Nature and Fortune are removed as buffers between man and God, and Alfred clearly expects the good man to find his reward in the here and now because God "sees the thought of each man, and distinguishes between his words and deeds, and rewards each one according to his deserts."[57] Resignation thus brings not philosophical acceptance of fate but the reward of God's soothing presence when things go wrong. In effect, immanent justice is reintroduced through the back door.

At the same time as Alfred, Remi, and the monk of St. Gall made Boethius accessible, they also deprived the *Consolation* of whatever

54. "Ostendit autem omnem rem suam retinere naturam et licet aliquid deviet adeandem tamen redire conatur. Demonstrat etiam omnia essentialiter esse bona quia dominus bonus omnia bona creavit. Non tamen iusta sunt omnia quae sunt bona. Bona enim in essentia et natura iusta vero sunt in actu et in opero. Hinc est diabolus dicitur bonus essentialiter non tamen iustus est in opere." B. N., Lat. 15090, 34 recto.
55. F. Anne Payne, *King Alfred and Boethius* (Madison, 1968), p. 31.
56. W. J. Sedgefield, *King Alfred's Old English Version of Boethius* (Oxford, 1899), p. 128 lines 17–20.
57. Sedgefield, *King Alfred's Boethius*, p. 141 lines 7–9.

challenge it might have offered to early medieval readers. In this their accomplishments are an image in miniature of the Carolingian period as a whole. For though great strides were made in the liberal arts and in education in general, the most learned men of the Carolingian period regarded themselves as no more than conservators and purifiers of tradition. Their efforts produced no revolution in mentalities; they were not intended to; and by the end of the ninth century the movement that produced them had spent all its energy.

The Tenth Century

The Carolingian era lasted little more than a century; the empire itself barely survived the death of Charlemagne in 814. Though Louis the Pious, Charlemagne's sole surviving son and his successor as emperor, was devoted to the idea of Christian unity, he was incapable of inspiring the fear on its behalf that Charlemagne had. He resisted with only partial and intermittent success the demands of his sons for kingdoms of their own, and three years after his death in 840 they formally partitioned the empire into three kingdoms. Though the imperial title survived, actual power fell to the kings and eventually into the hands of magnates whose interests rarely extended beyond their immediate districts.

The Carolingian revival of intellectual activity endured somewhat longer than the empire, but it too was showing signs of exhaustion by the last decades of the ninth century when Remi and Alfred wrote. There was, to be sure, no return to the levels of illiteracy that had existed before the Carolingians; Charlemagne and Alcuin had built too well for that. Yet a diminution of vigor is unmistakeable by the early tenth century, as the flood of commentaries and original works slowed to a trickle. The decline in quantity was accompanied by a falling off in quality: not only were there no more Erigenas; there were not even Hraban Maurs.

This slackening in intellectual activity has often been blamed on the assaults of the Vikings that began around 800. There is some truth to this charge: England in particular suffered a harsh occupation, and some religious houses on the continent were hard hit as well. But it also seems likely that by 900 the labors of several generations of scholars had left few questions unanswered that it would have occurred to the Carolingians to ask. It is hard to imagine, for example, what could be added to Remi's commentary on the *Consolation* without bursting the framework he established.

For the historian of mentalities, the chief interest of the tenth century lies in the adaptation of men to the void left by the collapse of the Carolingian empire. The orientation to rules and authority did not substantially change. Yet in the absence of a monarch able and willing to decide most issues, individuals were often left to their own devices in determining which rules and rulers ought to be obeyed. Though most of their solutions to this problem were conservative, at least in intention, the cumulative effect of their efforts was to undermine the unity the Carolingians had so painfully achieved.

In government the most remarkable feature of the tenth century was the durability of Carolingian traditions. Although the always fragile institutions of central government had virtually disappeared, the habit of obedience left over from the times of greatness was enough to secure the survival of the Carolingian dynasty for another hundred years. Italy, which lacked any monarchy of its own, proved ready to acknowledge as king whichever northern king could claim lordship as Charlemagne's heir. In west Francia, the territory roughly equivalent to modern France, Carolingians continued to rule until the end of the tenth century, despite occasional breaks in the succession and a thoroughgoing absence of any noteworthy abilities in the kings themselves. East of the Rhine, an illegitimate Carolingian succeeded in having himself recognized as king after the death of Charles the Fat; after the extinction of his line, many eastern Franks attempted to place themselves under the Carolingian king of west Francia. Though this project was abandoned and the family that eventually took control of the kingship was Saxon not Frankish, they looked back to Charlemagne as their predecessor, had themselves crowned at Charlemagne's capital of Aachen, and in midcentury revived the imperial title. Except for the Saxon Ottonians, the jurisdiction of these kings was not usually very great, for they rarely acted outside their personal territories. But this fact only emphasizes the extent to which their authority rested less on their actual power than on their legitimacy as Charlemagne's successors.[58]

The survival of Carolingian practices is equally apparent at the

58. On the reluctance of the Germans to abandon the Carolingians, see K. J. Leyser, *Rule and Conflict in Early Medieval Society* (Bloomington and London, 1979), pp. 1–7; Leyser's discussion of sacral kingship (pp. 75–107) traces the mutations of this idea in the tenth century.

local level. The Carolingian count had been charged with enforcing
the law, holding a court known as a *mallus* for the county he
administered, and generally carrying out whatever orders he was
given by the king. The weakness of central authority meant that
counts, who previously had been subject to transfer and removal by
the king, were able to make themselves hereditary lords, but otherwise changes came slowly. In most places counts freed themselves
from their connections with the monarchy only gradually and even
then continued to go through the motions of holding court in the
manner of their Carolingian predecessors.

This process can be observed in detail in the area around Mâcon
in southern Burgundy, one of the better documented and best studied regions of the tenth century. Though the office of count itself
became hereditary after 890 in the family of a man named Racoux,
for the first half of the tenth century the counts continued to acknowledge the superiority of the king of west Francia by permitting
him to invest them with their office and attending the royal court
when it met nearby. After midcentury, however, even these slender
bonds were broken: 949, when Louis IV visited Autun, was the last
occasion when the king of France came to the region, and 959 the
last time any count of southern Burgundy sought royal installation
into office. Since regional lords were no more successful in exerting
control over the counts of Mâcon, these were for all intents and
purposes independent sovereigns by 950. Henceforth the counts
held their office as private property and exercised the power of the
ban, originally a grant from the king to his representative, as a
personal possession.[59]

A similar history can be told for the comtal court. In Mâcon, as
elsewhere in France, the court appears to have preserved into the
tenth century much of its old character as a public forum. The term
mallus publicus was still occasionally used to describe it; magnates
other than the count attended regularly; and litigants who were not
personally dependent on the count brought their cases to the court
for trial. After midcentury, however, one begins to see signs that the
public peacekeeping functions of the court were being forgotten.
Instead of exercising its jurisdiction over cases as a matter of
course, the court's power to decide cases depended increasingly on
the accused's agreement by solemn oath to accept the judgment of
the court; and the assessors of the court, traditionally known as

59. Georges Duby, *La société aux XIe et XIIe siècles dans la région
mâconnaise* (Paris, 1971), pp. 89–93.

scabini, came to be described as the *fideles* or vassals of the count. While the new terminology may not, as Duby believes, mean the court's personnel had changed, the shift is significant as another indication that the court was being seen as a possession of the count.[60]

These transformations, of the count from official to lord and of the *mallus* from royal to comtal court, are found in most regions of Europe in the tenth century. (The chief exception is east Francia or Germany, where the strong Saxon monarchy kept alive the tradition of kingship as the sole legitimate authority.) This fragmentation of the powers of government is usually accounted for by the desire of nobles for independence. But while tenth-century magnates probably liked taking orders no more than most people, the demands made on them by their superiors were too slight and the process of gaining independence too drawn out for willful rebelliousness to have been more than a contributory factor. Instead, it is probably correct to see the main cause of these developments in the erosion of the belief that obedience was due. By 940 the experience of royal intervention in southern Burgundy was remote. To most observers, the count and the *mallus* must have seemed to exist entirely on their own, and possibly the counts themselves nearly forgot their own origins as royal officials. When unable to see the purpose of language and practices whose origins lay in a society far different from their own, people adapted their customs and terminology to reflect the situation they believed existed.

While the durability of Carolingian forms is probably the most remarkable fact of tenth-century government, the changes that did occur are not the less significant for that. Although the counts continued to hear cases brought before them, as their awareness of their public duties dwindled they seem to have acted less and less frequently as agents of peace; quarrels between magnates, which often led to armed conflict, met little check. Moreover, in a society where all authority came from above, once the count's connections with the king had been severed, there existed no alternate source of legitimacy for the count's right to rule. Shorn of all supporting ideology, the Carolingian legal order henceforth depended on habit and the military power of the counts. The entire structure of government was now vulnerable to the first occasion when a magnate's

60. Duby, "Recherches sur l'évolution des institutions judicaires pendant le Xe et le XIe siècle dans le sud de la Bourgogne," *Moyen Age* 52 (1946): 153–61; *La société mâconnaise,* pp. 93–98.

personal interest clashed with the custom of obedience to the count.

When we turn from secular to monastic institutions the picture is similar. The supremacy of the Benedictine Rule, established as the sole legitimate rule by Carolingian policy, remained unchallenged; no new rules were written in this period. Yet the impression of continuity is undercut by the destruction suffered by individual houses. Part of the damage was done by invaders, because monasteries—as settlements well-known to be rich in movable treasures—were favorite targets for the Northmen. Some monasteries were sacked several times, and in certain regions—notably England—organized communities virtually ceased to exist. Scarcely less serious was the collapse of central authority that left most communities free of outside supervision. Many houses fell into the hands of the local magnate who served as their lay protector, often with the result that the magnate took the title and office of abbot for himself. Discipline in houses under lay abbots was rarely severe: some monks are known to have moved their wives or concubines into the monastery with them, so that only their tonsures distinguished them from laymen. But even where the forms of monastic behavior were better preserved, observance of the rule was rarely complete and at best mechanical.

Much of what we know about the internal organization of monasteries comes from the complaints of ardent spirits, for there were a few of these to be found in the tenth century. One of them was Romuald of Ravenna, whose devotion to the Rule was perhaps typical of the type. Romuald entered a monastery more or less by chance when, in the early 970s at the age of twenty, he went to Saint Apollinaris at Classe to do penance for his share in the murder of his uncle by his father. A vision of St. Apollinaris inspired him to take monastic vows—he had first to obtain the support of the archbishop because the monks feared the anger of his father—and the enthusiasm one often finds in converts led him soon to be critical of his fellow monks. The basis of his complaints appears to have been that the monks' behavior did not conform to the Rule (Romuald's biographer Peter Damian tells us that he often quoted to them relevant portions of the Rule) and after three years of such criticisms some of the other monks plotted to kill him. After one of the conspirators, apparently moved by guilt, disclosed the plot to Romuald, Romuald fled to live as a hermit.[61] A subsequent return

61. Damian, *Vita beati Romualdi*, c. 3, ed. G. Tabacco, [*Fonti per la Storia d'Italia* no. 94 (Rome, 1957)].

to Classe as abbot, undertaken at the insistence of Emperor Otto III, ended no more happily. Again stressing the Rule, Romuald governed strictly, but according to Damian the monks reacted badly, "going from bad to worse."[62] Romuald resigned his abbacy to go back to his hermitage, though he subsequently had to escape a murder attempt by one of the succeeding abbots at Classe whom Romuald accused of simony.

Romuald was disappointed in his desire to live according to the Rule, but not all those eager for monastic life were so unsuccessful. One who found a spiritually satisfying existence was Odo of Cluny whose biography, written by his friend John of Salerno shortly after Odo's death in 942, reveals a search for rigor that bears many resemblances to Romuald's. Dedicated at birth to St. Martin by his father, Odo began at the age of sixteen to experience severe headaches that did not abate until he entered the chapter at Tours and thus paid the promised gift in full. Once tonsured, however, Odo soon found the life of a canon insufficiently strict and he, like Romuald, went to live with a friend in a hermitage. The two of them looked "throughout France" for a monastery to enter without finding one that met their standards until the friend, Adhegrinus, chanced to stay in the Burgundian monastery of Baume when on a pilgrimage to Rome. The customs of the place so impressed him that he established residence in a small cell nearby and sent for Odo who, as an educated man (he had studied with Remi of Auxerre), was made master of the school.[63] When Berno, the abbot of Baume, founded a new house near Mâcon at Cluny, Odo and Adhegrinus moved there; when Berno died in 926, Odo succeeded him as abbot.

While no customals survive from tenth-century Cluny, some idea of the discipline that attracted Odo can be obtained from John's biography. The Cluniacs attributed their customs to a legislator of an early age who is, although they had the name wrong, clearly Benedict of Aniane, but they, in fact, recognized as obligatory many practices that had no precedent in Anianian legislation. It was evidently a matter of great concern, for example, that at the end of a meal the monks gather all crumbs and consume them; John writes feelingly about the anxiety of a monk who, absorbed by the reading, let the time set aside for eating pass with the crumbs still in his hand.[64] Other rules mentioned by John required the use of a candle

---

62. Ibid., cc. 22–23; for Romuald's later accusation against an abbot for simony, see c. 41.
63. John of Salerno, *Vita Odonis*, i.31, 35 (*PL*, 133: 56–57, 58).
64. Loc. cit.

by the schoolmaster when taking a boy to the privy at night.[65] The overwhelming impression is of a community that felt considerable uneasiness when faced with actions not covered by rules.

The rules that governed Cluny had their origin in authorities of many kinds.[66] Scripture was one source of custom, particularly the example of Old Testament patriarchs. Another was Benedict of Aniane's *Concordia Regularum*,[67] a collection of monastic rules of all kinds, although whereas Benedict in good Carolingian form had collected these rules in preparation for standardizing monastic customs and omitted many when he issued his reforms, the Cluniacs treated the *Concordia* as a quarry to be mined for new rules. Still another source of authority was miracles: the rule requiring the eating of crumbs was lent force by two miracles concerning its observance. Often John, and one suspects Odo as well, did not know the origin of their customs, but as long as they could cite some kind of sacred authority for their actions the precise origins of a given custom appeared to matter little.

Cluny's eagerness to gather customs from all sources was motivated by a belief that actions performed in accord with rules were the only means to salvation. Odo himself emerges from John of Salerno's biography as a man obsessed with the ideal of literal obedience: John tells us that Odo always gave money to the poor, whether or not he had enough for himself, and that—in obedience to the Rule's command that monks cast their eyes down in humility—Odo looked at the ground to the extent that he was known by the other monks as the Digger. Odo justified this conception of piety by telling John the story of a refugee from a community where discipline had broken down; he came to Cluny dressed in a blue habit. Desiring to give Cluny all he owned, the monk had returned to his previous monastery to collect his possessions when he was stricken by illness. As he lay dying the Cluniac brother who accompanied him had a vision of St. Benedict in heaven turning away his soul because his habit was of the wrong color; only the quick action of the Cluniac in changing clothes with the dying man

65. Ibid., i.30; ii.23 (*PL* 133: 56, 73).
66. I have utilized in my discussion of Clunian custom the interesting article by Barbara Rosenwein, "Rules and the 'Rule' at tenth century Cluny," *Studia Monastica* 19 (1977): 307–20; and see now her *Rhinoceros Bound: Cluny in the Tenth Century* (Philadelphia, 1982). Professor Rosenwein disagrees with certain of my conclusions; cf. *American Historical Review* 84 (1979): 308–9. But see the next paragraph below.
67. *PL* 103: 713–1380.

enabled his salvation. "Attend therefore son," said Odo in conclu- 141
sion to John,
The Search
for a Rule

> to the word of the Apostle saying: *Faith if it have not works is
> dead* [Jam. ii, 17] and as it is written elsewhere: *He who saith
> that he knoweth Christ ought himself to walk as he walked*
> [I John ii, 4, 6.]. So he who professes to be a monk ought in
> work and word to imitate the Father Benedict, because it is
> written *Not the hearers of the law are just before God, but
> the doers* [Rom. ii, 13]. Purity of mind is not sufficient for a
> monk if indications or signs of other works are lacking.[68]

In the absence of the proper external behavior, therefore, good
intentions were not enough.

Foreign as this ideal seems to us today, there can be little doubt
it struck a responsive chord in the tenth century. The success of
Cluny itself is perhaps the best evidence for the popularity of a
disciplined external obedience: already in the 930s Cluny's customs
were being adopted by other communities—most notably Fleury in
the Loire valley and several Roman establishments which Odo was
invited to reform—and by the middle of the eleventh century Cluny
ruled a monastic empire numbering over a thousand houses. Moreover, though Cluny's success was unique, the desire to live entirely
according to rules led to the elaboration of detailed routines at
most reformed monasteries. At Gorze, for example, though the
emphasis was placed on physical labor and austerity rather than
the liturgy for which Cluny became famous, the calendar was filled
with fasts and vigils that consumed the monks' time. And when, in
the 970s, the council of Winchester met to reform the monasteries
of England, it proceeded by preparing a lengthy customal that was
to be binding on all English communities.[69]

In monasticism as in politics, therefore, the tenth century was
characterized chiefly by a proliferation of local customs. Though
the contrast with the Carolingians' efforts to impose uniform customs could hardly be greater, the underlying motive—to establish
perfect rules—was essentially the same. Under Charlemagne, re-

---

68. *Vita Odonis* iii.2. The translation is from Gerard Sitwell, *St. Odo of
Cluny* (London and New York, 1958), p. 73.
69. For the spread of Cluny's customs and for those of Gorze, see K.
Hallinger, *Gorze-Kluny* (Graz, 1970). The text of the *Regularis Concordia*
issued by the council of Winchester has been edited by Thomas Symons
(London, 1953).

forms had been shaped by the awareness that the growth of the Frankish empire had produced a disturbing variety in usages; in the tenth century, with the collapse of the empire, the lacunae in existing codes were felt more acutely. The destruction of Carolingian unity resulted not from changing mentalities but from the same mentality operating in changed circumstances.

FIVE

Conclusion to Part II

Mentality and Society in the Early Middle Ages

Governments must conform to the nature of the men governed. This axiom shows that in the nature of human civil things the public school of princes is the morality of the peoples.

—*The New Science,* 246, 247.

"Confronted by man," wrote Fernand Braudel at the end of his great work on the Mediterranean, "I am tempted always to see him enclosed in a destiny that he scarcely helps fabricate, in a landscape that stretches before and after him in the infinite stretches of 'long duration.'"[1] Braudel's view that human society is shaped primarily by external forces has been widely accepted by historians, but it will be apparent from the title of this book that I do not agree. The dominant mentality of an age does not simply mirror social and economic conditions. It can be a force in its own right.

In the foregoing chapters we have already seen several instances of this process at work: how the emergence of a new mentality under the Roman Empire caused the recasting of classical traditions and eventually the restructuring of government itself; how in the fifth and sixth centuries legal and religious institutions were brought into agreement with the morality of the period; and how, under the Carolingians, the activities of kings and scholars were directed by their ideas about the proper duties of men. Before leaving the early Middle Ages, however, it is perhaps appropriate to offer a few less obvious illustrations of the impact of mentality upon everyday life. The strength of these examples as evidence of mentalities is necessarily less great than the more discursive materials we have been using, for when evaluating behavior there is always room for uncertainty that one has correctly inferred the un-

1. *La Méditerranée et le monde méditerranéen a l'époque de Philippe II,* 2d ed. (Paris, 1966), 2: 250.

derlying motivation. Yet though difficult, analysis is by no means impossible, and in light of the emphasis usually given to the effects of social structure upon ideas, the opportunity to discuss the reverse process is well worth the risks.

Probably the clearest cases of the influence of mentalities are those that resulted from reliance on supernatural forces. Belief in magic is endemic in all primitive societies, and conversion to Christianity did—and does—little to alter this fact; the place of pagan deities and powers is simply taken by the Christian god, the saints, or their relics. The ordeal is perhaps the best documented instance of the baptism of pagan rituals, but in fact charms survived for practically every purpose. An early British manuscript contains a series of Christian charms for a variety of occasions, and the use of Christian fertility rites, such as sprinkling holy water on fields or beasts, is attested until well after the end of our period.[2] Prayers could even become a commodity of exchange: Lupus of Ferrières tried to obtain a quantity of lead from the king of England by offering him prayers in return.[3]

Perhaps the most interesting cases of Christian magic are the rituals used to blast enemies. The calling down of curses has good Biblical precedent, especially in the Old Testament, and Gregory of Tours alone provides several examples of the invocation of God's vengeance. (Divine justice could also work unbidden, of course, but this is a rather different phenomenon.) No particular form of prayer appears to have been thought necessary, however, until the tenth century, when care was being taken to give standard form to all kinds of activities. Several rituals survive from that period that illustrate nicely the relationship that existed between people and supernatural forces.

A malediction from the monastery of Saint Wandrille in Rouen has recently been studied by Lester Little. The curse actually seems to date from the ninth century, but true to the methods of that age the claim was made that the text derived from ancient and venerable authority: Saint Wandrille himself was said to have received the curse from Pope Martin I as a gift for the protection of the monastery, and its geneology went through a series of archbishops and popes all the way back to Pope Sylvester I (314–355). Cast in the form of an invocation to God, the malediction asks for the

2. Hugh Farmer, "The Studies of Anglo-Saxon Monks (A.D. 600–800)" in *Los Monjes y los estudios* (Abadia de Poblet, 1963), p. 99.
3. Duby, *The Early Growth of the European Economy*, trans. Howard B. Clarke (Ithaca, 1974), pp. 55–56.

damnation of the malefactors persecuting the monastery in terms that allowed few loopholes for escape:

> Let their part and inheritance be crucified by perpetual fire, with Dathan and Abiram, Judas and Pilate, Saphira and Anania, Caiaphas and Annas, Simon and Nero, with whom let them be tortured by perpetual crucifixion without end. . . . Let them be cursed in the cities. Cursed in the fields. Cursed in castles. Cursed in islands. Cursed be the fruit of their bellies. Cursed in their homes. Cursed entering. Cursed exiting. Cursed in all places. Let the lord cast over them hunger, famine, and rebukes, and on all the works they do. . . .

Technically the monks had no power to perform an anathematization; that right was reserved to bishops. Yet the form of this malediction leaves no doubt that the monks believed the ritual itself would be effective. A similar curse from the monastery of Saint Martial concludes with the words (presumably accompanied by the snuffing of candles) "and thus may all memory of them be extinguished forever and ever."[4]

Similar to maledictions both in purpose and in the confidence that the correct enactment of the ritual would itself have the desired result were the procedures for humiliating relics. The idea was that the saint should be made aware of the indignities suffered by the community by suffering some of his own—usually by having his relics placed on the floor in front of the altar, in the case of St. Martin of Tours by covering the saint's tomb with thorns. Thus alerted to the danger of the community (and to his own lapses as a protector), the saint could then be expected to seek out the malefactor named in the ritual and punish him for his misdeeds. One could hardly find a clearer expression of the belief that saints retained a physical reality through their relics, or of the personal relationship that was expected to exist between the saints and their worshippers.[5]

The willingness of people to utilize these rituals should not be seen as a harmless expression of anxiety about the uncertainty of life. The decision to call upon the saints often meant that other,

4. Lester K. Little, "Formules monastiques de malédiction aux IXe et Xe siècles," *Revue Mabillon* t. 58 (1970–75): 377–99; and, by the same author, "Le morphologie des maledictions monastiques," *Annales: Economies. Sociétés. Civilizations.* 51 (1979): 43–60.
5. Patrick Geary, "L'humiliation des saints," *Annales: E. S. C.* 51 (1979): 27–42.

potentially more productive solutions to problems were explored poorly or not at all. Thus, though maledictions themselves may have worked well enough in certain cases—monks not being the only people to believe in supernatural forces—more lasting and general barriers to violence might have been achieved through forming combinations with other people for mutual protection. And the reliance on charms in other areas may have had still graver consequences: fertility rites may have made people feel better, but manure has a more marked effect on agricultural yield.

A second area of interest is the influence of mentalities on government. Given the ineffective personalities of many kings of this period, the lack of any strong institutions to support them, and the many forces tending toward fragmentation, it hardly overstates the case to claim that the egocentric disposition to see authority residing in superiors provided the chief foundation of early medieval kingdoms. The belief that royal power came from God, widespread throughout all classes of society, proved a surprisingly good barrier to encroachment by magnates of nonroyal families. The long survival on the throne of both the Merovingians and Carolingians shows how effective a barrier this idea could be. Indeed, the history of Frankish politics from the sixth century on makes very little sense unless one accepts the fact that the prestige of kings had little to do with their actual power.

The influence of mentalities can be seen more subtly in the literalistic attitudes that both rulers and subjects brought to their duties. Kings shared their subjects' belief that their authority was divine in origin, and they also accepted the idea that God expected them to preserve the peace and protect the Church. But few kings brought to their office either the understanding of what those responsibilities entailed or the sincere desire to fulfill them that Charlemagne did, and they tended to carry out their duties in a fairly perfunctory manner. Most felt it was enough to exhort their subjects to obey the law and to refrain from breaking it themselves, often regarding with indifference the wrongs their subjects did to each other. Much of the disorder of the early Middle Ages can be directly attributed to the tolerance officials bore toward violence that did not affect them directly.

The literalistic conception of duty one finds in officials was matched, however, by that of their subjects. The mechanical, rule-following nature of loyalty in the early Middle Ages is well illustrated by the long list of obligations in which Charlemagne had all his subjects instructed: they were (according to the capitulary of

802) to obey God, abstain from seizing properties of the emperor, obey the call to the army without fraud, obey the *bannum* (authority) of the emperor, and pay the rents they owed the emperor. Charlemagne thought this catalog of rules a great improvement on previous definitions of fidelity, and perhaps it was. Before his time, Franks had been expected only to refrain from imperiling the life of the king, to refrain from introducing enemies into the kingdom, and to report instances of infidelity they witnessed in others.[6] Yet the fact that Charlemagne believed an oath of such detail could deter wrongdoing is the best evidence for the essentially passive obedience early medieval kings could expect.

The consequences of this orientation toward literal, external obedience can also be seen in the history of vassalage. Originally a tie between a magnate and the armed retainers who lived with him and whom he provided with arms and food (one thinks of the ring-giving kings of *Beowulf*, though the term is not used there), vassalage was adapted by the Carolingians to relations between the king and his counts. The motive for persuading counts to become vassals was undoubtedly to reinforce the official duties of the count by creating a personal tie to the king, because a personal relationship was, as Ganshof observed and Piaget would agree, "more meaningful to men of limited intellectual development."[7] But while this plan worked well enough for Charlemagne, the fear of whose vengeance could deter even the most hardened felon, its success was not lasting and by the tenth century vassalic bonds imposed at best the obligation to avoid doing direct harm that previously characterized relations between king and subject. Marc Bloch explained this development, which greatly contributed to the political fragmentation of the tenth and eleventh centuries, as an expression of "violent manners and unstable temperament; the men of this period," he wrote, "were in every way much more disposed to show formal respect for rules than to obey them consistently in practice."[8] Bloch thought of this phenomenon as an "inconsistency" that needed explanation, but we can now see that the contradiction is only apparent when one interprets tenth-century rules by our reasoning: for the egocentric mind, obedience to rules requires no more than formal respect.

The attitude toward duties of both rulers and ruled meant that it

6. On this oath, and the notion of loyalty in general, see F. L. Ganshof, *Frankish Institutions under Charlemagne* (Providence, 1958), pp. 13–14.
7. Ibid., p. 52.
8. *Feudal Society*, trans. L. A. Manyon (Chicago, 1961), 1: 235–36.

was difficult to get people to do anything out of the ordinary: mobilizing an army could take weeks or months; imposing a new tax might be nearly impossible. In most periods this rigidity may have made little difference, but in the ninth and tenth centuries the inability of government to respond flexibly to new circumstances greatly increased the vulnerability of Europe to the Vikings and other invaders. The speed with which seaborne invaders could strike would, of course, have been a problem for any society, but what is remarkable about the tenth century is the ease with which hostile forces could seize and hold large sections of territory. Bloch cites the example of Le Freinet on the coast of Provence, which was held by Saracens from 890 until 972, when their capture of the abbot of Cluny roused the count of Provence to expel them.[9] The success of these Saracens, and of the Vikings who settled Normandy, is due less to their own military superiority than to the incapacity of Christian magnates to recognize their obligation to provide a defense for their society and to exert themselves in a sustained fashion unless their personal interests were at stake.

Finally, a word must be said about the effects of mental attitudes on economic and social structures. Some of these I have already had occasion to mention in discussing beliefs about the supernatural, which altered economic behavior by making it possible to barter goods for prayers and modified agricultural techniques by encouraging reliance on charms. In the present context I shall confine my discussion to one of the most important sources for the social history of the Carolingian period, the polyptyque of St. Germain.[10]

This document, compiled in the early ninth century at the command of Abbot Irmion of the abbey of St. Germain, is the earliest and most extensive of surviving Carolingian estate inventories, covering 24 villages in the region around Paris. As one would expect from a landlord's inventory, a thorough accounting is made of the rents and services owed the abbey, but information is also provided on a surprising variety of additional subjects including the sex, age, and social status of the inhabitants, the number of buildings, the size and yields of the fields, and the number of livestock. The quantity and detail of the census have made the polyptyque valuable for determining family size, population density, and agricultural productivity for a period when other reliable sources are exceedingly rare.

9. *Feudal Society,* 1: 5–7.
10. For much of what follows, see C. E. Perrin, "Observations sur la manse dans la région parisienne au début du IXe siècle," *Annales d'histoire sociale* 2 (1945): 39–52.

A peculiarity of the polyptyque is the lack of correspondence between the register's division of land into accounting units called *mansi* and the actual structure of landholding. Since *mansus* means household, each unit may once have held a single family, but the actual situation described by the polyptyque is quite different. Some families hold several *mansi*. Other *mansi* are divided among several families. At the village of Neuillay there are no instances of a *mansus* held by one family; instead, every individual *mansus* is shared by two to four families, with other parcels described as half and quarter *mansi* paying dues separately. Whatever the reality the *mansus* may have had in earlier periods, by the ninth century it had become an accounting fiction.

If one asks why such an awkward system was preserved, one answer certainly was its convenience. Fixing payments once and for all spared administrators the need to reassess dues whenever property changed hands through sale or inheritance. One finds the same tendency, for example, in the polyptyque's descriptions as "servile" of certain tenements held by free men. Presumably these *mansi* had at one time been held by slaves—they are as a rule smaller than free *mansi*—and the status of the tenement had become merged with the status of the tenant.

Yet it is hard not to suspect that the complexity of the accounting scheme is due in part to an egocentricism that attributed reality to names and categories regardless of their current utility.[11] Bloch, commenting on this problem, observed that one rarely finds two manorial surveys, even from a single region, that use the same criteria for legal status. Some borrowed Germanic and Roman terminology indiscriminately; the polyptyque of St. Germain recognizes *lidi*, alongside Roman *coloni* and *servi*. Other surveys, which tried simply to describe reality, found they could not do so with precision, with the result that there is considerable overlap in the characteristics of different social classes. "Evidently," Bloch remarked, "to contemporaries the structure of the society in which they lived did not possess clear-cut contours."[12] The meticulous preservation of increasingly meaningless categories thus was more than an obstruction to the efficient collection of rents, though it certainly was that; it had the further consequence of rendering the legal organization of society virtually impossible to grasp intellectually, even for those few who might have been tempted to make the effort.

11. For comparably arbitrary systems of classification, see C. R. Hallpike, *Foundations of Primitive Thought* (Oxford, 1979), pp. 123–24.
12. *Feudal Society*, 1: 256.

The cultural history of the Middle Ages is often explained by reference to the poverty and political disorder of the times, but it is too often forgotten that those conditions were not visitations like plague or bad weather. People contributed to them by their actions, and their actions were the consequence of the reasoning by which they interpreted their world. The disposition to seek miraculous remedies, the inability to work together for common goals, the rigidity of mind that caused people to evaluate current conditions in terms of outmoded categories and traditions—these features of the mentality of the early Middle Ages were as important in shaping the society of the times as any economic force.

The Process of Enlightenment

These commonwealths gave birth to philosophy . . . and from the philosophies providence permitted eloquence to arise and, from the very form of these popular commonwealths in which good laws are commanded, to become impassioned for justice, and from these ideas of virtue to inflame the people to command good laws.

—*The New Science*, 1101.

The Making of
a New Mentality

Europe in the
Eleventh Century

*There ensued the third kind
of authority, which is that
of credit or reputation for
wisdom.*

—*The New Science*, 946.

In the foregoing chapters we have discovered a remarkable consistency in the way Europeans reasoned about their society and the world between the late Roman Empire and the tenth century. They looked for direction to the pronouncements of superiors—kings, abbots, or the ancients—whom they tended to regard as divinely inspired. They took little interest in relations between peers except to regulate exchange and reprisals, extending the system of vengeance and compensation even to dealings between men and God, and they had no sense of society as a community based on consent. They rarely concerned themselves with intention, whether they were assessing the morality of an action or interpreting the words of authority. And they believed their actions and wishes could influence the physical world either by the invocation of supernatural forces through ritualized prayer or by providing the occasion for the operation of divine justice.

In 1000 this mentality was still intact, but the next hundred years brought dramatic changes. Before midcentury, theologians and legists began to study the writings of authorities with a new critical spirit, aware that they had to choose the best among many available interpretations. In 1075 Gregory VII began the struggles with secular authority that within a few years would lead to a conception of relations between rulers and their subjects that placed both in the context of a human society. By 1100 the desire to live according to new ideals of interior spirituality had found expression in the creation of religious orders that differed in organization and purpose from the monasteries of the early Middle Ages. Separately each of these developments constituted a significant departure from the reasoning of the early Middle Ages; taken together they *153* signaled the origins of the mentality that became ascendant in the twelfth century.

How was this shift from one mentality to another accomplished? This must be a central question for any study of medieval culture as it is for this one, and the efforts of scholars to explain the process of change fall into two general classes. One is the group that begins with twelfth-century culture in its mature form and tries to trace its most obvious features back to their origins. The value of this approach depends entirely on the selection of features to be studied, however, and in practice historians have too often been mesmerized by the notion that what happened in the twelfth century was a "renaissance." This concept has undeniable value as a description of the twelfth century, and it has generated much valuable research into textual traditions, school curricula, and other issues essential to understanding the culture of the period. But the hypothesis of the renaissance as an engine of cultural change, with its attendant idea that the new ways of reasoning must have grown out of the recovery of classical learning, has not been as fruitful. Either we have been left with serious lacunae in tracing the process of change, as when the history of logic skips from Gerbert to Lanfranc to Abelard; or the new texts in science, law, and philosophy prove on inspection to have come into circulation only because intellectuals touched by the new mentality actively sought them out. The conclusion is unavoidable that people, not books, were the authors of the new culture.

The second approach to this period takes as its point of departure the growth of towns and commerce. No one can doubt the importance of towns as forums for the growth of learned disciplines, for the routines of monasteries and noble courts were generally incompatible with the intense study and specialized disputations through which critical methods are refined.[1] But the positive effects of urbanization or the growth of commerce on the development of reasoning are harder to discover. To begin with, if one mapped the areas where new kinds of reasoning first appeared, one would find that the cultural changes were by no means confined to the areas of Europe most affected by the revival of commerce. Chartres and Pavia, two of the centers to be discussed below, were perhaps not greatly different in the early eleventh century from what they had been before, and Chartres was not even situated in a region undergoing great economic change. A further difficulty is

1. The chief exception is St. Anselm, but he *is* an exception.

that within the towns those who were most involved in the new
culture had little apparent connection to the new economy. Merchants—the class most caught up in the new economic system—
played an insignificant role in the creation of the new culture, and
it is hard to see how commerce affected the jurists and clerics who
did make the essential contributions because in their work these
specialists tended to follow their own interests instead of attending
to the issues that might be useful to merchants. Perhaps this is only
to be expected; businessmen today make money not culture, and
there is no reason to believe that twelfth-century merchants were
any different. Yet for those who have wished to argue it was experience with money that generated the culture of the twelfth century,
it has been disappointing to find that those who handled money the
most otherwise contributed so little.

If instead of looking for specific doctrines or social conditions
one looks for departures from the reasoning of the early Middle
Ages, what emerges as the key to the period is the collapse of
traditional authority that occurred in many regions in the late tenth
and early eleventh centuries. In the early Middle Ages the habit of
looking to superiors had been reinforced by the ready availability of
authority: at first the texts of the ancients and later, when the
internal contradictions of tradition became clear, the decision of
kings or powerful church leaders. Thus the predestination controversy of the ninth century had been settled not by general debate
but by the actions of Hincmar of Reims and Charles the Bald. By
the eleventh century, however, the power of rulers was disintegrating in much of Europe. Unable any longer to count on their superiors to settle their disputes, disputants found it useless to cite rules
and authorities in support of their position; the other side simply
answered with citations of its own. Instead, people had to learn
ways of persuading their peers by showing their interpretation of
the texts was correct, by answering the arguments of their opponents, and in general by appealing to the good sense of their audience. The effort to adapt to this necessity stimulated the development of cognitive skills that had rarely been required since the time
of Cicero.

Saying that disorder sparked the development of advanced reasoning doubtless will strike many as peculiar. I will admit it was
not what I expected when I began research, and that I offer it as an
interpretation only because it fits the facts of where the new kinds
of reasoning can earliest be found. But it is not as paradoxical a
position as it may at first appear. Prosperity and security may favor

the development of intellectual disciplines along established lines, as they did in the ninth and again in the twelfth centuries, but they are not necessarily inducements for innovations. Learning to think in new ways is no easy task, and people undertake the labor only because circumstances drive them to it. Further, to say that disorder was productive of intellectual development in the eleventh century is not the same as saying that it always has this effect, because credit must also be given to the relatively high level of education achieved as a result of Charlemagne's reforms. By itself, as we have seen, Carolingian education produced no breakthroughs in reasoning. Yet its successes meant that debate would begin only at a level where solutions could not be found by reference to ancient authority, and that once begun there would be a sufficient body of scholars to sustain the discussion that stimulated the development of analytical cognitive skills.

The effects of this subtle transformation in the conditions of discussion and debate can be traced in three distinct movements of thought. The earliest was the resumption of philosophical and theological inquiry in northern France, of which evidence can be found in the first decades of the eleventh century. The second was the revival of legal studies in the middle decades of the century that can be traced to Pavia, the old capital of Lombardy, which was the seat of the kingdom's highest court. Last of all was the demand for church reforms, given special urgency by the growing diversity of society in the towns, which provoked continent-wide debate about the proper forms of Christian life. Only the last of these has received much attention from historians, because the other two produced little in the way of new ideas until the second half of the eleventh century. It is the use of this criterion, in fact, that is responsible for the impression that medieval culture changed suddenly in the few decades around 1100. But by looking at reasoning instead of doctrine, we can trace the development of thought generation by generation across the whole eleventh century. That in itself is a strong argument in favor of seeing changes in cognition as lying near the heart of the cultural transformation.

Dialectic and Debate in Eleventh-Century France

Since reliance on formal logic is the most distinctive feature of the schools of the twelfth century, historians have often taken the use of logic as the measure of what is important in the eleventh. Almost

invariably this attitude has led them to the work of Gerbert of
Aurillac.[2] Born a few years before 950, Gerbert was given as a child
to the monastery of St. Gerald of Aurillac, where he received his
early education. A chance encounter with the count of Barcelona
took him to Spain in 967 where he apparently became acquainted
with some Arabic learning on mathematics, and from that time
forward he enjoyed the patronage of some of the most powerful
men in Europe, including three emperors and the king of France.
His letters show him engaged in political intrigue at the highest
levels.[3] "Dangerous times do not allow one to commit all the things
to letters that can be entrusted to very trusty messengers," he wrote
to one correspondent. "Weigh carefully the many ideas in the few
lines of this letter," he wrote to another. "The dangerous times
have extinguished our freedom of saying clearly exactly what we
mean."[4] In the long run this policy paid off in his nomination to the
papacy by Otto III, but his career also suffered the reverses of a
man whose advancement depended on the favor of patrons: named
in 980 by Otto II to be abbot of the great monastery of St. Colum-
ban of Bobbio, he was driven out at Otto's death three years later;
in 991 he was elected archbishop of Reims with the support of
Hugh Capet and lost that position when Hugh deserted him; and
in 997 he went to Sasbach to take possession of an estate given him
by Otto III only to find the property taken from him by another
official acting in Otto's name. Although Gerbert's frequent remind-
ers of his services and loyalty in his letters to the Ottonians reveal
the personal costs of these experiences, in an age when traditional

2. For a convenient summary of Gerbert's career see Harriet Pratt Lattin's
introduction to her translation, *Letters of Gerbert* (New York, 1961);
R. W. Southern, *Making of the Middle Ages* (New Haven, 1953), pp. 175–
79; and Uta Lindgren, *Gerbert von Aurillac und das Quadrivium. Untersuchungen zur Bildung in Zeitalter der Ottonen* (Wiesbaden, 1976).
3. Auerbach rightly observed of Gerbert "that his adroitness and calculation did not serve a cause in which he deeply believed, but his own advantage. It can scarcely be denied that almost throughout his life Gerbert was
a political intriguer without ideas. He was capable of personal affection
... but within these limits he was an ambitious gambler who made use of
ideas for the personal advantage they seemed to hold out to him. . . . At
times, especially in the struggle over the archbishopric of Reims, we have
the impression that, like so many lesser minds, this wonderfully gifted
man, with a naivete that was almost sincere, looked on what served his
purposes as right and proper." *Latin Literary Language and Its Public*,
trans. Ralph Manheim (New York, 1965), p. 173.
4. *Die Briefsammlung Gerberts von Reims*, ed. Fritz Weigle (Berlin/Zu-
rich/Dublin, 1966), letters 38, 41.

hierarchies were crumbling there cannot have been many men as dependent as he on the patronage of great men.

Despite Gerbert's varied and interesting life, his historical significance lies chiefly in his contributions to learning. He introduced Europeans to the abacus and the astrolabe, which he had encountered while in Spain, and he constructed devices for the observation of the stars that were much in demand among his contemporaries. He wrote treatises on arithmetic and geometry, subjects that had received little attention in Latin Christendom since antiquity. And he was the first to lecture systematically on the logical works of Boethius. R. W. Southern, who took the beginning of Gerbert's career as the starting point of *The Making of the Middle Ages*, is just one of those who have celebrated these accomplishments.

When we ask, however, not what Gerbert studied but how he studied it, the significance of his contributions becomes more doubtful. Too often his expertise is turned to purposes that are pedantic or trivial. The treatise *De Rationali et Ratione Uti*, for example, Gerbert's only writing on logic, addressed the problem of whether the statement "rationality involves the use of reason" contradicts Porphyry's rule that greater or more universal things can be predicated of lesser but not the reverse.[5] To solve this problem Gerbert worked from Aristotle's distinction between necessary and possible actions to the distinction between power and action, finally concluding that "the use of reason is an accidental fact and since accident may be an attribute of the subject, it is legitimate to say that the rational being makes use of reason." Gerbert's ability to manipulate the principles of logic to reach this conclusion is undeniable, but the reader of the treatise must come away wondering whether the issue on which he spent so much energy was of importance to any conceivable audience. Gerbert himself draws no broader lessons from his proof—he does not, as Abelard might have done, use the question to penetrate the workings of language —and it is difficult to see why Otto III, to whom the treatise is dedicated, would have been at all interested in this question. Philippe Wolfe hardly overstates the case when he describes the *De Rationali et Ratione Uti* as a "lifeless" exercise in "mental gymnastics."[6]

One might expect Gerbert's ability in logic to be displayed to better effect in his letters, where he dealt with issues of urgent

5. A. Olleris, *Oeuvres de Gerbert* (Paris, 1867), pp. 310 ff.
6. *The Cultural Awakening* (New York, 1968), p. 181.

importance to himself and his contemporaries. But though he does
occasionally employ logical terminology in his correspondence, when he gets down to business he bases his argument on citation from authority in the manner we found in the Carolingian period. A good example of Gerbert's method is found in a letter (the longest in the surviving collection) written to Bishop Wilderode of Strasbourg for the purpose of justifying the deposition of Arnulf as archbishop of Reims that enabled Gerbert himself to take the title. Gerbert's discussion of law and authority shows a bare trace of formal logic (he mentions "the judicial genus of cases"), and his rhetorical training comes out in a flowery prologue praising the rule of law, but the great bulk of the letter is given over to quotations, including a ten-page section devoted to passages from Hincmar of Reims. Gerbert's discussion touched the authority of canons and of synods and the legality of a bishop's resigning his office, issues that could have been addressed in the context of a conception of the archbishop's role in Christian society; yet Gerbert turns out to have nothing original to say about any of these topics. Because Gerbert's important personal stake in this issue serves to warrant the fact that this is the best case he could make, one is led to the conclusion that his mastery of formal logic simply did not extend to the construction of an argument for practical purposes or to the analysis of a given text.[7]

FULBERT OF CHARTRES

While the study of logic would become an important feature of high medieval thought, the causes of the change in mentalities are to be sought not in the classrooms but in the nearly universal collapse of public order. The precarious foundation of late tenth century government has already been noted, and even a slight shock was capable of bringing the entire structure down. In Mâcon, for example, where the habit of obedience had sustained the count and his court after the demise of effective royal authority, the event that finally shattered the structure of government came around 982 when Otto William, an outsider to the region, became count by marrying the widow of Aubry II. Within a few years of Otto William's succession, the other magnates of the region ceased to attend

7. *Letters of Gerbert*, pp. 236–63. Weigle does not give the Latin text, which may be found as no. 217 in Julien Havet, *Lettres de Gerbert* (Paris, 1889).

the comtal court, and after the count was deprived of the prestige of their attendance it was not too long before the castellans who held his fortresses also freed themselves of his authority. By the early eleventh century, the comtal court was left entirely to the count and his immediate dependents, and the last judgment pronounced against a castellan dated from 1019.[8] Elsewhere the cause of disruption might be different—the accession of an ineffective count or the aggression of a neighbor—but the consequences were duplicated in most parts of France: counts lost the obedience of their fellow magnates and often of the castellans who held the fortresses on which their power depended; the holding of courts became more a matter of physical force than of right, with previously free men losing their independence in the process; and rivalry between lords became a source of constant warfare and usurpation. The results bore a strong resemblance to the distribution of power in other societies, such as that of modern organized crime, where a person's authority extends only as far as the arms of his or her personal retainers can make it effective.

The society produced by this collapse of centralized political authority can be seen in one of the most eloquent testimonies to the age—the letter collection of Fulbert, bishop of Chartres from 1006 to 1028. Of the 103 letters in the collection written by Fulbert, well over half mention or are primarily concerned with instances of lawlessness and disorder, including horse theft, simony, disobedience by an abbot of his bishop, disputes over the legality of canonical elections, the violent seizure of a bishopric, attacks on peasants and churches, and outright warfare. The sheer number of these issues, and the amount of Fulbert's time they must have taken, is impressive. Yet what is perhaps most important about these incidents is the difficulty Fulbert had getting anyone in positions of authority to take corrective actions. One such episode, typical of many, occurred in 1025 when Fulbert, finding his lands beseiged by Geoffrey viscount of Chateaudun, wrote to King Robert for aid. Earlier letters to Robert's son Hugh, to Odo, count of Chartres, and perhaps to Richard, count of Normandy, had gone unanswered; and though Fulbert thought the letter to Odo might not have gotten through (he asked Robert if Odo were with him), he was also afraid that Hugh and Odo might have given their consent to Geoffrey's activities "for otherwise it is hard to believe he would have entered into them." Hugh later cleared himself of this suspi-

8. Georges Duby, *La société aux XIe et XIIe siècles dans la région mâconnaise* (Paris, 1971), pp. 137–48.

cion by explaining that he was too far distant with too few men to help, but two more letters had to be sent to Robert before we hear the last of the affair.[9]

These conditions were probably not much worse than those Gregory of Tours had faced. In the late tenth and eleventh centuries, however, people responded differently, by appealing to peers and learning ways of reasoning with people on the basis of rough equality—what Piaget called reciprocal respect. The earliest manifestations of this trend came not far from Chartres in the peace associations of southwestern France. Organized by prelates, these associations required their members to swear oaths to each other as well as to God, and to come to each other's aid against those who broke the peace. The novel feature, as Mackinney observed, was that these associations were "based upon the idea of willing cooperation in the interest of public welfare rather than upon fear of spiritual punishment."[10]

Fulbert was certainly aware of these movements, and his letters reveal how such peer-directed reasoning could work at the personal level. Men like Robert and Odo were not bound to him by close personal ties, nor had he any power to intimidate them. In dealing with them, therefore, and in dealing with other church dignitaries, Fulbert had to be able to understand their circumstances and to persuade them that their interests or duties corresponded to his. The letter collection as a whole testifies to Fulbert's skill at this difficult task. In one of the letters discussed above, for example, Fulbert threatens that if Robert or Odo do not act to contain Geoffrey, he would go into exile with consequent damage to their reputation: "Heaven forbid," he wrote, "that you should compel us to confess to a foreign king that you were unwilling or unable to protect the spouse of Christ, the holy church which was entrusted to your guidance."[11] The subservience one sees in Gerbert's letters is totally lacking here, as is the bombast Gerbert directed toward his inferiors. Fulbert is willing to pay respect where it is due and to explain thoroughly the reasons for his opinions, but he is consistent in refusing to compromise his own dignity or his demand that his concerns be taken seriously.

The attitude of reciprocal respect that guided Fulbert in his deal-

9. *The Letters and Poems of Fulbert of Chartres*, ed. and trans. Frederick Behrends (Oxford, 1976), letters 98–101.
10. L. Mackinney, "The People and Public Opinion in the Eleventh Century Peace Movement," *Speculum* 5 (1930): 184.
11. *Letters*, p. 183.

ings with others found theoretical expression in his most famous work, a definition of the relationship between lord and vassal contained in a letter to William, duke of Aquitaine. Previously, all of the responsibilities of fidelity had been thought to flow toward the lord. William himself, for example, in an incident that may have prompted him to seek Fulbert's advice, tried to dupe his vassal, Hugh of Lusignan, out of a valuable marriage while insisting at the same time on Hugh's complete obedience. (A contemporary judicial record reports William told Hugh, "You are so greatly in my debt that you ought to do anything I say.")[12] Fulbert, however, defined the obligations between lord and vassal in these words: "He who swears fidelity to his lord should keep in mind these six terms: safe and sound, secure, honest, useful, easy, possible." And after defining what these terms mean for the vassal, Fulbert continues: "The lord in turn should be faithful to his vassal in all these matters. If he does not do so, he will rightly be considered unfaithful, just as if the vassal, if he is caught violating any of them by his own actions or by giving his consent, will be considered perfidious and perjured."[13] Fulbert's exposition was to become a classic, the most copied of all his nonliturgical works, and what was important about it, as Bernard Bachrach notes, "is the reciprocal nature of *forma fidelitatis.*"[14]

Fulbert's political abilities, as manifested in his letters, have long been recognized by historians, and whatever importance he has for the history of thought is usually attributed to his ease in dealing with a society of men not too different from himself. Current opinion is probably well expressed by Southern when he remarks that "it is doubtful whether Fulbert added anything to the sum of knowledge" and added that Fulbert's contribution to learning was limited to "his sensitivity to what was going on around him . . . and his genius for drawing men to him."[15] But just as historians have overestimated Gerbert's originality because of the excessive attention they pay to formal logic, they have missed the fact that, by applying to scholarship the intellectual skills he developed in poli-

12. M. Garaud, "Une problème d'histoire: à propos d'une lettre Fulbert de Chartres à Guillaume-le-Grand, comte de Poitou et duc d'Aquitaine," *Etudes d'histoire du droit canonique dédiées à Gabriel Le Bras* (Paris, 1965), 1: 561.

13. *Letters*, no. 51, pp. 90–93.

14. "Toward a Reappraisal of William the Great, duke of Aquitaine (995–1030)," *Journal of Medieval History* 5 (1979): 18.

15. *Making of the Middle Ages*, pp. 197–201.

tics, Fulbert was blazing a trail away from the pedantic and ultimately sterile reasoning of the early Middle Ages. Without staking out any strikingly new positions, he was changing the whole way people talked and argued with one another.

The sophistication of Fulbert's argumentation can be seen most clearly in his three treatises against the Jews, which were probably written around 1009.[16] The choice of subject is itself significant, for the impossibility of relying on Christian authorities meant Jews had to be persuaded by arguments addressed to them as rational people. (There were always attempts to argue for Christianity from miracles, but these obviously belong to a different mental world from that of Fulbert's treatises.)[17] The relevance of this problem to the development of reasoning was to make defenses of Christianity against unbelievers a popular genre for the next hundred years: Anselm and Abelard were among those who devoted major works to the subject. While Fulbert's contribution does not bear comparison with theirs, it is important to notice his awareness of the approach that had to be taken.

Fulbert's method can be illustrated by the third of the treatises. Here, as in the others, Fulbert premises his argument on Gen. 49:10—a source whose authority he could expect Jews to accept because it was part of their own holy writings—which states that the sceptre will remain in the hands of Judah "until he comes to whom it belongs and to him shall be the obedience of the peoples." Although this text had long been regarded by Christians as a prophecy of Christ, who was born shortly after the institution of the Herods by Rome ended Jewish self-government, Jews had denied this interpretation on two grounds: that each Jewish father was like a king, and that Jewish kingdoms had existed elsewhere than the Holy Land.

Fulbert gives the traditional Christian position an interesting twist by undertaking to refute these arguments. To the first objection, that each Jewish father was like a king, Fulbert replied with gentle ridicule, commenting that the diaspora had not been a hardship since the Jews now had many kings where previously they had had only one. Then, with greater seriousness, he argued that since

16. PL 141: 305–18; see also B. Blumenkranz, *Les auteurs chrétiens latins du moyen âge sur les juifs et le judaisme* (Paris, 1963), pp. 237–43.
17. For a virtually contemporary debate between a Christian and a Jew, but one entirely different in tone from that of Fulbert's treatise, see Anna Sapir Abulafia, "An Eleventh-century exchange of letters between a Christian and a Jew," *Journal of Medieval History* 7 (1981): 153–74.

no one now had the authority to anoint kings there could be neither kings nor people under them, "for where the efficient cause is
missing, there cannot be the effect." In any case, Fulbert concludes,
is one to believe the Messiah will come only when all Jewish fathers
have died?

Fulbert answered the contention that there were somewhere ru-
mored to be Jewish kings whose existence proved the sceptre of
Judah had not fallen by observing that as a house needs a foundation, walls, and a roof, so a kingdom requires a king, a country
(patria), and a people *(populus)*; if any of these is missing there is
no kingdom "for where a part is absent the whole cannot exist. . . .
The kingdom of Judah, however, has lost its land, which has come
into foreign hands; and it lacks a people, since the people are dis-
persed into all nations; and there has long been lacking a truly
legitimate king. Since the kingdom of Judah has thus lost all its
parts, the kingdom has ceased to be."[18]

The originality of Fulbert's arguments has been commented upon
by scholars, but for our purpose the central point is that Fulbert's
approach to his text betrays an awareness that several different
interpretations are possible. He does not merely cite the text and
draw the conclusions that support his case, as Carolingian authors
usually did; he actually argues that his interpretation is the only
viable of the many readings that might be offered. In defending his
interpretation, moreover, Fulbert draws on formal logic with a
sureness that Gerbert never displays. His description of unction as
the "efficient cause" of kingship drives in a point already made.
And his description of a kingdom—in analogy to a definition of
a house that he may have found in Boethius's *De Topiciis Differen-
tiis*[19]—is not rhetorical fluff but addresses the meaning of a key
word in the text under discussion. Whereas Gerbert used his

18. "Nam sive patria, sive populus, sive rex desit regnum esse non possit.
Ubi enim pars deest, totum esse non potest; et contra, ubi totum est, partes
quoque esse necesse est. . . . Regnum autem Juda terram suam perdidit,
quando ipsa in manus extraneas venit; populo caruit, postquam in omnes
nationes dispersus est populus; rege vero legitimo longe ante caruerat:
sicque regnum Juda, omnibus partibus suis amissis, regnum esse desivit."
PL 141: 316B.

19. The suggestion that Fulbert may have found his definition of a house in
Boethius is made by Behrends (p. xxvii), but he gives Fulbert too little
credit for developing what is a single sentence in Boethius into a coherent
argument relevant to a specific subject. Of greater interest, perhaps, is a
comparison between Fulbert and Isidore, who in a piece against the Jews
also based on Gen. 49:10 contended that there could be no Jewish king
because the Jews lacked priests, altar, and temple. Thus while Isidore saw

knowledge as an instrument for impressing patrons and bludgeoning underlings, Fulbert appears to regard debate as a contest in which an opponent's thrusts are parried and his defenses systematically stripped away.

Fulbert's remaining works, including sermons on why God became man and on the eucharist, do not present completed arguments, so it is not possible to assess the reasoning he used in dealing with other issues. But the impetus he gave to the growth of an intellectual community can be perceived indirectly in the character of his students. The most famous of them, Berengar of Tours, shall claim our attention shortly. Less brilliant, and therefore more typical, was Adelman of Liege, a teacher and in his last years bishop of Brescia, who is known to us primarily for a letter he wrote to Berengar near the beginning of the latter's notoriety. The actual effect of this letter was negligible; Berengar, far from being deflected from his course, rejected Adelman's plea with a cruel insult. Yet the letter does offer a rare glimpse of the kind of discussions that, by the mid-eleventh century, were emerging from the schools to transform the nature of public debate.[20]

The immediately arresting feature of Adelman's letter is the gently personal tone in which he addresses Berengar. This had rarely been seen in the early Middle Ages and is not the result of youthful acquaintance alone. Auerbach observed of Servatus Lupus's letters that "the concrete personal touches that bring the correspondents and the persons mentioned in their letters to life are nowhere to be found," that Lupus never includes "sidelights . . . of particular interest to the addressee" that make the narrative "clear to him by relating it to his own experience."[21] Adelman, however, unmistakably is writing to Berengar alone. He begins by addressing him as *conlacteus* (foster-brother), explaining that he uses that term on account of "that most sweet fraternity" which they shared under Fulbert, and he proceeds to remind Berengar of the evening conversations in the garden with Fulbert in which Fulbert, "his sight obscured by tears which broke out while he spoke," urged them to follow the road marked out by the Fathers. It was to

---

kingship in sacral terms, Fulbert shifted to a conception that recognized the relation between king and people as central to the character of a kingdom. Cf. Blumenkranz, *Juifs et chrétiens dans le monde occidental 420–1096* (Paris, 1960), pp. 231–33.

20. The text is given in R. B. C. Huygens, "Textes latines du XIe au XIIIe siecle," *Studi Medievali* 8 (1967): 476–93.

21. *Literary Language*, p. 132.

Adelman's distress, therefore, (he wrote) that he heard of the scandal Berengar had provoked by his statements. The specific arguments Adelman then urged upon Berengar must not detain us here, though he made his case with as much cogency as the more famous disputants in the controversy and with considerably less in the way of personal abuse. The important fact is that this obscure schoolmaster felt confident enough to make those arguments in his own voice, appealing to Berengar as one reasonable man to another, without adding to his letter a heavy burden of patristic citations.

Fulbert had been dead over twenty years when Adelman's letter was written, but the influence of the give and take of his own mind is unmistakable. One need only read this letter alongside the cold and abrupt letters Lupus wrote to Gottschalk when rebuking him for his views on predestination to see the distance that already had been come from the mental world of the early Middle Ages. We are already entering the society that saw the first great scholarly debate of the high Middle Ages.

BERENGAR OF TOURS

The statement that, as Adelman wrote, disturbed "not only Latin but also Teutonic ears" was Berengar of Tours's assertion that the bread that is consecrated at the altar during mass was not the true body of Christ but an image or symbol. In taking this position Berengar was addressing an issue that had not existed for the Latin fathers; for them the eucharist was significant chiefly as a ceremony that united the Christian community in a common meal. The first formally to argue that the bread was physically changed was Paschasius Radbertus, a monk of Corbie in the ninth century. Paschasius was answered within a few years by Ratramanus, another monk of Corbie, who upheld the proposition that the words "body and blood" in the mass were used figuratively; but, in the manner of many Carolingian debates, the question was left hanging.[22]

Evidence that the argument continued comes from a little known treatise written at the end of the tenth century by Heriger of Lobbes (d. 1007).[23] Heriger himself believed in the real presence as defined by Paschasius, but he recognized that some of the Fathers held

22. This section was written before the publication of Brian Stock, *The Implications of Literacy* (Princeton, 1983). Stock discusses the key texts along lines different from mine, but since literacy for Stock is not the ability to read or write but an attitude toward texts I do not believe our views are fundamentally incompatible.

23. *De Corpore et Sanguine Domini*, printed Olleris, *Oeuvres de Gerbert*,

other views and he proposed to show that their positions were
logically equivalent to Paschasius's. Heriger argued that his project was legitimate because "that art of dividing genera into species and resolving species into genera is made not by human machinations but by the Author of all arts that are true arts."[24] Unfortunately, as with Gerbert, the argument fairly bristles with logical terminology. A typical passage reads:

> Let there be constituted two extreme end-points and the middle of them, different proportionally by equal differences. To this likeness again let two extreme end-points be constituted, predicate and subject, and a subaltern middle of them; that as the first can be predicated of the middle, and the middle of the end, and thus the first of the end.[25]

Later in the eleventh century the power of this kind of reasoning would be revealed by St. Anselm, but in Heriger's hands the effect is still mechanical and unpersuasive: having run through his formulas, he considers the case proven without attempting to show that the Fathers actually did believe in the real presence or that the doctrine itself had any basis in physical reality.

It was, then, to a society where the nature of the eucharist was already debated that Berengar's opinion became widely known around 1049. What helped make the resulting controversy important for the development of reasoning, however, was the absence of effective authority we have already noticed. Berengar was four times condemned for his views by councils (in 1049, 1050, 1059, and 1075) without really being silenced. It was only when he was cornered at the council held by Pope Gregory VII in 1079 that he was finally forced to swear an oath he could not wriggle out of and compelled to give up his views. The difficulty of obtaining a final judgment meant that both sides were under pressure to refine their arguments in hopes of winning supporters, and nearly every leading scholar in northern France was sooner or later drawn into the dispute.[26]

For most historians the chief interest of the eucharistic debate is

---

pp. 279–88; for correct attribution, see Morin, *Revue Bénédictine* 20 (1908): 1 ff.

24. Olleris, *Oeuvres de Gerbert*, p. 286.

25. Ibid., p. 287.

26. For Berengar's final defeat and the events leading to it, see Robert Somerville, "The Case against Berengar of Tours—A New Text," *Studi Gregoriani* 9 (1972): 55–75.

the application to theology of formal logic by Lanfranc of Bec, Berengar's chief opponent, who "was allowing new science to give clarity and definition to a view which had been only adumbrated before."[27] Viewed from the perspective of the schools of the twelfth century, this judgment is understandable. Yet if the debate is placed instead in the context of the history of mentalities, it becomes apparent that Berengar was not only the more adventurous thinker but the one whose methods and presumptions more closely anticipated the directions of later medieval thought.

The central issue in the debate was the sense in which the bread and wine of the eucharist could be said to be the body and blood of Christ. The proponents of a real presence held the opinion that the words "hoc est corpus meum," which were pronounced in the mass, made sense only if taken literally. Cardinal Humbert, who led the attack on Berengar at the council of 1059 before Pope Nicholas II, expressed this view when he proposed that "the bread and wine which are placed on the altar after consecration are . . . the true body and blood of our lord Jesus Christ which not only sacramentally but also in truth are physically taken up and broken by the hands of the priest and crushed by the teeth of the faithful."[28] The position was stated with greater subtlety by Hugh of Langres—significantly, another student of Fulbert—when he wrote Berengar that

> you have this choice: either you change the nature of the
> bread entirely, or you do not dare to call it the body of Christ.
> If you were to say that the bread retains its own nature, and
> yet is not powerless as a sacrament, you would be speaking
> against reason; if you add nature to it, you alter its inherent
> qualities. For all things, while they persist in their nature, do
> not recede from the things inherent in their nature.[29]

To this and similar arguments, however, Berengar replied that the literal reading is just one of the meanings the words might have. "When that Humbert of yours [he wrote Lanfranc] says that the bread which is placed on the altar after consecration is the body of

27. R. W. Southern, "Lanfranc of Bec and Berengar of Tours," *Studies in Medieval History Presented to Frederick Maurice Powicke*, ed. R. W. Hunt, W. A. Pantin, and R. W. Southern (Oxford, 1948), p. 39.
28. M. Gibson, *Lanfranc of Bec* (Oxford, 1980), p. 81, citing Lanfranc, *Liber de corpore et sanguine Domini*, PL 150: 405–42, cap. 2.
29. Gibson, *Lanfranc of Bec*, p. 79, citing PL 143: 1327.

Christ, . . . the 'body of Christ' is to be taken tropologically (i. e., figuratively)."[30] Berengar defends this reading by showing there are many passages in the Bible that are meant to be read figuratively, and that the Fathers treated them as figures of speech. It is in this context, to defend the superiority of a figurative reading, that Berengar made his famous argument that if the words of the mass are taken literally, as the doctrine of transubstantiation requires, then the statement is self-contradictory because the bread to which *hoc* refers would cease to exist.

Thus far the structure of Berengar's argument resembles that of Fulbert on Gen. 49:10: both endeavor to establish the best interpretation of a text out of the many possible. And Berengar's own doctrine, that the bread becomes the body of Christ not in nature but in the mind of God and is recognized as such by the heart of the believer,[31] is perhaps not distant from Fulbert's ideas or those of the Fathers. Margaret Gibson, Lanfranc's most recent biographer, conceded that Berengar may well have been closer than Lanfranc to the meaning of a text of Ambrose that was bitterly debated in the course of the controversy.[32] But the heart of Berengar's argument lay elsewhere, less in texts or grammatical doctrines than "the nature of physical reality."[33] Anyone, he wrote Ascelin of Chartres at the beginning of the controversy, can see that "words of consecration do not cause the matter of the bread to withdraw. . . . That is so plain that to experience this suffices to convince even a schoolboy who does not understand that the force of a combination of words is not strong enough [to produce this effect]." To believe otherwise, to accept the position of Paschasius, "is to judge against the reasons of all nature."[34]

30. *De Sacra Coena*, ed. A. F. Vischer and F. Th. Vischer (Berlin, 1834), p. 86.
31. "Quantum enim ad naturam, panis est, quod tu vides oculis corporis; quantum ad divinam benedictam, ipse panis est corpus Christi, quod attendere debes oculis cordis, oculis fidei." *De Sacra Coena*, p. 177.
32. *Lanfranc of Bec*, p. 92.
33. The term is used by Hugh of Langres in his letter to Berengar ("Rerum existentium . . . si bene perspiceres"). *PL* 143: 1326D, cited by Gibson, *Lanfranc of Bec*, p. 94.
34. "Ipsa verba in consecrationem panis institutam non decedere sacramento panis materiam. . . . Ita planum est ut sufficiat hoc sentire et convincere etiam puerulus in schola constitutus, qui vim juncturae verborum non instrenue callet." *PL* 150: 65C. At the beginning of the same letter Berengar wrote that if you believe with Paschasius "sapis contra omnis rationes naturae." 65B.

In taking this position, Berengar was arguing from a conception of nature that had been absent from Latin Christendom since Boethius. But because Berengar's ideas were the product of his own cognitive processes, not of conscious reflection and thought, he could not believe that others did not perceive the world in the same way. The impatience he displayed in his letter to Ascelin is the first sign of this incomprehension, and it turned to fury when Lanfranc, his own student, joined the contest against him. Over and over in *De Sacra Coena*, the work that replied to Lanfranc, Berengar repeated what was obvious to him, that Lanfranc wrote "against his learning, against his reason."[35]

Yet what was obvious to Berengar was by no means obvious to others. To Berengar's opponents, Berengar's insistence that a miracle does not occur with the consecration of the bread could only mean that he did not believe in miracles at all. Ascelin spoke for many when he wrote Berengar that "nature is nothing other than the will of God. Anyone in sane mind who calls nature the cause of things . . . admits the will of God to be the origin of nature of every kind."[36] It was in vain that Berengar argued that when Moses' staff turned into a serpent, it did so "manifeste" by a transformation of the matter of the staff, "while the bread and wine on the altar patently experience" no such transformation.[37]

It was Lanfranc's contribution to the controversy to answer Berengar's challenge to this old conception of the world. Much of his

35. See Southern's comments, "Lanfranc of Bec," p. 39, with references; but similar comments can be found on almost every page of *De Sacra Coena*.

36. "Sed neque hoc, ut dicis, contra naturae rationes ago, neque enim aliud naturam dixerim quam Dei voluntatem. Quis enim sane sapiens causam naturam vocet, aut non potius omnium naturam, et ex natura sui generis nascentium voluntatem Dei esse fateatur." *PL* 150: 67D. Similar arguments were made by Adelman and by Guitmund of Aversa, who expressed doubt that Berengar believed in the miracles of the Fathers.

37. "Revera manifestissimum habere debuit eruditio tua, rem gestam de Moysi virga et de aquis Aegypti nulle prosus similitudine convenire cum conversione panis et vini mensae dominicae, nulla similitudine res gestas illas ea, quae de pane et vino pre consecratione geruntur altaris, contingere, quia solum quiddam in manu Moyses virga est, serpens de ea faciendus nunquam extiterat, virga manifeste per corruptionem subiecti desitura erat esse virga, serpens per generationem subiecti virga in terra proiecta tunc primo incipere esse habebat. Panis autem atque vinum nullem patitur corruptionem subiecti, sed potius consecrationem suscipit." *De Sacra Coena*, p. 163.

Liber de corpore et sanguine Domini consists of patristic quotations that had long been familiar, and much of the rest of rather
trivial displays of his expertise in logic.[38] But at the crucial point, in
explaining the miracle, Lanfranc was able to bring to bear the
technical language of eleventh-century scholarship. The consecration, he argued, changes the elements of the bread in their *essentia*
while leaving intact the external properties of the bread. It did not
matter that Berengar was not one whit convinced. ("How," Berengar asked, "can one speak of flesh where there are to be seen none
of the properties of flesh? Bread cannot be destroyed by transformation of its matter unless that by which it was not stone, not
flesh, but bread departs.")[39] The success of Lanfranc's book was
assured by the elegant, modern expression it gave to old and still
dominant attitudes.

Lanfranc's formula and Berengar's condemnation determined
Catholic doctrine on the eucharist for all time. Yet it is one of the
ironies of history that the question should have been settled when
it was, for within a few decades Berengar's conception of nature
was itself to become a commonplace. Around 1120, in words that
might almost have been intended for Lanfranc, William of Conches
criticized those who

> Ignorant themselves of the forces of nature they don't want
> people to look into anything; they want us to believe like
> peasants and not ask the reason behind things. . . . Could
> anything be more wretched than saying that something exists
> because God can make it, and yet not seeing that it does not
> exist, or having any reason why it should exist, or showing
> the usefulness for which it would exist. God does not do ev-

38. Though Lanfranc in his own time was considered a master of dialectic,
the examples of his learning that have come down to us are almost always
pedantic exercises in the manner of Heriger or Gerbert. In his biblical
commentaries, for example, he is usually content to classify arguments or
rework the biblical text into a formal syllogism. Cf. Gibson, *Lanfranc of
Bec*, pp. 50–61; Southern, "Lanfranc of Bec," pp. 36–37.

39. "Nisi enim his panis proprium aliquid accepisset, per quod illum non
lapidem, non carnem, sed panem esse constat, nulla ratione panis esse
coepisset; nisi caro haec individua proprium acciperet aliquid, per quod
eam non lapidem, non panem, sed carnem esse oculis corporis appareret,
nullo modo vel de nichilo, vel de alio aliquo, ut esset caro, institui po-
tuisset. Contra nunquam quilibet panis esse per corruptionem subiecti
desinet, nisi id per quod non lapis, non caro, sed panis erat, forte amiserit."
De Sacra Coena, pp. 92–93.

erything he is able to. To use a peasant's words, Can God make a calf from a tree trunk? Has he ever done it?[40]

The vehemence of William's language leaves no doubt that the ideas of Lanfranc and his contemporaries were still to be found. But they were no longer in the ascendancy. Had the doctrine of the eucharist not already been settled, it is likely that the twelfth century would have decided the issue the other way.[41]

For our present purposes, however, the outcome of the controversy is less important than the manner in which the participants consistently addressed and tried to answer the arguments of the other side. Lanfranc's book contains passages of an earlier work by Berengar that is now lost; and Berengar's surviving treatise is in parts almost a line by line answer to Lanfranc. The contrast with ninth-century debates, whose treatises rarely took notice of opposing views except to heap abuse on them, could not be more striking, and it cannot be accounted for by observing (as Southern does)[42] that eleventh-century scholars were more used to the give and take of the lecture room. Lanfranc, Berengar, Ascelin, and the others lived in a society where respect for the intelligence of one's fellows—in Fulbert's time a skill essential for survival—was becoming an attitude valued in its own right; it is perhaps not by chance that most of the men who prosecuted Berengar before the papal court at the end of his life were not schoolmasters of the type we have been discussing but monks used to living in accord with the dictates of authority. Berengar's claim that reason alone should determine the truth was not, to be sure, entirely accepted by his adversaries. But it was not entirely rejected either. Within a few years of Berengar's death, the appeal to reason was to become one of the distinguishing characteristics of the mentality that shaped twelfth-century intellectual life.

40. "Sed quoniam ipsi nesciunt vires naturae, . . . nolunt eos aliquid inquaerere sed ut rusticos nos credere nec rationem quaerere. . . . Quid miserius quam dicere istud, est! quia Deus illud facere potest, noc videre sic esse, nec rationem habere quare sic est, nec veritatem ostendere ad quem hoc sit. Non enim quidquid potest Deus facere, hoc facit. Ut autem verbis rustici utar, potest Deus facere de trunco vitulum? Fecitne unquam?" *Philosophia mundi* i.23 (PL 172: 56–58). The translation is from Chenu, pp. 11, 12.

41. For the doubts of Aquinas and Bonaventure about some of the arguments used against Berengar, see Somerville, "Case Against Berengar," p. 58 n. 15. By then, of course, the issue was beyond discussion.

42. "Lanfranc of Bec," p. 38.

The Development of Jurisprudence before the Digest   *173*
*The Making
of a New
Mentality*

The revival of jurisprudence took place in Italy a little later than the revival of logic, and here, too, the inclination of historians has been to regard twelfth-century developments as a result of a recovery of ancient learning.[43] The hero in this case is not a teacher but a book for, as one leading scholar remarked, "it is unthinkable that a science of law could have taken shape in the medieval West without the rediscovery of Justinian's Digest."[44] The work for which this extraordinary claim is made was not the only book of Roman law available to medieval people. Yet while the Code and Novels emphasized individual laws, and the Institutes was an introduction for beginners, the Digest preserved the opinions of classical jurists on some of the basic issues of jurisprudence. This unique subject matter meant, it is argued, that it alone was capable of stimulating medieval readers to critical thought on the law.

The biography of the Digest fits well with these claims for its importance. Compiled in the sixth century, it disappeared from sight soon afterward; the last reference to the Digest in the West dates from 603, and by the eleventh century only one copy seems to have survived in Europe. The first evidence that it was being read again comes from 1076, when it was cited in a Tuscan law court. Then, in the early twelfth century we hear of the study and teaching of Roman law at Bologna, from which the influence of the Digest was then disseminated throughout the rest of Europe.

One might well ask whether the rediscovery of the Digest after so many years of neglect was entirely a matter of chance, as this interpretation seems to suppose: it is a tribute to the belief that books are a greater influence on culture than people that this question is not raised more often. I ask it here for two reasons. The first is the fact that, far from occupying a central place in the new jurisprudence as this interpretation would seem to require, the Digest was treated by the early glossators no differently from those of Jus-

43. This section was written before the publication of Harold J. Berman, *Law and Revolution* (Cambridge, Mass., 1983). Berman traces the development of jurisprudence to the Gregorian reform, but because he is unaware of the Pavese jurists and offers no new evidence linking the Gregorians to formal jurisprudence I have felt no need to alter my comments. In any case, I agree with Berman's main point, that the eleventh century marked the beginning of the modern western legal tradition.
44. Stephan Kuttner, "The Revival of Jurisprudence," in *Renaissance and Renewal in the Twelfth Century*, ed. Robert L. Benson and Giles Constable (Cambridge, Mass., 1982), p. 299.

tinian's compilations that had never been out of circulation. All were carefully glossed by the first medieval masters of Roman law, Irnerius and his successors at Bologna; but longer works were generally devoted to the Code or the Institutes. And if a twelfth-century jurist wished to address more theoretical issues—including those which the Digest is famous for raising—he generally chose to cast his thoughts in the form of introductions *(exordia* or *materia)* to one of those works. The Digest does not appear to have emerged as a separate topic for the writing of summas until around 1200, and only by slow degrees thereafter, as Maitland observed, did it come to its rights.

To explain my second objection, it is necessary to begin with the curious fact that the vulgate Digest which was the standard Bolognese text during the middle ages differs at a number of points from the manuscript (now known as the Florentina) that in the eleventh century was the sole surviving copy. The text at D. 36.1.71 can illustrate the kind of differences that exist. The Florentina gives the following reading:

> De evictione praediorum vel mancipiorum vel ceterorum cavere heres, cum restituit hereditatem, non debet.

The vulgate inserts "rerum" after ceterorum, greatly clarifying the meaning and giving a reading close to that which is widely accepted today: "vel ceterorum rerum hereditarum cavere heres." Because a comparison of the vulgate with the Florentina shows many emendations of this type, it was for a long time assumed that the vulgate was prepared by collating the Florentina with another manuscript that was now lost. When Mommsen disproved this assumption in his edition of 1870, he made inescapable the conclusion that an editor working from the Florentina alone had prepared an archetype later used in preparing the Bolognese vulgate. The Florentina itself was then largely ignored until the fifteenth century.[45]

But if the Florentina was edited sometime in the late eleventh century, by whom was this work done? Our only clues lie in the character of the emendations themselves. Some of them make grammatical corrections, and some were apparently arrived at by comparing the Florentina with the Institutes or with fragments of the Digest that were still in circulation in the eleventh century. Both

45. Theodor Mommsen, "Ueber die kritische Grundlage unseres Digestentextes," *Juristische Studien*, vol. 2 (Berlin, 1905). H. Kantorowicz, *Ueber die Entstehung der Digestenvulgata* (Weimar, 1910).

these techniques, we have seen, were used by text editors in the
Carolingian period and require no talent or training that would not
have been widely available in the eleventh century. Yet there is
another class of emendations, including the one given above, that is
more revealing because it consists of conjectures apparently made
by the editor. Corrections of this type can only have been made by a
person who has a good idea of what the text *should* say; and that is
precisely the problem. It stretches credulity to suppose that the
legal learning of an editor capable of making these emendations
was minimal before he encountered the Digest. But if he must himself have had a sophisticated understanding of the law before he
could put the Digest into circulation, the Digest itself cannot be
held responsible for the revival of legal thought.

This conclusion is less paradoxical than it seems, for there is
ample evidence of serious legal studies at Pavia by the mid-eleventh
century, well before the likely date for the editing of the Digest.
Legal historians have been quick to dismiss the importance of this
school because its interest was in Lombard law; no prototype of
Bolognese Romanism is, they conclude, to be found here. But the
Pavese glosses on the Lombard law, extending over more than a
century, amply reveal the development of legal reasoning from the
simplest grammatical glosses to the careful inquiry into the intention of the law and the elaboration of sophisticated analytical techniques that later would be applied to Roman law. That the history
of this development is the proper business of the historian of mentalities no one will doubt, and before it is done it will lead us back
to the problem with which I began: the eleventh-century origins of
the study of Roman law.

As the main residence of the Lombard kings Pavia had been the
home of *scriptores* and *iudices* and other men learned in the law as
early as the sixth century, but the school in which I am interested
probably has its origins in the mid-tenth century. The preceding
period, dating back to the disintegration of Carolingian authority
in the mid-ninth century, had been one of increasing particularism
in Italy as well as elsewhere in Europe, and this had meant for the
law that each locality developed increasingly distinctive sets of formulas for common notarial documents and often wildly varying
customs. In some places, for example, oral agreement to sell property alone sufficed to pass title in the property to the buyer; in
others payment of the price might be needed; in still others neither
payment of the price nor delivery passed title until a document had

been drawn up to record the fact. Law became, for all practical purposes, "the customs of a single *piazza*."[46]

This period ended in the mid-tenth century when Otto I conquered Lombardy. Otto did not entirely restore Pavia to its former place as capital, for he preferred to have administrative offices scattered throughout the kingdom. He did reassert the position of the court located in Pavia, however, and it is around the officials of this court that the Pavese school of law must have grown up. The exact nature of the school, whether it was an educational institution or merely the intellectual circle of jurists, is uncertain and perhaps unknowable. But it is clear that the interests of the jurists grew out of their experience with the practical business of government.

Given the diversity that had arisen while centralized rule was in abeyance, it is not surprising that the first task of these jurists was determining which were the rules of law. The *Quaestiones ac monita*, for example, consists simply of thirty-two brief notes or memoranda on subjects ranging from criminal procedure to the laws of inheritance. Because it is likely that these memoranda were prepared in response to questions that arose in the course of litigation, the fact that elementary rules such as the age of legal majority had to be looked up is telling evidence of the confusion that surrounded the operation of the courts at this time. Much more ambitious than the *Quaestiones*—but otherwise in the same vein—is the work that has come to be known as the *Liber Papiensis*. Apparently drawing on the resources of the palace archives, the jurists gathered into this book all the laws then in force in Italy, including the enactments of the Frankish and Saxon emperors as well as the Lombard codes of the sixth and seventh centuries. Manuscripts of

46. U. Gualazzini, "La scuola pavese, con particolare riguardo all'insegnamento del diritto," *Atti IV Congresso Studi Alto Medioevo* (Spoleto, 1969), pp. 64–67; for the general background of Pavia, see also B. Pagnin, "Scuola e cultura a Pavia nell'alto medio evo," *Atti IV Congresso Studi Alto Medioevo*, pp. 75–106; D. A. Bullough, "Urban Change in Medieval Italy: the Example of Pavia," *Papers of the British School at Rome*, n.s. vol. 21 (1966), pp. 82–130; and P. Vaccari, *Pavia nell'Alto medioevo e nell'età communale* (Milan, 1966). Vaccari's contribution to *Ius Romanum Medii Aevi* (I, 4 b *ee*) is the most recent survey of legal studies at Pavia, though from the point of view of Roman law. G. Diurni, *L'Expositio ad Librum Papiensem e la scienza giuridica preirneriana* (Rome, 1976), is a recent study of a key manuscript. The best discussion in English of Pavese legal studies is still P. Vinogradoff, *Roman Law in Medieval Europe*, 3d ed. (Oxford, 1929), pp. 48–55.

the *Liber Papiensis* survive from as early as the 1010s, and later recensions kept the work up-to-date until 1056 when the death of Henry III marked the end of effective imperial legislation for Italy.[47]

Both these works probably had their origins in the late tenth century, and their purpose places them clearly within the mentality that we have seen was predominant at that time. Their authors made no new law and, in general, performed no intellectual operations on the laws they preserved. Not only do the memoranda in the *Quaestiones* offer no interpretations of existing law, they follow no discernible logic, so that notes four and five discuss Frankish and Roman succession while Lombard succession is left to nearly the end. Similar problems afflict the *Liber Papiensis*, for by leaving ancient codes intact and arranging them in a rough chronological order the jurists produced a work in which legislation relevant to a given subject might be scattered throughout the text. In the twelfth century the owner of one manuscript was to make his book more useful by preparing an index to direct a reader to all the laws on theft, for example, or contract.[48] But the idea of such an endeavor was foreign to the Pavese of the late tenth and early eleventh century. For them as for generations of lawyers before them, law was a set of rules to be followed rather than an intellectual construct to be manipulated and understood.

What urged the jurists of Pavia into new ways of thinking about law was a withdrawal of royal authority from Pavia that compelled them to rely more and more on their own judgments. Already in the last years of Henry II a Pavese writer was complaining about the dismantling of financial offices in the city.[49] This affront may have fed the resentment the Pavese felt at rule by a German emperor, for when news came in 1024 that Henry II had died they took the opportunity of an interregnum to destroy the royal palace. Pavese emissaries to the new king, Conrad II, argued the lawyerly point that the rioters had offended no one since they had no king at the time, but Conrad was not appeased[50] and he proceeded to

47. *Quaestiones ac monita* and *Liber papiensis* together with the *Expositio* to be discussed below, are published in MGH *Leges* 4 (ed. Boretius), cited as Boretius.

48. For a description of this manuscript, British Library Additional ms. 5411, see Boretius, pp. lv–lvii.

49. *Honorantie Civitatis Papie*, c. 21, in MGH *Scriptores* 30: 1450ff.

50. The first sentences of Conrad's reply has often been taken to show the emergence of a new political idea, that of a kingdom distinct from the

lay siege to the town. The devastation of the countryside forced the Pavese to submit, but when the royal palace was rebuilt it was situated outside the walls and subsequent emperors often had themselves crowned in other cities. Though the Pavese court continued to function, its administrative importance appears to have declined from this time forward.

Behind the surface of these events it is possible to discern the rise of the new social and economic classes that were soon to earn for Italian towns a reputation for riot and turbulence. Yet for the Pavese jurists the growth of commerce was less important than the transformation of their working conditions caused by the loss of regular association with the king and the rest of the royal administration. Their work had little to do with issues that might have interested a merchant or artisan, for their texts remained the traditional ones collected in the *Liber Papiensis*: they discussed wergilds and morning-gifts, pledges, and compurgation. Yet deprived now of their regular contact with authority, they had no way to determine the correct interpretation of the laws except by debate among themselves.

The earliest evidence of the effects on reasoning of these changed circumstances is found in a set of glosses to the *Liber Papiensis* prepared in the late 1030s by the jurist Gualcoso. For the most part, these glosses take the form of dialogues summarizing or rather dramatizing the glossed *lex*. Here, for example, is the gloss to Rothar 164 in its entirety:

---

king. "I know that you have not destroyed the house of your king since you had none at the time; but you cannot deny that you destroyed a regal house. Even if the king died, the kingdom remained, just as the ship remains whose steersman falls." But the rest of his answer makes clear that his purpose was simply to show that the death of Henry gave the Pavese no right to destroy the palace, for he charges them with simple trespass, not treason or lèse majesté. "They were public, not private buildings; they were under another law, not yours. Those who invade the properties of others are liable to the king. Therefore you who were invaders of the property of others are hateful to the king." [Scio, inquit, quod domum regis vestri non destruxistis, cum eo tempore nullum haberetis; sed domum regalem scidisse, non valetis inficiare. Si rex periit, regnum remansit, sicut navis remanet cuius gubernator cadit. Aedes publicae fuerant, non privatae; iuris erant alieni, non vestri. Alienarum autem rerum invasores regi sunt obnoxii. Ergo vos alienae res invasores fuistis, igitur regi obnoxii estis.] Wipo, *Gesta Chuonradi II imperatoris*, ed. Harry Bresslau (Hanover, 1878), pp. 22–23. See also the translation by Theodor E. Mommsen and Karl F. Morrison, *Imperial Lives and Letters of the Eleventh Century* (New York, 1962).

Peter, your uncle Martin appeals against you, because you hold land that is his in such a place.—This land is my own from my father Albert.—You ought not to succeed to him, since you were born of adultery.—Let him swear with his oath-helpers, as the law says.

To the reader accustomed to the technical glosses of the twelfth century, this form is as odd as the content is simple. Yet in some places the gloss goes farther—into an assessment of the possible circumstances that might occasion an action (e.g., Rothar 9 or Wido 6) or into a discussion of different opinions as to the meaning of the law (e.g., Rothar 2). Gualcoso's apparatus, simple though it was, thus marked a turn away from the purely linguistic or grammatical glosses found in some of the earliest manuscripts of the *Liber Papiensis*.

Gualcoso was not the only jurist of his generation whose work survives. Glosses of several of his contemporaries are to be found in manuscripts of Lombard law from the period, the most important of which preserves an *Expositio* to the *Liber Papiensis*.[51] The date of this manuscript has been the subject of much controversy.[52] Yet the date of the *Expositio* is unimportant for my immediate purposes because it is possible to single out the comments of early jurists whose careers can be dated by charters they witnessed. Of these early commentators, three in particular stand out: Bonifiglio, who was active roughly between 1015 and 1055; Guglielmo, his perhaps younger contemporary; and Ugo, Guglielmo's son, who often appears in disputes with both his father and Bonifiglio. Guglielmo and Ugo, who from the number of times their opinions were cited were probably the teachers of the author of the *Expositio*, belonged to a group the author knew as *moderni*. Opposed to them were the *antiqui*—adherents of a strict and often crudely literal style of interpretation whose opinions are rarely cited except to

51. Biblioteca nazionale (Naples) *Brancacciana* I.B.12.
52. Boretius, the nineteenth-century editor, thought the *Expositio* was written in the late 1070s, but historians protective of the originality of Bologna have argued for a twelfth-century date because an early date could make the *Expositio*'s eight citations of the Digest as early as any. Their evidence on this point seems to me unpersuasive, resting as it does on the curious notion that the *Expositio* so resembles the work of early Bolognese glossators that it must be late enough to have been influenced by them. On the whole, a date in the last two decades of the eleventh century is the most likely, especially since the last generation of jurists cited by name were active well before 1070.

be refuted. The gap that divides the *antiqui* and *moderni*, however, is as much one of mentality as of legal doctrine.[53]

The character of the debates between these jurists is captured by the following exchange, remembered today less for its subject matter than for the identity of one of the participants. Lanfranc *archiepiscopus* posed the following question to Bonifiglio *iudex*:

> "If the bearer wished to validate a charter that had been challenged, and the notary and all witnesses are dead, how ought it to be done?" Bonifiglio answered him: "By custom the bearer of the charter should validate it with 12 compurgators and with two other charters." . . . Lanfranc: "Then custom is against law; for it is this custom that the prologue to the legislation of Otto I has in mind where it says that 'a detestable and dishonest custom has grown up in Italy.'"

Archbishop Lanfranc has to be Lanfranc of Bec, who though he left perhaps before 1030, indeed came from Pavia,[54] and some slight corroboration of this attribution may be found in the fact that here, as in the debate with Berengar, Lanfranc is an *antiquus* clinging to the literal meaning of the text. His reasoning persuaded Bonifiglio who withdrew, we are told, "with an embarrassed smile and his head bowed." But Guglielmo, "of no little ingenuity," settled the matter *(sic determinavit)* by showing Lanfranc had misunderstood the legislation he cited:

> Otto said "a dishonest and detestable custom has grown up" not in respect to the aforesaid custom but respecting this, that certain greedy men were drawing up false charters of alienation and defending the charters by perjury, thus acquiring the goods of others. Thus Otto gave the challenger of the charter the choice of battle or letting the bearer swear.[55]

Guglielmo's position depends entirely on a clear and undeniable exposition of Otto's intention, an attitude toward texts that is practically never to be found in the sources of the preceding six centuries and which was thus re-emerging in Pavia as it was in the France of Fulbert.

This exchange is typical of the times because whereas the *antiqui*

---

53. The evidence is discussed by Boretius, pp. xciii–xcvi. There are 12 comments attributed to Bonifilius, 58 to Guglielmo, 57 to Ugo (of which only 16 overlap with those of his father), and 82 to the *antiqui*.

54. Gibson, *Lanfranc of Bec*, pp. 7–8.

55. Boretius, at Wido 6.23.

often tried to argue (as Lanfranc did) that one law superseded or "broke" (*rumpere*) another, the inclination of the *moderni* was to preserve all the laws (*salvare*) by reconciling (*solvere*) contradictions.[56] Their underlying assumption was the premise basic to any jurisprudence—that the laws were internally consistent and knowable by reason. This assumption was defended in a number of ways in addition to the argument from intention used by Guglielmo: by making careful distinctions between the areas where two laws applied; by showing that one's opponents' reasoning led to absurd and insupportable conclusions; and, what is particularly significant in view of the history of the Digest, by proposing an emendation of the text based on a conception of what was needed to make sense of the law. Most of these emendations were relatively simple, such as substitutions of *aut* for *et*, though it is certainly important that the legists were willing to suggest such changes independent of any manuscript authority.[57] But the text of Liutprand 4 is subjected to more substantial changes. The law, which deals with inheritance in default of male heirs, begins in the oldest manuscripts of the Lombard law with the words: "Si qui Longobardus sorores et filias in capillo" (If a Lombard leaves sisters or unmarried daughters in his house they shall share his inheritance equally.) This wording, with the phrase "in capillo" (unmarried)[58] modifying "daughters," would, as the *Expositio* observes, lead to the "iniquity" of excluding unmarried sisters from the inheritance if there were married daughters, "which does not seem rational" (*Quod non videtur ratio*). This consideration, the gloss continues, led Guglielmo to propose the reading "Si quis Longobardus filias (married or unmarried the gloss says) et sorores in capillo." Most of the manuscripts of the *Liber Papiensis* in fact give this reading, which since earlier manuscripts of the Lombard law give "sorores et filias" suggests the jurists had enough confidence in their logic simply to alter the text accordingly.[59] The contrast with Bede or the editors of the Carolingian age could not be plainer.

56. So, for example, at Grimoald 2 where a divergence from Louis the Pious 55 is noted, Guglielmo comments that Louis's law "non erat ruptura immo addicio."
57. Cf., for example, the comments at Grimoald 2, Karolus Magnus 129.
58. Literally "with hair" for, as Katherine Fischer Drew explains, only unmarried girls wore their hair hanging down. *The Lombard Laws* (Philadelphia, 1973), p. 251.
59. Boretius, p. 405. The gloss continues to show that the proposed reading parallels the wording of Liutprand 145.

Though the main energy of the *moderni* was spent on the task of elucidating the Lombard law, their comments reveal a comfortable familiarity with Roman law as well. There is nothing surprising in this; as early as the *Quaestiones ac monita* Pavese jurists had collected Roman rules of law, probably because the actions of clerics were governed by them.[60] But comments of the *moderni* often show they have mastered Roman categories of analysis as well as individual rules. Guglielmo and Ugo, for example, dispute whether Liutprand 8 ought to be regarded as covering contract (*contractus*) or crime (*maleficium*), and in other places Ugo casually relies upon the distinction between bona fide and male fide (Grimoald 2.2) or *possessio* and *proprietas* (Rothar 362.4). Even in these early glosses, moreover, recourse is sometimes had to Roman law where the Lombard law is obscure because, as Ugo and Guglielmo agreed, Roman law "omnium est generalis" (Otto I 4.3).

By the time of Guglielmo, then, the jurists had entered the mental world that made possible the growth of legal studies at Bologna, and the *Expositio* itself reveals a still more sophisticated conception of how law ought to be studied. First, the laws are taken from the chronological format of the *Liber Papiensis* and rearranged according to subject, with the various titles grouped into books on the model of the Code. This arrangement would remain the standard one for Lombard law for the rest of the Middle Ages. Second, the *Expositio* is prefaced with a brief exordium introducing the reader to the study of law. The text reveals clearly its roots in the schools of liberal arts by explaining, as Boethius prescribed, the intention, utility, and part of philosophy to which the work belonged. It also explained, through quotations of the Digest and Institutes, the purpose of the law itself. None of this corresponds exactly to any of the *exordia* of Irnerius and his followers, but the desire to make a general statement and much of the context is unmistakably similar.[61]

60. At Rothar 226 the observation is attributed to Guglielmo that two brothers could be governed by different rules of manumission since if one was a clerk Institutes 1.5.3 would apply to his acts. For instances of *antiqui* citing Roman law, cf. the *Expositio* at Rothar 1 and 7.

61. See the examples in H. Kantorowicz, *Studies in the Glossators of the Roman Law* (Cambridge, 1938), pp. 233–40 and his discussion pp. 37–67; on introductions in general see Edwin A. Quain, "The Medieval Accessus ad Auctores," *Traditio* 3 (1945): 215–64. The independence of the *exordium* of the *Expositio* from influence by those of Bologna is partially attested by what Quain calls its "defective" character, for what is left out was the section which for the Bolognese was the most important—the one describing the matter (*materia*) of the work.

But the most important point about the *Expositio* is the quality
of the glosses themselves, many of which are quite elaborate and
include exhaustive categorizations of issues that might arise in
court or discussions of hypothetical difficulties. The commentary
to Rothar 1, for example, which legislates against those who would
plot against the life of the king, contains five parts. The first poses
the question of how the law can say "plot" *(cogitaverit)* when only
God can know anyone's thought. The answer shows the increasing
interest of the jurists in dealing with intention (an interest apparent
in other glosses as well)[62] and also their inclination to base a judgment on evidence instead of relying on ordeals as earlier jurists
might have done:

> [The question] is solved in this way: it is known through indi-
> cations, for example if someone is discovered in the king's
> chambers after hours having a naked sword under his cloak,
> or with a knife in his sleeve, or if the cupbearer of the king
> while near him is seen to prepare poison, . . .

The next two sections show that, against the assertions of the
antiqui, the law applies to slaves; the fourth discusses whether the
malefactor's goods are to be confiscated if he dies between forming
the plot and executing it; and the fifth whether alienations made by
the malefactor before he is charged are valid. (The last two sections
are both resolved by explicit reference to Roman law.) Still more
complex is the gloss to Wido 6, of which the debate between Lanfranc and Guglielmo is the twenty-third and last section. The earlier sections analyze the cases in which, if there is conflict between
charters, the later will prevail (three cases by law and two by custom); how prior charters can be denied; the penalty paid by him
who offers a false charter in support of his claim; how long a
period is to elapse before a challenge to a charter goes to trial; what
is to be done if the bearer is the notary who drew up the charter;
and so on. Whether one notices the playful attitude that imagines
complicated (though purely hypothetical) problems, the care with
which opinions are attributed to their author so the reader can
assess their authority, or the technical mastery of the commentary,
the difference between the *Expositio* and law books of the early
Middle Ages is unmistakable.

We have seen that the conditions of free debate compelled Pavese
jurists to abandon the rule-oriented learning of the late tenth century, and we have traced, generation by generation, the refinement

---

62. For example, at Rothar 200.

of critical methods until they attained a level of skill in interpretation that well deserves the title of jurisprudence. All this recalls what has already been said for the France of Fulbert and Berengar, as do the facts that the innovations involved no new texts and were not, so far as we can tell, motivated by the revival of commerce. But while for the purpose of understanding the processes of intellectual change our story is now complete, a few words must be said about the origins of the Romanism that marks twelfth-century jurisprudence.

The first question concerns the relationship of the Pavese school to the rediscovery and editing of the Digest. Hermann Kantorowicz considered this question in his magisterial study of the vulgate Digest, and he rejected the likelihood of a relationship between the Lombard jurists and the Digest on the grounds that the Romanism of the *Expositio* was inferior by the standards of 1100—the year when he supposed it to have been written.[63] I myself am not persuaded that Romanism is the standard by which the competence of specialists in Lombard law ought to be judged nor that, given the fast-changing nature of the period, one ought to downgrade lawyers of the 1070s for failing to measure up to those of 1100. What must seem the main issue to anyone who approaches the 1070s from 1000 instead of from 1100 is the fact that whoever edited the Digest employed methods that had not been used on texts for at least 600 years and which were still rare in the eleventh century. Whatever the date of the *Expositio* as we have it, the glosses it preserves show conclusively that by the third quarter of the eleventh century the Pavese jurists had the legal training, attitudes toward texts, and demonstrated interest in Roman law to do the job of editing the Digest: no other group can be named in Italy where a similar combination of abilities was to be found.[64] It is always possible, of course, that as with Cain's wife there was somewhere a second creation that left no records. Otherwise, however, the case that the Digest was put into circulation by Pavese-trained lawyers,

63. Kantorowicz, *Digestenvulgata*, p. 75.
64. The claims of Ravenna, often cited as a center of Roman legal studies in the eleventh century, rest entirely on the citations of the *Digest* made by Peter Crassus of Ravenna in a polemic on the investiture contest. There is not only no other evidence of Roman law being studied there, but Crassus himself undertook no juristic analysis of the texts he cited, which for him were important only as authorities. See the comments of Ernst Genzmer, "Die justinianische Kodifikation und die Glossatoren," *Atti del Congresso Internazionale di Diritto Romana* (Pavia, 1934–45), Bologna, 1: 371–72.

whose studies of the Lombard law led them to the Digest, though
circumstantial nonetheless seems strong.

Because virtually nothing is known of Irnerius or his back-ground, the same considerations apply to the question of Bologna's relationship with Pavia, and here they are supported by other, more substantial indications. Of obvious importance is the fact that the basic varieties of Bolognese gloss—the cross-reference, *distinctio*, and *quaestio*—are all to be seen in Pavese writings from the mid-eleventh century though without the formal terminology that was later to be borrowed from twelfth-century dialecticians.[65] Yet for me the most persuasive evidence is the continuity in minor points of scholarly style of the kind that students learn from their master and carry on in their own work through force of habit. One such point is the use of *sigla* (for example, *B.* for Bonifiglio, *a* for *antiqui* or *y* for Irnerius) to identify the origins of a gloss or opinion. Another, and still more distinctive, is the curious style by which the jurists cited laws to which they wished to refer. A Pavese would not cite a law by king and number, as we do today, but instead would give the first words of the text; Liutprand 1 becomes "lex Liudprandi que est 'Si qui Longobardus se vivente.' " They used similar forms to refer to Roman law ("legitur enim in nono libro Codicis in lege, quae est 'meminisse oportebit.' ")[66] and it is in the same style that Bolognese jurists later referred to titles or *Leges* in their own writings.[67] Because the style itself is cumbersome and not likely to be arrived at spontaneously, the conclusion must be that some of the early Bolognese masters had studied long enough with Lombard jurists to acquire the style from them.

The picture of a Romanist jurisprudence arising spontaneously out of the rediscovery of a great book and the labors of a few great masters has long been an attractive one for historians. Yet it takes nothing away from the real and important achievements of these masters to recognize the accomplishments of their predecessors: to do so can only help us understand the processes by which intellec-

---

65. Ibid., pp. 381–84, and Genzmer, "Vorbilder für die Distinctionem der Glossatoren," *Acta Congressus Iuridici Internationalis VII Saeculo a Decretalibus Gregorii IX et XIV Saeculo a Codice Justiniano promulgatis. Romae 12–17 novembris 1934* (Rome, 1935–1937), 2: 343–58, and Gerhard Otte, *Dialektik und Jurisprudenz* (Frankfurt, 1971).

66. Both from *Expositio* to Rothar 1. One might note that the Pavese showed considerable familiarity with Roman law to be able to give citations in this form.

67. Vinogradoff, *Roman Law*, pp. 60–61.

tual change occurred. Men did not come to the study of law because a fascinating book fell off a shelf into someone's lap, nor (as
is sometimes proposed) because they wanted to score points in the
debating contest between pope and emperor. To suggest that they
did is seriously to underestimate the effort required to think juris-
tically. Instead, as we have seen, it was the press of daily circumstances that first moved the lawyers of Pavia out of traditional ways
of thinking, and then it was the desire to stump their colleagues
that stimulated their desire for learning.

Mentality and Church Reform:
Hierarchy to Community

In coming to the church reforms of the eleventh century, we leave
behind the intimate confines of classrooms and courts for the councils where the great issues of the day were debated. The chief interest of historians has understandably been in the conflict over investitures between Gregory VII and Henry IV. The pope was the
aggressor, attempting to upset the long-established status quo, and
the claims made before and during the contest mark the beginning
of the movement that would lead to papal control of the church by
the thirteenth century. But the impulse that inspired Gregory and
his partisans was by no means as new as these outcomes make it
appear. From the standpoint of cognition they had more in common with the early Middle Ages than the twelfth century, and they
saw themselves, much as had reformers of the tenth or eighth centuries, as enforcing established rules or restoring the original order
of the church.[68]

This self-image is nowhere more clearly revealed than in their
industry in making collections of church canons. The numbers
alone tell the story: well over thirty eleventh-century collections
survive, with the vast majority of them being from the period after
1050 when reform activity was greatest. Quantity has, in this case,
nothing to do with quality; none of these collections shows the
intellectual rigor already to be found at Pavia. But the fact that so
many were made, and that the reformers were so familiar with
them, shows the importance they attached to the problem of defining and enforcing the law of the church.[69]

68. For a general treatment of this theme, see Giovanni Miccoli, *Chiesa
Gregoriana* (Florence, 1966), chapter 7 [" 'Ecclesiae primitivae forma' "].
69. P. Fournier and G. Le Bras, *Histoire des collections canoniques en*

This desire to return to ideal, God-given rules was the driving impulse of all eleventh century reformers. It is expressed, for example, in the monastic reform movement, which continued the program that had already been set forth by Romuald of Ravenna and Odo of Cluny. The appeal that Cluny's strict round of liturgy and ritual held for an age chiefly concerned with indiscipline helped Cluny reach the peak of its importance in the eleventh century,[70] but even where, as in the hermitages of Italy, more emphasis was placed on private meditation and prayer, the Benedictine Rule was in force and the basic ideal was still one of rigorous obedience to the Rule.[71] Thus Peter Damian, the age's most eloquent advocate of the interior life, though preferring his hermitage at Fonte Avellana could offer the highest praise to Cluny,[72] because interiority was for him, as it had been for Gregory I, a matter of perfecting obedience that had first to be expressed in action. The idea that acts were meaningless without inner spirituality was still remote from his thought, and he viewed with equanimity both the hiring of substitutes to do penance and the oblation of boys to monasteries.[73]

The call for monastic rigor was not always well received by the monks, but the most explosive consequences of the reforming impulse came when the rules regarding the secular clergy were invoked. Though this campaign took many forms, from attacks on married clergy to demands that cathedral canons live according to a common rule, nearly everywhere the greatest controversy surrounded the issue of simony. The practice of selling church offices was itself nothing new, for the revenues and prestige high offices carried had always made them attractive, although there may have been some increase in its frequency in the eleventh century. Why this should have happened is not at all clear; possibly it was simply that, as a consequence of the general increase in fertility, wealthy families found themselves with more younger sons to find livings

occident depuis les fausses décrétales jusqu'au Décret de Gratian (Paris, 1931). J. Joseph Ryan, St. Peter Damian and His Canonical Sources (Toronto, 1956); Hennig Hoesch, Die Kanonischen Quellen im Werk Humberts von Moyenmoutier (Cologne/Vienna, 1970).

70. For Cluny in the eleventh century, see Noreen Hunt, Cluny under Saint Hugh 1049–1109 (Notre Dame, Ind., 1969); H. E. J. Cowdrey, The Cluniacs and the Gregorian Reform (Oxford, 1970).

71. PL 145: 327–36, especially 332.

72. PL 145: 371–86; 145: 873.

73. For Damian's views of penance, see R. W. Southern, Western Society and the Church in the Middle Ages (London, 1970), pp. 226–27; for oblation, PL 145: 318–21.

for and ended up with a bidding war for desirable positions. But whatever the reason, simony was the most explosive single issue in most parts of Latin Christendom from the middle of the eleventh century to the first decades of the twelfth.

The earliest denunciation of simony that survives is a letter by Guido of Arezzo written to the archbishop of Milan around 1030. Guido is best remembered as a musician, because he invented the notation of pitch by line and staff that is still in use today, and his objectives there shed valuable light on the workings of his mind. His invention was soon to make it possible to write polyphonic music and indeed to undertake careers as composers, but Guido himself was apparently unaware of these revolutionary implications. What he stressed himself in his writings on the subject was the value of notation, an inspiration (he felt) from God,[74] as a means to improve the quality of prayers for souls by making chant easier to learn and remember. A dangerous state of affairs existed, he wrote in one letter on the subject, because monks and other religious had not been learning to chant their prayers properly and often made mistakes. "Who would not weep that there is such a grave error in the holy Church, and such perilous discord that in celebrating divine offices . . . we often seem not to praise God but to struggle among ourselves."[75] It is in many ways typical of the eleventh century that what soon proved to be an important innovation was motivated by the desire to preserve inspired archetypes.

This theme of restoring correct order links Guido's musical invention with his letter against simony. Having heard, he wrote the archbishop, that the sacred orders in his jurisdiction were torn into pieces by money, he wished to remind him of the rule "pronounced by the Holy Spirit through Gregory I" that those who were ordained through money ought to be removed. Such heretics were, Guido argued, using an image that was soon to become standard, like the moneychangers Christ threw out of temple. They were, moreover, not only dangerous to themselves; because everyone who heard their masses should be understood to undergo excommuni-

74. *PL* 141: 423.
75. *PL* 141: 413. "Et quod super omnia mala magis est periculosum, multi religiosi ordinis clerici et monachi psalmos et sacras lectiones . . . negligunt; dum cantandi scientam, quam consequi numquam possunt, labore et stultissimo persequuntur. Illud quoque quis non deleat, quod tam gravis error est in santa Ecclesia, tamque periculosa discordia, ut quando divinium officium celebramus, saepe non Deum laudare, sed inter nos certare videamur."

cation, they are worse than Arians and Manichees for they "steal
upon all in the holy church by diabolical fraud as if to contaminate
the chastity of the church by the foulest pollution." Unless, therefore, the archbishop extirpated this practice "innumerable people
must meet eternal death."[76]

This made for a harsh doctrine, one that contemplated the damnation of parishioners who might well be quite unaware that the
priest whose mass they heard was a simonist. But it was not necessarily a revolutionary doctrine, nor one at odds with lay society.
Many prominent lords, including most notably Emperor Henry III,
gave the campaign against simony their full support, just as, in
other circumstances, they supported monastic reform. They could
afford to do so because while those reforms attacked abuses they
left their basic position in society, and their control of certain ecclesiastical offices, unaffected. Even Peter Damian, who offered a
broad definition of simony that included cases where the appointee
offered service or favors instead of money, saw nothing to criticize
in the action of kings who selected bishops for worthy motives.[77]

Our first task, then, is to understand how the Gregorians, utiliz-
ing the reasoning that had been dominant for nearly a millennium,
arrived at the conclusions that had such revolutionary implications. We will then be in a position to trace how, as the conflict
between pope and emperor compelled propagandists on both sides
to find more sophisticated and persuasive arguments, they articulated the ideas about society and authority that were to dominate
the rest of the Middle Ages.

Southern has described one principle that underlay the Gregorian
movement as the desire to end the mingling of sacred and secular
things. This attractive formulation captures the revulsion against
pollution of the church that is evident, for example, in the letter of
Guido of Arezzo. But it is important not to conclude from it, as
Southern himself seems to do, that the reformers considered recourse to supernatural forces crude or unspiritual. Ordeals, indeed,
almost from the beginning, were one of the favorite tools for the

---

76. MGH *Libelli de Lite* 1: 5–7. The attribution to Guido has been challenged on stylistic grounds by Anton Michel, "Die antisimonistischen Reordination und eine neue Humbert Schrift," *Römische Quartalschr. für
christliche Altertumskunde* 46 (1938): 19 ff.; but Michel's attribution has
not met wide acceptance. Cf. Hoesch, *Kanonischen Quellen*, pp. 33–34;
G. Miccoli, *Chiesa Gregoriana*, p. 40.
77. PL 145: 463–66.

conviction of simonists, and after the dispute began with the emperor, Gregory VII looked constantly for a sign that would prove the iniquity of his opponent in the eyes of God. Instead of a reduction in reliance on miracles, the reformers seem to have had in mind rather a monopoly for the priestly order whose sacramental role was never far from their thoughts. The ability to administer sacraments—and one must always remember that Humbert, who pursued Berengar with an implacably literal interpretation of the mass, was one of the earliest of the Gregorians—stood for the reformers as proof of their most extreme claims for the rights of the priesthood.[78]

This point can be illustrated by one of the most important works of the time, the *Libri III Adversus Simoniacos* of Cardinal Humbert.[79] This work was occasioned by a debate among the reformers over whether it was necessary to reordain priests whose original ordination came at the hands of a simonist bishop.[80] By calling into question the sacraments performed by innumerable priests and attended by many innocent parishioners, this proposition would have made the well-being of the church dependent on the character of individual bishops, and already in 1051 Peter Damian felt it necessary to refute it. Humbert's treatise began with the purpose of answering Damian. Yet in the course of it his own position evolved, and he found himself led to the enunciation of more and more radical doctrines.

The treatise itself is very much a work in the old style. It is not just that each point is hammered relentlessly home; that is true of all medieval polemic. Rather, it is the habit of fastening on to words

---

78. Hildebrand's own position is uncertain, but Berengar's own opinion—that he leaned in his direction—though often cited is unreliable; after all, Berengar also thought Lanfranc had, secretly, to agree with him. (I might note that this kind of incomprehension is what one expects of dialogues between people with different cognitive structures.) More weight should be given to the views of Beno (one of the cardinals who later broke with Hildebrand), who charged that the pope had sought a miracle to confirm the position of the Roman church. The gravamen of the charge was that the pope had been weak in faith, but the nature of the miracle sought—that the bread should take the shape of fingers in imitation of a miracle worked at the behest of Gregory I—makes it clear that he was not seeking support for Berengar. *Benonis aliorum cardinalium scripta i,* in MGH *Libelli de Lite* 2: 370–71.

79. MGH *Libelli de Lite* 1: 95–253.

80. On this dispute in general, see G. Miccoli, "Le ordinationi simoniache e le sinodi lateran del 1060 e 1061," *Studi Gregoriani* 5 (1956): 33–81.

or phrases and using them without regard for other possible meanings or honest differences of interpretation. Humbert makes no effort to persuade his opponent; he merely batters him to the ground.

This style makes for difficult reading today, but in the eleventh century Humbert's work must have found an interested readership because it addressed all the theological concerns of its time. In the first place, the treatise bristles with citations of canon law and precedent: a letter of Leo I on baptism (c. 2); a passage from the Pseudo-Isidorian collection of canons (c. 8); council decrees (cc. 11, 18); excerpts from Ambrose and Augustine (cc. 16, 17); and, especially, letters of Gregory the Great (c. 13). Much of the argument, moreover, centers on the question of how the miracle of the sacrament takes place, and in particular whether heretics could work valid sacraments of any kind. Contending that because it is the action of the holy spirit that cleanses sins in baptism, Humbert concluded that "it is obvious that the baptism of heretics, which is made without the sanctification of the holy spirit, effects neither remission of sins nor renovation of the old man but only a washing of the body."[81] So too, he says, in a crucial passage that depends almost entirely on a play on words, it is impossible for a simonist bishop to bestow grace because, since grace cannot be bought, he does not have it. "For grace (*gratia*), unless accepted freely (*gratis*), is not and cannot rightly be said to be grace. Simoniacs, however, do not accept freely what they accept. Therefore, what is at work in ecclesiastical orders they do not accept; if they do not accept it, they do not have it; if they do not have it neither freely nor not freely can they give it to anyone."[82] The state of mind of the priest or of the bishop, for Humbert, means nothing. Ordination was for

81. "Si autem baptismum domini Iesu secundum baptistae sui testimonium in Spiritum sancto fit et igni, ut omnium remissio peccatorum ex illo valeat fieri et vetus homo noster renovari, apparet baptisma hereticorum, quia sine sancti Spiritus sanctificatione constat, nullam peccati remissionem, nullam veteris hominis renovationem, sed solam visibilem absolutionem operari." MGH *Libelli de Lite* 1: 105.

82. ". . . gratia, nisi gratis accipiatur, gratia non est nec dici recte potest. Symoniaci autem non gratis accipiunt quod accipiunt. Igitur gratiam, quae maxime in ecclesiasticis ordinibus operatur, non accipiunt; si autem non accipiunt, nec habent; si non habent, nec gratis neque non gratis cuiquam dare possunt." MGH *Libelli de Lite* 1: 108. The same play on words appears elsewhere, e.g., MGH *Libelli de Lite* 1: 132: "Gratia autem, nisi gratis accipiatur et deture, gratia nec est nec vere dicitur. Nam si venditur et emitur, iam non esse gratia merito concluditur."

him, as was the eucharist, practically a physical event, the convey-
ance of a property that the bishop either had or had not.[83]

Thus far Humbert was only repeating arguments that he must
often have made before in the circles to which both he and Damian
belonged. Writing the third book of his treatise, however, led Humbert away from simony to the issue of lay control of the church and
ultimately to the question of lay investiture. How this was accomplished can be illustrated by comparing two passages from his treatise. The first, from book one, describes the rules governing canonical election in these words:

> Whoever is consecrated bishop, according to the rules decreed
> by the saints first is elected by the clergy, then demanded by
> the people, and finally consecrated by the other bishops of the
> province with the judgment of the metropolitan.[84]

There is little in this definition that would have struck Humbert's
contemporaries as exceptional; Leo IX had said much the same
thing ("Let none be provided to the rule of the church without
election of the clergy and people"),[85] and he himself had, after his
selection by Henry III, presented himself to the people and clergy of
Rome to comply with this requirement. Humbert added only the
words (*prius, deinde,* and *tandem*) that specified in what order
these events ought to take place, an addition that in context is an
innocent embellishment of his argument that simonists could not
be bishops. When, however, Humbert returns to this theme in the
third book these innocent words take on ominous significance.

> Although it is decreed by men venerable throughout the
> world and supreme pontiffs speaking at the inspiration of the
> Holy Spirit that the choice of the clergy ought to be con-
> firmed by the judgment of the metropolitan and the petition
> of the people and nobles by the consent of the prince, to the
> rejection of the holy canons and the contempt of the whole
> Christian religion everything is done in preposterous order so

83. Humbert specifically addresses the question of what kind of *possessio*
the bishop's powers are in book three, MGH *Libelli de Lite* 1: 199–200.
84. "Quicumque consecratur episcopus, secundum decretales sanctorum
regulas prius est a clero eligendus, deinde a plebe expetendus, tandemque a
conprovincialibus episcopis cum iudicio metropolitani iudicio consecran-
dus." MGH *Libelli de Lite* 1: 108.
85. "Ne quis sine electione cleri et populi ad regimen ecclesiasticum pro-
veheretur." *Sacrorum Conciliorum nova et amplissima collectio*, ed. J. D.
Mansi (Venice, 1774–75), 19: 741.

that the last are first and the first last. For the secular power is
first in electing and confirming, and then come the consent of
the nobles, people and clergy, whether or not they are willing,
and finally the judgment of the metropolitan.[86]

It was but a short step from this position to the condemnation of
lay investiture, which was the visible symbol of both the violation
of canon law and of the disrespect for the boundaries dividing
those who have the power to baptize and those who do not.[87] By
the time he was done Humbert had virtually equated simony and
lay investiture, and he had rendered even conscientious use of royal
authority an intolerable usurpation of clerical rights.[88]

The immediate impact of these ideas ought not to be overstated.
A compromise over the issue of reordination was reached in 1060
and 1061, with the theological questions left unresolved. And
though a canon was issued against lay investiture in 1059, higher
offices were not included in its scope and well into the 1070s the
most ardent reformers continued to accept investiture at the hands
of laymen without complaint.[89] But in denying lay rulers a role in
the governance of the church, Humbert attacked a conception of
ecclesiastical organization that had held sway in the West since the
conversion of Constantine. How the papacy argued its right to fill
the void that resulted is the next subject we must consider.

The basic materials for the doctrine of papal supremacy came
readily to hand, and, as with the case against lay investiture, they
comprised both supernatural and canonical elements. The supernatural component came from the identification of the living pope
with St. Peter that was still, in this time, taken quite literally. The
popes thought of themselves not so much as the heir to Peter's
office as Peter's living representative, and none felt this more

86. MGH *Libelli de Lite* 1: 205. One should not mistake such passages for
a consistent doctrine; Humbert's description of the forms of election shifts
from passage to passage even within book three, with the role of the
metropolitan a particular source of confusion. Cf., for example, MGH
Libelli de Lite 1: 205 where the judgment of the metropolitan is portrayed
as giving consent to the desires of clergy, people, and nobles.
87. See, for example, MGH *Libelli de Lite* 1: 205, 217, where Humbert
argues that as laymen do not perform baptisms neither do they perform
investitures.
88. MGH *Libelli de Lite* 1: 211.
89. G. Borino, "L'investitura laica dal decreto di Nicolò al decreto Gregorio VII," *Studi Gregoriani* 5 (1959–61): 348–52.

strongly than Gregory VII who could, in his struggle against the emperor, assure potential allies that if they supported him St. Peter would be their debtor, that he was, in some sense, the incarnation of Peter.[90] Sources to support this position were equally abundant, coming partly from statements made by earlier popes, and partly from Carolingian forgeries that had, by now, acquired the patina of authenticity. Even so, there was little so clear that it could not be improved upon, and Tellenbach has rightly observed that by extending old laws the Gregorians created new ones.[91] Where, for example, previous popes insisted only that the consent of the pope was needed to depose a bishop, Gregory VII was prepared to assert that he could depose bishops on his own, without consulting a synod. And where tradition had held that important matters be reported to Rome, Gregory VII took this to mean that subordinates could, with papal consent, bring accusations against their clerical superiors.

This kind of bending and pruning of sources could be shown for nearly all of the statements that make up the *Dictatus Papae*, the list of propostions (apparently a plan for a book of canon law), that may be taken as a fair statement of Gregory VII's view of his own powers. He claimed, in the first place, "that the Roman church was founded by God alone" and proceeded from there to assert both a general inerrancy for the Roman church and sainthood for himself. This is strong stuff, even if we cannot be quite certain exactly what Gregory meant. The rest of the list is more specific, spelling out in some detail an administrative jurisdiction over all western churches and asserting the right to depose emperors and absolve men of their oaths of fealty to their lords. Taken as a whole, this is a conception of Christian society every bit as hierarchical as any of the early Middle Ages, differing only in placing the pope rather than the king or emperor at the top. This impression, moreover, is confirmed by Gregory's correspondence. Two themes predominate there: the identification of the pope with St. Peter to whom "God has given the rule of the whole Church,"[92] and the

90. I. S. Robinson, *Authority and Resistance in the Investiture Contest* (Manchester, 1978), pp. 19–20. See also, Southern, *Western Society and the Church*, pp. 94–104.
91. *Church, State and Christian Society at the Time of the Investiture Contest*, trans. R. F. Bennet (Oxford, 1940), pp. 140–42.
92. *Registrum* i.15 (MGH *Epist. Sel.* 2: 15). An English translation of selected letters has been made by Ephraim Emerton, *The Correspondence of Gregory VII* (New York, 1969).

duty of obedience all Christians owed the Roman church. The chief text quoted in support of this second proposition was drawn from Gregory the Great's *Moralia*, where he compares disobedience to idolatry, concluding that "only obedience has the merit of faith." No mention is made in this passage of the pope, and indeed Gregory was writing for monks; but it is typical of Gregory VII's method that he did not hesitate to see the passage as showing "how great is the alienation from Christian law not to exhibit to the utmost obedience to the apostolic see."[93]

The Gregorians' use of sources was undeniably tendentious, but I do not believe them guilty of deliberate falsification. Their underlying modesty is perhaps best expressed by the works of art commissioned. In vain one looks for representations of the popes, replete with the insignia of power, such as would become common in the early twelfth century; indeed, no contemporary portrait of Gregory VII survives.[94] What one finds instead are basilicas built, often at great effort and expense, on the model of early Christian churches. Desiderius of Monte Cassino, for example, a member of Gregory VII's intimate circle and later himself pope as Victor III, imported Byzantine craftsmen to adorn his new church with mosaics such as he saw in early Christian churches, and his example was followed by others. Ernst Kitzinger has well argued that this artistic desire expressed a deliberate policy, one of looking back to the Constantinian and post-Constantinian age when originated so many of the statements of papal primacy that the Gregorians quoted repeatedly in their writings.[95] This earnest desire to return to a model of the early church can be reconciled with their grandiose claims only when one accepts the fact that the Gregorians were no more capable of seeing that one could honestly arrive at different interpretations of his favorite texts than were other writers of the early Middle Ages. Gregory VII in particular did not so much weigh and reject other readings as fail to consider them at all: however tortured his interpretations seem to us he felt no need to justify them. His distortions were the product not of cunning but of mentality: it

93. *The Epistolae Vagrantes of Gregory VII*, ed. and trans. H. E. J. Cowdrey (Oxford, 1972), p. 24. See also, on this theme in general, Robinson, *Authority and Resistance*, pp. 22–24.

94. But see G. Ladner, "The Commemoration Pictures of the Exultet Roll Barberinus latinus 592," in *Paradosis: Studies in Memory of Edwin A. Quain* (New York, 1976).

95. "The Gregorian Reform and the Visual Arts: A Problem of Method," *Transactions of the Royal Historical Society*, 5th ser., 22 (1972): 87–102.

made sense to him that authority, which he always conceived of as coming from above, should pass from Christ to Peter to himself as pope, and so that is what he understood his texts to say.

It was also the inherent persuasiveness of the Gregorian program to men of the same mentality that explains the reformers' success in compelling obedience outside their circle. The administrative apparatus of the papacy was still primitive, and the pretensions of legates to interfere in local matters was often resented. Many bishops, moreover, read canon law differently than the Gregorians, and they spoke out against the implication that their own ministry was inferior or subordinate to the "pope's."[96] Yet such was the logical force of the Gregorian position that, in the beginning at least, few—even of those who thought the pope exceeded his authority—were willing to stand against him. It was Henry IV's misfortune to discover this only when, in March 1076, he tried to rally the bishops among his followers to denounce Gregory: at Utrecht, for example, of the three bishops who agreed to pronounce the sentence of excommunication against the monk Hildebrand, two stole away under cover of darkness.[97]

The conflict between Gregory and Henry was, therefore, not a struggle between old and new mentalities but one between two versions of the old. Both sides claimed to receive their authority from God, to enforce the right order of the church, and to exact the obedience of all Christians. Yet on the central issue of who stood at the top of the social hierarchy there was no room for compromise, and because neither side was able to overcome the other, positions quickly hardened. The stalemate that resulted provided the stimulus to cognitive development that the reform itself had not, and in the polemical literature that abundantly survives it is possible to trace the emergence of new attitudes toward texts and new conceptions of society.

The trend toward increasingly critical reading of texts can be illustrated by the course of the debate over the right of the pope to depose an emperor. Gregory VII justified his position by quoting the following passage from the correspondence of Gregory the Great: "If any king, priest, judge or secular person shall disregard

96. Tellenbach, *Church, State and Christian Society*, pp. 142–47. On the weaknesses of the papal chancery, see Alexander Murray, "Pope Gregory VII and His Letters," *Traditio* 22 (1966): 149–202.
97. Augustin Fliche, *La réforme grégorienne* (Louvain/Paris, 1926), 2: 291.

this decree of ours [in favor of a hospital] or act contrary to it, he shall be deprived of his power and his office and shall learn that he stands condemned at the bar of God for the wrong that he has done."[98] Within a few years, however, the cardinals who broke with the pope were quoting the whole letter of Gregory I to prove that the passage in question was merely a general anathema pronounced against those who violated the privileges that Gregory was confirming. Gregory VII, they wrote, cut out only the text that suited his own intention: he quoted it correctly, but he did not interpret it correctly.[99] Bolder still was the reply of the anonymous *Liber de unitate ecclesiae conservanda*. The author of this work, probably a monk of the monastery of Hersfeld, does not seem to have had at hand the collection of Gregory I's correspondence. But he knew enough of Gregory's relations with secular authority to see that the passage, at least as interpreted by the reformers, was out of character. "Certainly Gregory called the Roman emperors his lords and himself their servant, . . . and out of fear of God he did nothing even against the Lombards who were pagans and persecutors of the church."[100] In developing such standards of interpretation, these proimperial writers were following the path that had earlier been taken by the masters of France and the jurists of Pavia: they were evaluating the text by the intention of its author.

Just as the pope's deposition of Henry IV provoked Henry's followers to careful scrutiny of Gregory's sources, the need to defend Gregory provided the stimulus for Manegold of Lautenbach to enunciate a new conception of civil authority. Manegold did not attempt to defend what was clearly Gregory's main idea: that any king who failed in obedience to the papacy lost favor with God. Instead, his approach was to argue that a schismatic king (for that was how he described Henry) failed in his duty to his subjects. The people (*populus*), Manegold wrote, "raise a king or emperor over them so that he can rule and govern them by reason of his just authority, giving to each his own, fostering the pious, destroying the impious, thus distributing justice to all. But if sometime he

98. Gregory VII to Hermann of Metz, 15 March 1081, trans. from Emerton, *Correspondence of Gregory VII*, p. 168 (*Regestrum* viii.21).
99. "Hoc recte optulisti, sed no recte divisisti [the second person is because the pamphlet is addressed to Hildebrand]." *Benonis aliorumque cardinalium scrita iii*, in MGH *Libelli de Lite* 2: 391. A similar passage (p. 400) criticizes the basis of the pope's claim to sanctity. On this and what follows, see Robinson, *Authority and Resistance*, pp. 41–42, 138–41.
100. MGH *Libelli de Lite* 2: 199. For a similar critique of Gregory VII's use of Gelasius, see pp. 230–31.

infringes his compact (*pactum*) by which he was chosen, . . . reason justly considers the people absolved of their obligation of submission."[101] It is noteworthy that in this passage, as in others where he pursues this theme, Manegold feels free to make his case without benefit of citations from authorities. The chapter just quoted begins, in fact, with an explicit appeal to reason and ends in the same way.[102] But the chief interest of Manegold's argument must be that, in assuming that civil authority comes from consent of the governed, Manegold was giving voice to a conception of society that had not found expression for a millennium. Whether in this he drew inspiration from ancient sources is not really important. Augustine had, as we saw, been familiar enough with this idea to quote it, but even he had not reasoned out (as Manegold did) the consequences of this idea for a complex argument.

The concept of a *pactum* between king and people is sufficiently striking that its orginality has long been recognized. But more important than any specific formulation was the shift from God to human society as the source of law, and as the investiture contest dragged on this idea was stated more and more frequently. Around 1100, for example, one finds Bishop Ivo of Chartres dismissing the notion that lay investiture was against divine law: if it were, rulers could never have instituted the practice. Law is not for Ivo, as it would become, a matter of social convention; it is still the rulers who make the laws. Yet in attributing to secular rulers such discretionary powers, Ivo moved well beyond the early medieval attitude that saw all law as coming from God.[103]

It was this desacralization of society, however tentative it may have been, that opened the way for the eventual settlement between emperor and pope. As long as the issue was seen as one of divine law the possibilities for compromise were limited: how could one knowingly transgress the commands of God? When, however, the issue had ceased to be seen as one of orthodoxy against heresy, both sides were better able to acknowledge the legitimacy of some at least of the other's concerns, and strive to reach a mutually

101. *Liber ad Gebhardum*, MGH *Libelli de Lite* 1: 391–92. For a comparable passage, see p. 365.

102. The same is true, for example, of p. 365. For a wider perspective on Manegold's attitude toward *ratio* see Wilfried Hartmann, "Manegold von Lautenbach und die Anfänge der Frühscholastik," *Deutsches Archiv für Erforschung des Mittelalters* 26 (1970): 47–149, especially pp. 110–29.

103. MGH *Libelli de Lite* 2: 642–46. Interestingly, Hugh of Fleury, a royalist where Ivo was a reformer, was willing to see the organization of the church was a matter of mores. Ibid., 2: 472.

acceptable bargain.[104] While the terms of the eventual settlement were not quickly reached, the process of negotiation itself marked the beginning of an age in which agreement and not obedience would be the dominant concern of political life.

The eleventh century has in common with the seventeenth the fate of forever being overshadowed by the fruition of developments its achievements made possible. This is easy to understand. Compared to Abelard's writings, Berengar's are groping and confused, just as the progress of the Pavese jurists was painful and gradual compared to the achievements of the Bolognese only a little later. But we can appreciate these earlier thinkers if we understand that their task was of a different order. They had not only to clear new territory. They had to invent the mental tools by which the clearance could be done.

104. See, for example, Paschal II's letter renouncing involvement by clerics in worldly affairs, MGH *Const.* 1: 141 (no. 90).

SEVEN

A World Remade

European Society in
the Twelfth Century

*Now since this world of
nations has been made by
men, let us see in what
institutions all men agree
and always have agreed.
For these institutions will
be able to give us the
universal and eternal
principles (such as every
science must have) on
which all nations were
founded and still preserve
themselves.*
—The New Science, 332.

Because each generation educated its successor into the new mentality, the new attitudes toward tradition, society, and nature were well established by 1100 even though the actual numbers who shared it were still very small. For the twelfth century, therefore, the historical problem shifts from the social conditions that produced cognitive change to the impact of the new cognition on society. By this I have in mind no abstract force, but the actions and thought of individual men and women. The libraries of Europe were little different in 1100 than they had been 100 or even 200 years earlier. To people who came with new questions, however, and read with an eye not only on the words of the ancients but their meaning, the familiar texts yielded new answers and prompted new lines of inquiry. So too with social institutions which, as people saw them in different terms, became in fact different. Kingship and serfdom, monasticism and marriage meant greatly different things in 1200 than they did in 1100 not because anyone decided to rebel from tradition, but because old practices could not be bent to new thoughts without experiencing a fundamental transformation.

In what follows I shall consider first educational institutions and attitudes toward learning, next the restructuring of monastic and legal institutions to conform to the new mentality, and finally the

200

effects of that mentality on attitudes toward the physical world. In part because of my own background, and in part because I believe that the test of a new interpretation is what it can tell us new about already familiar materials, I have drawn my examples from a relatively narrow geographical area—England and northern France—and even my discussion of that area has been selective. Thus I discuss Abelard and not the Victorines, monastic constitutions but not spirituality, science but not imaginative literature. My selections, however, are meant to be suggestive rather than exhaustive, for I believe that the influences which I discuss were equally to be found elsewhere in Europe and in authors who, at first glance, might appear opposed to those I discuss. The intensely emotional spiritual lives of Bernard, Francis of Assisi, or the mystics, though based on values different from those of the schoolmen, reflect the awakened interest in intention no less than Abelard's *Ethics*. Similarly, the historian Otto of Freising and the prophet Joachim of Fiore are easily contrasted to Parisian schoolmen on a number of doctrinal and philosophical issues. Yet from the standpoint of cognition, they clearly belong to the era after 1050, for they both display a willingness and ability to impose an intellectually coherent vision that is unlike any writer of the early Middle Ages.

The Schools

ABELARD

No one figure dominates the first half of the twelfth century as Augustine does the last years of the Western empire, and given the complexity and speed of developments this is hardly surprising. But my choice of Abelard to illustrate the character of these times is not an arbitrary one. To begin with, none of his works was greatly influenced by the translations that, from the beginning of the century, were being made from Greek and Arabic; this means that his ideas, where they are new, are the product of his reflections and the academic debates of the time and not merely the consequence of the availability of new sources. Abelard's range of interests, moreover, was exceedingly wide: a catalog of his surviving works would include, in addition to his formal writings on dialectics, ethics, and theology, an innovative textbook (the *Sic et Non*), an autobiography, several letters to Heloise, poetry, and two Biblical commentaries. Certainly none of his contemporaries wrote so extensively.

Finally, there is the very longevity of his career in a time when the conditions of education and sophistication of discussion were changing more quickly than they ever have since. As a youth in the early 1100s, Abelard was the student and then the competitor of Roscelin, William of Champeaux, and Anselm of Laon; in the 1130s, when he returned to Paris, he held his own alongside the likes of William of Conches, Thierry of Chartres, and Gilbert of Poitiers. The first group lived and taught in isolation from one another and were concerned with issues not too greatly different from those of the generation of Berengar of Tours; in the second are to be seen for the first time both the intensely competitive environment of discussion and many of the specific theological and philosophical issues that later characterized the medieval university. The length of time dividing the two periods was not great, really only twenty years. Yet only Abelard spanned it with equal influence at both ends, and if the meagerness of our evidence does not always permit us to gauge his personal influence on developments, the bare fact of his survival as a scholar to be reckoned with attests to the special attunement of his interests with those of his age.

It is appropriate to begin with Abelard as a dialectician, for he was nowhere more typical of his time than in his preoccupation with logic. Yet if we are to understand the fascination this discipline held for men of the twelfth century, we must first of all rid ourselves of the notion that what occurred was chiefly a renaissance, that is, a recovery of old but previously unappreciated knowledge. The traditional view is well put by Southern, who argued that in a society where both nature and human affairs defied understanding, logic "opened a window on to an orderly and systematic view of the world and of man's mind."

> The student began with Porphyry's *Introduction* to Aristotle, translated with a twofold commentary by Boethius, and learnt there the art of classifying the objects external to the mind. He learnt to play with the terms *genus* and *species*, *differentia*, *property*, and *accident*, and to apply these conceptions in argument and discussion. He proceeded then to Aristotle's *Categories*, and learnt to classify the remarks which can be made about any object whatsoever. . . . From this point the student progressed to Boethius's translation and commentaries on Aristotle's *De Interpretatione*. Once more he met the same miraculous order and simplicity—this time in the classification of the kinds of statement which we can make on any subject.

Such indeed was the school curriculum, down to Abelard's time. But to conclude as Southern does, that the attraction of logic lay in the usefulness of its classifications for organizing experience, and that "the digestion of Aristotle's logic was the greatest intellectual task of the period,"[1] is to mistake libraries and textbooks for living culture. One has only to read what Abelard's generation themselves wrote on logic to see that their interest was not (as it had been for tenth-century logicians) in classifications, nor even as it would be later, in syllogisms. Their concern was with the workings of language itself.

An illustration will make this clear. In *De Interpretatione* Aristotle concluded his brief discussion of the verb (the entire section requires only about fifteen lines in Boethius's translation) with the remark that the verb *to be* does not convey any meaning (*non signum est rei*) unless it is joined to other words. His point here is a simple one, that unlike the verb *run*, for example, *is* does not convey an image to the hearer unless in statements such as "Socrates is" or "Socrates is white." Abelard is, on this issue, in general agreement. Yet his gloss on this sentence fills six closely printed pages of his commentary to *De Interpretatione*, because he took this opportunity to discuss the entirely different problem of what relationship is posited when two terms are joined by the verb *to be*. A typical section (somewhat abbreviated) reads as follows:

> Because the substantive verb (i.e., to be) signifies anything whatever in essence, the copulation of essence is never absent from it, for it invariably frames the proposition one thing is another. Even when it is adjoined to adjectives, as when one says "Socrates is white". . . nevertheless as a consequence of the substantive verb the substantive *album* [white thing] is conjoined with Socrates in respect of essence. So much, indeed, is to be understood in this substantive force that "album" can be substituted for Socrates in any proposition to give propositions such as "a white thing runs."

Abelard is contending in this passage that the relationship between *white* and *Socrates* established by the proposition "Socrates is white" is not one of accident to substance but the identity of two things; put another way, if the statement is true then Socrates cannot be other than white. To grasp the implications of this position it is necessary only to consider (as Abelard, prudently, does not) that one sentence of the form "A is B" is this one: *Hoc est corpus meum.*

1. *Making of the Middle Ages* (New Haven, 1953), pp.180–81.

Abelard, moreover, would go further and apply his arguments to statements not of the form "A is B" by converting "Socrates runs" to "Socrates is a running thing."[2]

Around such issues reputations were made and broken in the late eleventh and early twelfth centuries, and one may well ask what it was that made this kind of abstruse linguistic analysis seem so important. For though logic was to occupy a secure place in the school curriculum for centuries to come, during most of that period it was a discipline that students passed through on the way to more exciting subjects. It was uniquely at the period we are discussing that logic seemed so central to the pursuit of knowledge, and that moment passed as quickly as it came. It was perhaps already on the decline in Abelard's own lifetime, as he himself shifted the focus of his interests to theology by the 1120s.

To answer this question we need to recall what had happened to intellectual discourse as a consequence of the cognitive changes we have been discussing. The old practice had been to settle disputes by citing authority; such had been the approach taken, for example, by the participants in the predestination controversy of the tenth century (with the exception always of John the Scot). But this approach could not survive the realization that many of the texts inherited from antiquity were capable of more than one construction. One scholar might cite a text only to find that his opponent disagreed about its meaning. By 1100 it was even increasingly the case that the very authority of a text's author might be denied or disregarded.

To those outside academic life, these stances could be understood only as the product of pride or impiety, attitudes that threatened to reduce the uncertainties of the past to an anarchy of subjective interpretations. For them, the solution seemed to be a return to established truths; certainly this was St. Bernard's position when he criticized the schoolmen (and Abelard in particular) for being unwilling to acknowledge the authority of the Fathers. He made this complaint in 1140. But no better answer could be made to it than the one Abelard had already given in the Sic et Non.[3] It was not

2. The commentary on De Interpretatione is part of the Logica Ingredientibus, ed. Bernhard Geyer in Peter Abaelards philosophische Schriften (Beiträge zur Geschichte der Philosophie und Theologie des Mittelalters, Bd. 21, hft. 1–3; Münster, 1919–27). The relevant pages are 358–63. The text of Boethius's translation is found in L. Minio-Paluello, ed. Aristoteles Latinus 2.1–2 (Bruges/Paris, 1965).
3. Sic et Non, ed. Blanche B. Boyer and Richard McKeon (Chicago, 1976–77), p. 103.

just that Abelard makes clear that he does not believe authority can solve all problems, that sometimes the doctors of the Church really are in disagreement and that even the apostles and prophets occasionally erred where they were not recipients of direct inspiration. Nor is it that, far from despairing at this conclusion, Abelard encourages the student to regard such uncertainties as a challenge: "for by doubting we come to inquire, and by inquiring we perceive the truth."

The real lesson of the *Sic et Non* is that any use of authority, no matter how apparently simple, is an act of interpretation. The structure alone tells the story. The work is arranged as a series of propositions with opinions from authorities quoted both for and against, and though many of these propositions are serious enough, Abelard's purpose is perhaps best revealed in the apparently more frivolous sections. One of these, for example, posed the question whether sin is pleasing to God. Not even the dimmest student can have been in doubt as to the correct answer to this question, but Abelard found to support the proposition passages taken from, among others, Augustine and Gregory the Great. The danger of uncritical reliance on authority could hardly be plainer, and Abelard makes this lesson explicit in his preface. His constant reminder is to attend to the intention of the author rather than the apparent meaning of the text: sometimes the same word is used with different meanings, sometimes for variety authors used different words to mean the same thing; some passages are to be taken literally, others figuratively; some authors cite passages they disagree with, for the purpose of refuting them, so the passage is not to be taken as representing their own opinion; some opinions were later repudiated by their authors; and sometimes apocryphal works are cited as if they had the authority of scripture. (Abelard emphasizes these last two points by including in the text of the *Sic et Non* Augustine's *Retractions* and Pope Gelasius's letter on the canon of the Bible.) The elementary character of this advice should not deceive us: all that we have seen of the reasoning of the early Middle Ages attests to the fact that such errors really were made. By thus parodying a style of debate that had only in his time begun to seem old-fashioned, Abelard drove home his main point that accepting the authority of the saints did not excuse one from the use of one's own judgment.

The *Sic et Non* testifies to the collapse of the world of discourse in which citation of authority had been the alpha and omega of debate. By 1100 no amount of skill in resolving contradictions could put this world back together again: once the act of interpretation had become a conscious one, attention inevitably shifted from the ancient texts to the modern interpreter.[4] Not just certainty but the means of reaching certainty were threatened, and it was this pressing need that led to the importance of logic in the intellectual life of the time. The hope seems to have been that by studying language one could learn what statements were of necessity true, that on such truths a new kind of discourse could be built. This aspiration is not as fanciful as it might sound; a similar collapse of certainties at the beginning of this century also caused a renewed interest in logic. From the eleventh and early twelfth centuries, moreover, we possess a number of works that seem to have been written with the purpose of illustrating how this claim could be made good.

The works which I have in mind are a group of dialogues and treatises written to defend Christian doctrine against the attacks of nonbelievers. The form itself was, of course, a very old one; one thinks of Fulbert's little tracts against the Jews. But it was given an important new twist by setting up as the adversary of Christianity not a Jew or a pagan but a "fool" (for Anselm) or a "philosopher" (for Abelard) who accorded no value at all to scripture or revelation.[5] To understand the appeal of this genre we need not assume that such radical skeptics actually existed in any numbers. There was sufficient intellectual challenge in the fact that the premise of the form excluded authorities, which were so troublesome at this particular time, and required that the authors proceed by a process of defining terms and drawing out the consequences of mutually accepted truths. Anselm's ontological proof of the existence of God is the most famous example of this kind of argument, but there are others in Anselm's oeuvre and also in Abelard's dialogue of a philosopher with a Christian and a Jew. What all these works show, however, and were meant to show, is that logic alone could form the basis of discussion and agreement.

In the late eleventh and early twelfth centuries, then, the study of logic was the study of discourse. Certainly this was how Abelard saw the issue. Logic was, he wrote, the science of distinguishing

4. This is a point that I believe is missed by interpreters who see the *Sic et Non* as a return to authority. Cf., for example, Martin Grabmann, *Geschichte der Scholastischen Methode* (Freiburg, 1909–11).

5. *Dialogus inter Philosophum, Iudaeum et Christianum*, ed. Rudolf Thomas (Stuttgart, 1970), lines 1341–48, pp. 91–92. An English translation by Pierre J. Payer (Toronto, 1979) is now available.

true and false arguments or, alternatively, of speech and its mean-ings.[6] The restrictiveness of his definition should be noted; indeed, many of the inquiries that ancient logicians had taken as their own Abelard specifically excluded, among them the study of thought itself or the question of how speech relates to the external world. In practice, of course, this boundary could hardly be sustained, and it is in one of the places where it was breached that we come face-to-face with one of the areas where the shift in cognition was resulting in new relations between humans and their world.

To explain this point, a brief digression is necessary. For Plato, Aristotle, and indeed every thinker whose views survive down to John the Scot, thinking—and seeing or hearing—meant some kind of union of the senses with the source of sensations. Augustine, for example, could write that "intellection is composed of the knower and that which is known, just as in the eyes what we call seeing consists of the sense itself and the sensible"; elsewhere he refers in similar terms to the "conjunction of the regarding soul with that which is regarded."[7] Professor F. Edward Cranz, from whose research I take this summary, refers to these conceptions of experience as "conjunctive." But for my purposes what must be striking is that children today often express the same views of thinking or seeing. This is not surprising; there is much intellectual realism in the ancient views, and it does not, of course, suggest that one ought to consider Aristotle or Augustine childlike.

The break with this tradition came at the time of Anselm and Abelard. According to Cranz, and this view is borne out by others, it was they who first set forth the modern position that sees a dichotomy between the knower and what is known, so that mental images are regarded as imaginary or fictitious. Abelard, in particular, works out these ideas with great clarity. It is in his earliest logical works, for example, that one finds the following:

> But perhaps one will say that this image is the idea itself, as Aristotle says in this passage: "These and their likenesses are the same things." But we do not accept this either. The idea, which is a form of the indivisible mind, cannot exceed its own subject, so it cannot fit itself to the quantity of all things nor

6. *Logica Dialectica*, ed. L. M. de Rijk (Assen, 1956), p. 286; *Logica 'Nostrorum Petitioni Sociorum'*, part of Geyer's 1919 edition of Abelard's philosophical works, p. 506, lines 26–28.
7. *Soliloquia* i.6.13; *De immortalitate animae* i.6.10. The translations are from F. Edward Cranz, "1100 A.D.: Crisis for Us?," in *De Litteris. Occasional Papers in the Humanities* (New London, 1978), pp. 84–107.

transfigure itself into all forms, just as the mind cannot. Thus we concede that completely nothing is an image of this sort or one of the likenesses of things which the soul makes for itself in order to contemplate in it a thing which is absent.[8]

It is this view, of course, that continues to prevail today.

Tracing the implications of this shift is a difficult task. One feels intuitively that such a change in the experience of the outside world must have profound implications for science, but though this period also saw the revival of scientific thought, it is hard to establish the connection. One place, however, where the effects can clearly be seen is in the eleventh and twelfth centuries' handling of the classic problem of universals. This was an old and difficult issue in logic. Simply stated, the question was what a word refers to when it is of the sort that can be used to describe two different things, as, for example, *animal* is used in these two statements:

> Socrates is an animal.
> Brunellus is an animal.

The ancient view of this problem was profoundly affected by the conception of thought discussed above, because philosophers began from the premise that if an idea existed it had to have its origins outside the mind. This did not mean that there was a consensus about a solution. For Plato, the source of ideas was the world of forms, which he distinguishes carefully from the world of physical objects. For Aristotle, the characteristics that are described by universals have in some sense a real existence in individual objects. Both of them would have agreed with Boethius that a universal had to be some thing because "an idea cannot be made from no subject."[9]

Such was the shape of the problem as it was handed down to the Middle Ages. Yet as soon as serious philosophical study began again in the eleventh century, one finds philosophers working from entirely different premises: the problem of what things are the source of universals has disappeared altogether. Garlandus Com-

8. *Logica Ingredientibus*, p. 315. The translation is from Martin Tweedale, *Abelard on Universals* (Amsterdam/New York/Oxford, 1976), pp. 169–74.

9. "Cum intellectus aut ex re subjecta fiat ... venus est qui de nullo subjecto capitur, nam ex nullo subjecto fieri intellectus non potest." *PL* 64: 84A. For introduction to the problem as it appeared to Abelard's generation, together with an illuminating discussion of Abelard's own solution, see Tweedale, *Abelard on Universals*.

postista, writing sometime in the middle decades of the century, already took for granted the position that universals are words not things. Soon afterward one finds Roscelin, one of Abelard's teachers, expressing the still more radical view that universals were mere puffs of air—the transitory physical sounds produced by speaking. I believe that such statements are evidence that philosophers were already taking for granted some kind of disjunction between thought and external reality. This reading of eleventh-century philosophy, moreover, defines an intellectual milieu that helps explain why it was St. Anselm who at this time first formulated explicitly the conceptions of thought and vision that have been the source of subsequent philosophy.[10] Given the absence of specific texts, my interpretation of this point perhaps cannot be proven. But what must be obvious to any reader is the confidence with which now forgotten scholars such as Garlandus were sweeping away centuries of philosophical tradition, knowing full well that they were doing precisely that.[11]

The destruction worked by eleventh-century logicians was very great, but there was in these early nominalists little in the way of constructive theory. Even if the universal *man* is, as Roscelin said, mere breath, statements such as "Socrates is a man" undoubtedly convey some meaning and other statements, such as "Socrates is an animal" and "Socrates is mortal," are deducible from it. The problem inescapably posed was how language can make true statements about the world of things even though ideas themselves are not things but mental figments.

It was this problem that Peter Abelard addressed in his dialectical works. The details of how he accomplished this task must not concern us here; suffice it to say that some of Abelard's theory has become intelligible only in this century as modern logicians have begun working along similar lines. But it is significant for our purposes that his underlying assumption was that the meaning words have comes not so much from external reality, as from the processes of language and discussion. Universals were, for him, expressions (*sermones*) that owe their existence to the meanings people

---

10. Since Anselm also joins those such as Berengar who treat miracles as exceptions to natural law, it is likely that there is a connection between the new conceptions of nature and thought. Cf. *De conceptu virginali et de originali peccato*, in F. S. Schmitt, *S. Anselmi Cantuariensis archiepiscopi Opera omnia* (Edinburgh, 1938–61), 2: 153–54.

11. Garlandus Compotista, *Dialectica*, ed. L. M. de Rijk (Assen, 1959); see the discussion by Tweedale, *Abelard on Universals*, pp. 135–40.

establish in them. They are therefore products not of reality but of discourse, or (it might better be said) of the intentions of those who establish them by participating in discourse.[12]

The reconceptualization of the relation between the human mind and the world of things was probably the most revolutionary product of the new cognition of the high Middle Ages, because there is to be seen a break not only with the early Middle Ages, but classical antiquity as well. Yet Abelard's surviving works testify equally to the revival or, it might better be said, the reinvention of two other ideas that were already in the process of reshaping European society. One of these, implicit in the concerns of the logical works, was the use of intention as the touchstone of morality. The other was the idea of nature itself.

Intention

Abelard's mature ethical theory is contained in the first medieval treatise on the subject, his *Scito Teipsum* or *Ethics*. Written in the 1130s, during the period following Abelard's return to Paris after years as an abbot in Brittany, this book amply reveals the transforming effect of logic on twelfth-century discourse. It begins as follows:

> We consider morals to be the vices or virtues of the mind which make us prone to bad or good works. However, there are vices or goods not only of the mind but also of the body . . . Hence to distinguish these, when we said "vices" we added "of the mind." . . . There are also however some vices or good things of the mind which are separate from morals and do not make human life worthy of blame or praise, such as dullness of mind or quickness of thinking, forgetfulness or a good memory, ignorance or learning. . . . Hence rightly when above we presented "vices of the mind" we added, in order to exclude such things, "which make us prone to bad works."[13]

Abelard's purpose in this passage is to create a language for the philosophical discussion of ethics, and he proceeds in quick order

12. Tweedale, *Abelard on Universals*, pp. 140 ff.
13. *Peter Abelard's Ethics*, ed. and trans. D. E. Luscombe (Oxford, 1971) p. 3. The place of the *Ethics* in twelfth-century thought is discussed by Luscombe in *The School of Peter Abelard* (Cambridge, 1969); Robert Blomme, *La doctrine du péché dans les écoles théologiques de la première moitié du XIIe siècle* (Louvain, 1958); P. Anciaux, *La théologie du sacrement de pénitence au XIIe siècle* (Louvain, Gembloux, 1949).

to distinguish vices, such as lust, from the consent of the mind to

the vice and both of these from the forbidden act itself. What
resulted, however, was not just a technical vocabulary but a conception of psychology that surpassed earlier ones by differentiating
between natural desires and the conscious mind that consents to
them or rejects them.

The thesis for which Abelard assembled this apparatus was that
neither vice nor the act are themselves sinful but only the sinful
intention. The importance of this stress on intention needs no emphasis here. We have already seen that confusion between action
and intention was endemic in the early Middle Ages, whose most
eloquent interpreters of interior life—men such as Gregory I and
Peter Damian—tended to regard internal obedience as a heighten-
ing of good actions rather than a primary good itself. This view still
had to be refuted with great care, and Abelard devotes several
pages to this purpose. He begins by imagining an innocent man
pursued by his lord, who means to kill him; the man flees as far as
he can until, cornered and without other resort, he kills in self-
defense. The fact that the man, at the end, acted intentionally
Abelard does not deny, arguing instead that the will was not to kill
his lord but to save his own life. "If perhaps someone says that he
wanted to kill his lord for the sake of avoiding death, he cannot
therefore infer that he wanted to kill him. For example, if I were to
say to someone: 'I want you to have my cap for this reason, that
you give me five solidi' or 'I gladly want it to become yours at that
price,' I do not therefore concede that I want it to be yours."[14] Yet it
is typical of Abelard that he does not content himself with this
sober case, but in subsequent pages develops his thesis through
frivolous and often sexual instances. Thus to distinguish between
the willed sin and the act that results, he remarks that "it often
happens that when we want to lie with a woman whom we know to
be married . . . yet we by no means want to be adulterous with
her—we would prefer that she was unmarried."[15] And to argue
that sexual pleasure itself is not sinful he invites us to consider the
case of a monk, bound in chains on a bed with a woman on each
side, and so brought to pleasure but not to consent. "Who may
presume to call this pleasure, made necessary by nature, a fault?"[16]
The flippant tone of such passages doubtless served to irritate
Abelard's monastic enemies, but reading them today it is easy to

14. *Ethics,* p. 9.
15. *Ethics,* p.17.
16. *Ethics,* p.21.

hear an echo of Master Peter's lecture style: witty and teasing, brilliant and provocative, all while never losing sight of the serious point at issue.

The cognitive achievement that underlay Abelard's *Ethics* was his ability to apply to the relationship between men and God the expectations of reciprocal respect that had been taking shape at the human level in the eleventh century. God thus became less the enforcer of rules and more engaged in a mutually loving relationship with human beings, thus more willing to forgive actions that, by being without malice, left that relationship intact. Evidence for such a shift begins to become abundant around 1100: in Anselm's work on the incarnation of Christ, in the occasional references to sin by theological masters of the generation before Abelard, and—most notably—in the whole direction of monastic reform.[17] But though Abelard clearly belonged to this wider movement, it would be mistaken to regard his *Ethics* as merely another statement of the new attitude, because the statement of a general principle is always a long step from preliminary specific applications.[18] In the case of the *Ethics* this gap between specific issues and general theory—what Piaget would call a *décalage*—is most apparent in the reaction of Bernard of Clairvaux and William of St. Thierry. Both these men were famous in their time and since for their eloquent works on inner spirituality, but they had given little thought to propositions that Abelard was ready to put forward in total seriousness: that there was sin neither in desire nor pleasure; that actions themselves are morally indifferent; that anathemas and excommunications, if they are undeserved, do not exclude the believer from God's grace. Abelard's position on these matters must have seemed to them an attack on monastic asceticism and the status of the priesthood in general, and they responded with the persecutions that led to Abelard's condemnation at Sens in 1140.[19]

Yet the importance of the *Ethics* does not come solely from the

17. See, in general, Southern, *Making of the Middle Ages*, chapter 5; Colin Morris, *Discovery of the Individual* (New York, 1972), pp. 65–77, which is particularly interesting for its juxtaposition of Abelard with his accusers, St. Bernard and William of St. Thierry.

18. Blomme relates the incomprehension and hostility with which Abelard's *Ethics* were received to his being too far advanced: "Bref, cette incomprehension . . . est révélatrice. Pierre Abélard avait manifestament certains préoccupations de moraliste que échappaient à ses contemporains." *La doctrine du péché*, pp. 339–40.

19. For the text of the accusations see J. Leclerc, *Revue Bénédictine* 78 (1968).

intellectual effort needed to reach a higher level of abstraction. Abstract statements have a power of their own. They reveal inconsistencies and problems that had not been felt before and that often threaten established institutions and assumptions. It was natural for Abelard, having set forth his general principles, to consider how his definition of sin affected contemporary customs of penance and confession. Toward the practice of requiring penance for bad actions he is surprisingly tolerant, offering as justification two considerations: that perhaps, as in the case of the woman who smothers her baby trying to keep him warm, the punishment will warn others to be more cautious; and that in any case it is foolish to expect of human procedures the perfection that only God can achieve.[20] Both arguments implicitly regard penance and confession as essentially human institutions, and this idea becomes explicit in later sections where Abelard contends that contrition alone, with or without the intervention of the priest, is enough to win reconciliation with God. Strikingly absent is any consideration of penance as a sacrament or as a ritual of the Church at which divine power is invoked.[21]

What is perhaps most important about these arguments, however, is the way they reveal the tension, typical of twelfth-century intellectual life, between new ideas and established customs. It was not conceivable that the institutions of confession and penance should be overthrown; there was too much respect for tradition for that to take place. But neither was it possible to ignore the discrepancy between new attitudes and practices that were rooted in very different kinds of reasoning. Abelard was not alone in feeling this tension. His ideas were taken seriously and debated, and later in the century there did emerge a form of confession that gave a greater role to the analysis of intention and psychological life in general.

Nature

The concept of consent or intention in all its forms, whether powerfully expressed as in the *Scito Teipsum* or quietly put into practice, was one of the main solvents of the early medieval mentality. Another was the idea of nature as a system of necessary forces and unvarying phenomena. Zither, machine, world-soul, and especially

---

20. *Ethics*, pp. 38, 42–44 for the first justification; pp. 38, 44–46 for the second justification.

21. See also the passages of Abelard's poetry cited by Morris, *Discovery*, pp. 71–73.

Lady Nature—these are some of the images which twelfth-century authors used to capture the unity and homogeneity of the universe, and their importance as evidence of a new outlook has been justly acknowledged. The world of marvels and miracles that had dominated Western thought since the second century was forced to recede somewhat, at least in intellectual circles, and the way was open for the more scientific inquiries of later in the century.

This movement of thought has traditionally been associated with the activities of the school of Chartres. Some of the claims of this school have been weakened in recent years, as Southern has shown that many of the leading Chartrain masters actually centered their teaching in Paris.[22] But enough sense remains of the distinctiveness of the masters themselves, as Platonists and natural philosophers, to interfere seriously with our understanding of the intellectual developments of the early twelfth century. The idea of nature was not confined to a handful of specialists weaned on certain books and instructed by particular masters. It was a commonplace of the times, the product of the same kinds of critical reasoning that were transforming other areas of thought.

Abelard is well suited to illustrate this point because, as a dialectician and theologian, he is often contrasted with the leading Chartrain thinkers. And here too, Abelard's ideas are clearly distinct from those of the early Middle Ages. For him, ritual of whatever kind holds no magical powers; indeed he ruthlessly pilloried Bernard of Chartres for venturing to suggest that the words of the mass might suffice to change bread to the body of Christ regardless of who said them.[23] Nature, moreover, he conceived of as being both regular and necessary. It was on this basis, for example, that he rejected the claims of astrology: if the stars truly caused events to happen, then the effects would be invariable as death following poisoning or rain following thunder.[24] Even apparent wonders,

22. "Humanism and the School of Chartres," in *Medieval Humanism and Other Essays* (Oxford, 1970), pp. 61–85. Southern was answered by Peter Dronke, "New Approaches to the School of Chartres," *Anuario de estudios medievales* 6 (1969): 117–40; and N. Häring, "Chartres and Paris Revisited," *Essays in Honour of Anton Charles Pegis*, ed. J. Reginald O'Donnell (Toronto, 1974), pp. 268–329. Southern's restatement of his position, which seems to me decisive, is found in "The Schools of Paris and the School of Chartres," *Renaissance and Renewal in the Twelfth Century*, ed. Robert L. Benson and Giles Constable (Cambridge, Mass., 1982), pp. 113–37.

23. *Theologia Christiana* iv.80 (CCCM 12: 302).

24. *Expositio in Hexaemeron*, PL 178: 754. The passage occurs in a discussion of the formation of the stars on the fourth day of Creation. An

such as those worked by demons, Abelard was prepared to argue are not properly speaking miracles but result from the demons' superior knowledge of the forces of nature.[25]

Abelard's interest in natural explanation finds its most explicit expression in his *Expositio in Hexaemeron*, or commentary on the creation.[26] Together with creation allegories inspired by Plato's *Timaeus*, commentaries on Genesis formed a popular genre in the middle of the twelfth century, in large part because they offered an opportunity to explore the extent to which natural forces could account for apparently miraculous events. Today the best known of these commentaries is probably that of Thierry of Chartres, whose opening sentence makes the claim to explain the creation "secundum phisicam et ad litteram"—according to the laws of nature and the letter of the text.[27] This commentary, indeed, is central to the whole conception of the school of Chartres as Platonist and scientific, because it is by similarities to Thierry's treatise that many twelfth-century thinkers have been assigned to the school by historians. In comparison with most of these "Chartrain" works, Abelard's exposition is very traditional in appearance. Begun as a commentary for Heloise and her nuns, it still retains the form appropriate for such a work, proceeding line by line and sometimes phrase by phrase, considering interpretations offered by previous commentators, even appending moral or mystical readings. Yet, read carefully, the *Expositio* reveals an interpretation of the creation that parallels at all key points that of Thierry of Chartres.

The similarities between Abelard's and Thierry's commentaries

---

instructive contrast is available with Augustine, who, at a corresponding point in his commentary, had also addressed this question. For Augustine the issue was an urgent one because attributing power over events to the stars seemed to imply that God (who made the stars) was the source of evil, not man; his refutation consisted of a discussion of the different fates of Isaac and Jacob, twins born at the same time. "De Genesi ad litteram," ii.17 (*CSEL* 28 pt. 1: 59–62). For Abelard, however, the issue is one of causality and epistemology.

25. *Ethics*, pp. 36–39. For general and somewhat contradictory views of Abelard's conception of nature see the essays by Luscombe and Jean Jolivet in *La Filosofia della Natura nel Medioevo* (Milan, 1966).

26. *PL* 178: 731–84. A new edition has now been prepared by Mary F. Romig (unpublished Ph.D. dissertation, University of Southern California, 1979). In preparing an early version of these comments I benefited from Dr. Romig's kind provision of an early version of her edition and also from the comments of Professor John Benton.

27. The text of Thierry's commentary is available in N. Häring, *Commentaries on Boethius by Thierry of Chartres* (Toronto, 1971), pp. 553–75.

go beyond a general interest in natural causation to the readings they give for specific passages. In the first place, both men define heaven and earth created on the first day as a kind of primordial soup of the four elements, and both trace the evolution of matter from that unformed state to the earth as it was known. All this is done, moreover, by reference to the action of natural forces: the tendency of earth to sink, for example, or of air to cool. Perhaps most important, however, both Abelard and Thierry define nature as the forces formed during creation, and Abelard in particular is insistent that the miracles God worked then do not apply to the world as men know it. "If indeed He should act now as He did then, we should assuredly say that these things were being done against nature, just as if the earth should produce plants spontaneously without any seed."[28] The explanation of these resemblances is not far to seek: both Abelard and Thierry were Parisian masters when they wrote their works in the late 1130s. In such a small community, it would be impossible for one man to lecture without his opinions becoming widely known, and, in fact, there are passages where one writer appears to address the views of the other.[29] It is worth insisting upon these resemblances because of the tendency to divide natural philosophy from other philosophical movements of the twelfth century.

The main differences between Abelard's and Thierry's commentaries lie less in the area of attitudes toward nature or even specific readings of Genesis than in the personal styles and orientations of the two scholars. Thierry is much more interested in speculation about the characteristics of matter itself, usually in a rather pre-Socratic way. For example, he devoted several paragraphs to assessing the qualities of the different elements (the "quickness" of fire for example) as a means of understanding the process of creation. Abelard, without being less interested in the creation as a physical event, is much more attuned to the text of Genesis itself and its

28. *PL* 178: 749; the translation is from Richard C. Dales, "A Twelfth Century Concept of the Natural Order," *Viator* 8 (1978): 183. Dales contrasts Abelard and Thierry on this issue, but the differences between them seem to me minor ones, questions of Aristotelian terminology more than basic substance. There is no doubt, however, that Thierry's statements are much more explicit about his purposes.

29. For example, Thierry (sections 22–23) was at some pains to refute the notion that the *spiritus Domini* of Gen. 1:2 was the wind. Abelard, as I show below, took this position, which was not otherwise prominent in the literature; Ambrose explicitly rejected it and Augustine's commentary went in another direction altogether.

possible meanings. The result is a rather discursive commentary, less focused than Thierry's though more complete. For our purposes, however, this discursiveness has the advantage of permitting us to observe the kind of reasoning that sustained the twelfth-century conception of nature.

Both these characteristics can be illustrated by the long gloss on the second verse of Genesis. In Latin the text reads: *Et Spiritus Domini ferebatur super aquas.* ("And the spirit of the Lord was borne over the waters.") Abelard's first order of business was to note that another translation used the verb *fovebat* (warmed) and that the original Hebrew read "flew *(volitabat)* over the face of the waters." Then, recalling that "waters" in this context had to be understood as the fluid mixture of the four elements he had already described as existing on the first day, Abelard disposed of the reading with *ferebatur* rather quickly: it refers, he says, to the ordering power of God working on this shapeless mass. More attention is given to the reading that would have the spirit of the Lord warming the waters, "that is like a bird who sets upon an egg to warm it or bring it to life." The image itself came from St. Basil, but Abelard developed it in a new direction by comparing the mixture of elements in the primeval soup to the components of an egg:

> For an egg not yet vivified or formed may well be compared to that confused heap [during the creation] in which the four elements were comprehended just as they are contained in the egg. . . . In fact the center of the egg, which we call the yolk, is like the earth in the world; the white like water adhering to the earth; the membrane like the air; and the shell like the fire. . . . Therefore just as the bird brooding on the egg and devoting herself to it . . . warms it with her own heat, forms the chicken and brings it to life, so divine goodness . . . is said to be set over that still fluid and unstable mass as over waters, that presently it might bring forth living creatures from it.[30]

Peter Dronke believes that in this passage Abelard is telling a fable, a creation myth,[31] but Abelard is not usually a storyteller and I do not believe him one here. For there is no reason to doubt that Abelard is doing in this passage just what he says he is: show-

30. PL 178: 735–36.
31. *Fabula: Explorations into the Uses of Myth in Medieval Platonism,* Mittellateinische Studien und Text, vol. 9 (Leiden and Köln, 1974), pp. 94–96.

ing how life could arise out of the materials present during the creation.

Abelard's endeavor to interpret Genesis in such terms provides an instructive contrast with early medieval attitudes toward natural processes. For Augustine, as we saw, nature itself was miraculous, so much so that he could in writing to Volusianus sweep away doubts about the creation by arguing that there was an equally great miracle in the power of seeds to produce plants. Every event thus became an expression of God's will in a very direct sense. Abelard, however, not only regarded the identity of God's will and nature as temporary, ending with the work of the creation, but treated natural events as a means of understanding even the undoubted miracles of that time. This reversal of emphasis is typical of the twelfth century, but it is all the more impressive to see it in Abelard who borrowed so much theological terminology from Augustine that it has even been argued that he was Augustinian in his attitude toward nature.[32] But the similarities in language ought not to deceive us. Abelard integrated Augustine's terminology into a logical structure very different from Augustine's own, and by reasoning differently with the concepts caused the concepts themselves to change.

One meaning, then, of Gen. 1:2 concerns the shaping power of God's goodness over the unshaped heap of matter. Abelard was not satisfied with this reading, however, because it left uncertain what physical event the verse refers to, and he went back again to the original Hebrew. *Ruauh*, he notes, which the Vulgate rendered as *spiritus*, could also mean "wind." The literal sense of the text, therefore, was that a wind blew *(volitibat)* across the face of the waters, agitating and mixing with the lighter elements on top. A brief defense of this as a plausible reading leads to the following significant passage: "So anyone could refer this text to the natural order of the elements, as he could say air surrounds water just as water does the earth. . . . This reading too agrees with the natural order of things."[33] Again, this time explicitly, Abelard tried to defend his reading of the creation as consistent with nature.

32. Tullio Gregory, "Considerations sur *ratio* et *natura* chez Abélard," *Pierre Abélard/Pierre le Vénérable: Les courants philosophiques littéraires et artistiques en occident au milieu du XIIe siècle*, Colloques internationaux du Centre National de la Récherche Scientifique, no. 546. (Paris, 1975), pp. 569–84.
33. *PL* 178: 737: "Videtur haec quoque sententia naturali rerum ordini consentire."

It would not be difficult to add other examples, but the main features of Abelard's exposition are already apparent. To begin with, the central principle of his exegesis was that the literal meaning of the text was a history of physical events. This principle justified what would otherwise seem rather questionable readings. In the foregoing passage, for example, it meant taking "waters" as a generic term for liquids instead of actual water, and going back to the Hebrew for an alternative translation to *spiritus*. The desirability of this approach is so obvious to Abelard that he does not even mention or attempt to justify it. Further, once the historical facts have been discovered Abelard preferred, when possible, to explain them in terms of natural causes. He was by no means rigid about this. Twice he denied that there was any need to explain the creation in terms of natural forces because those forces were in fact prepared during the work of the six days.[34] But in practice (including those two passages) he generally did manage to suggest natural causes for the events that Genesis describes.

This last point is worth underscoring because it directs our attention to the cognitive shift that made possible the reconstruction of the concept of nature. In the early Middle Ages it was enough for an event to be associated with relics or ritual or merely to be unusual for it to seen as a miracle. Just as in interpreting texts there was only limited capacity to defend a reading as the best of many possible, in dealing with natural phenomena or human events there was neither the inclination nor the ability to seek alternatives to miraculous explanation. The effect of this kind of reasoning on the concept of nature we have already seen: indeed, it hardly goes too far to say that for practical purposes the line between natural and supernatural dissolved. The *Expositio* is typical of the twelfth century in reversing this process. The act of asking rigorously what explanations were possible was enough to make the realm of natural explanation grow. Natural forces became distinguished from supernatural ones by being those always at work; this, in essence, was Abelard's point in his critique of astrology. It does not greatly matter that some twelfth-century thinkers included in their list of natural forces some—such as animism—considerably at variance with our own. Once the distinction was made it was but a short further step to the concept of nature as the system of all these forces, and that Abelard himself had made this step is quite clear from the *Expositio* as well as his other works.

34. PL 178: 745–46, 749.

I do not mean to exaggerate the importance of the *Expositio*. It by no means constitutes a turning point in scientific thought, as the *Ethics* arguably does in its field, and Abelard was not a scientist. But what the *Expositio* can do is remind us that interest in science was not the product of a school—at Chartres or elsewhere—nor of a distinct body of scientific and Platonic writings. Such an interpretation, however important for emphasizing the significance of natural philosophy in this period, only obscures what we have already seen to be the origins of natural philosophy with Berengar in the eleventh century and prevents our understanding of one of the most important developments of the twelfth. For as with the concern with intention, the idea of nature was not the possession of a few but the common property of all educated people, the product of the same cognitive changes that were transforming conceptions of relationships between people and of human society itself.

AFTER ABELARD

Abelard occupies what is in many ways an ambiguous place in the history of medieval thought. His doctrines and methods all mark a departure from early medieval attitudes: there is no work of his that could be mistaken for one written before 1100. But his works are equally distinct from those of the later twelfth and thirteenth centuries, and indeed, with the exception of the *Sic et Non*, surprisingly few manuscripts of any period survive at all. Only one copy remains of the *Dialectics* and that is incomplete; only five of the *Ethics*. Such figures do not suggest he was widely read for long after his death, and his direct influence on later developments appears to have been slight except for that exercised through his (admittedly numerous) students.[35]

In part this fate is that of the genius whose own work, however revolutionary in its time, is subsumed into the commonplaces of his successors. Yet in part what is reflected is less the elementary character of Abelard's own work than the unformed condition of European education in his time. In Abelard's time, entire disciplines, as well as doctrines, remained in flux, and it is this experimental quality that both gives the academic life of the early twelfth century its special excitement and explains the short life of some of its greatest works. A century later scholars would work with the assurance that their ideas would not quickly be forgotten because the issues they addressed had a fixed place in the school curriculum.

35. On this problem in general, see Luscombe, *School of Peter Abelard*.

If new ideas are to have a sustained impact, this amorphous
situation cannot endure for long, and around and following Abelard we can observe the forces that gave lasting institutional form
to the new trends of thought. The chief of these, perhaps, was
simply the growing numbers of masters and students. When Abelard first tried to establish himself near Paris, in the first decade of
the twelfth century, there were no more than a handful of masters
and the antipathy of one was enough to force him to keep his
distance. By the early 1140s, when he at last retired, there were by
Southern's count at least fifteen.[36] This is already a sizable change
—the number of students presumably had grown accordingly—but
it was just the beginning, and it seems safe to assume that by the
middle of the thirteenth century the academic community at Paris
alone numbered in the thousands. Such numbers inevitably entailed
a standardization of the curriculum because students had to be able
to move with ease from one master to another, and this meant also
a concentration of the energies of the masters on certain issues to
the exclusion of others. The results were not always exciting; academic debate rarely is. Yet over the long run the routine of the
medieval university proved a healthy environment for the survival
of higher learning, for though the flashes of insight may have been
rare, so, too, were the losses and periods of indifference that had
been the consequence of the absence of formal institutions in the
ancient world. This later history lies beyond my present concerns,
but before leaving the subject, it is appropriate to point out several
features of the medieval curriculum on which the imprint of the
interests and outlook of the new mentality was especially deep.

One was the systematic effort to reconcile conflicting traditions.
Abelard had noted the lack of agreement among authorities, but
for him as for others of his generation these areas of uncertainty
were places where they could develop their own ideas. He made no
effort to resolve them either in the *Sic et Non* or elsewhere. Respect
for tradition was too great in the twelfth century to permit this
situation to endure indefinitely, however, and by the middle decades of the century there came to be made collections of sources
that were actually intended for study. Gratian's *Decretum* from
around 1139 was one of these; the *Sentences* of Peter Lombard
from the early 1150s was another. Neither the compilers nor the
scholars who took these works as their texts expected the answers
given there to be definitive. They worked more in the manner pio-
neered by the Lombard lawyers of a century before, seeking out

36. "Schools of Paris," pp. 129–33.

the intention of the author and trying to resolve apparent contradictions. What resulted was often more original, perhaps, than
the scholars themselves knew, intellectual constructs vastly surpass-
ing their sources in subtlety. But the method itself tied scholars
more firmly to tradition and—especially in matters concerning the
Church—discouraged any effort to think matters through from
first principles.

A second area where cognition permanently altered the work
habits of the schools was in the proliferation of what Richard and
Mary Rouse have called "finding devices."[37] The *Decretum* and the
Sentences were themselves finding devices of sorts because, as Peter
Lombard claimed, they cut short the work of research by offering
what is sought "without effort" (*sine labore*). Other finding devices
developed in the twelfth century included many still in use today:
cross-referencing glosses (though ours are in footnotes instead of
the margins); simplified page layout including running headlines,
chapter titles in different lettering, paragraphing, and punctuation
to mark off quotations; indexes; and, ultimately, alphabetized reference books. One source of the impulse for the creation of these
tools was provided by the needs of teachers and preachers for quick
access to information. Another came from the increasing suspicion
of excerpts taken out of context, which meant that except for collections like the *Decretum* that had their own authority scholars
relied increasingly on integral texts. But what is important for us is
that such tools reveal an attitude toward authorities that supposes
that texts are to be arranged and intellectually manipulated for
various purposes instead of quoted with reverence as the final word
on a subject.

At the same time as these attitudes were leading some scholars to
transform the study of familiar texts, other scholars were enriching
the scholarly resources of Latin-speaking Europe with translations
of works from Greek and Arabic. Historians have tended to regard
these works as important chiefly for their influence on later medieval thought, and there is no doubt that this was considerable. The
thirteenth-century university would have been very different without works such as Aristotle's *Physics* or Ptolemy's *Almagest*.[38] Yet

37. For what follows, see the fascinating article by Richard and Mary
Rouse, "*Statim Invenire*: Schools, Preachers, and New Attitudes to the
Page," in *Renaissance and Renewal*, pp. 201–25. To the list of early examples of finding devices one could add the organization of Lombard law
into the *Lombardia* which had been accomplished before 1100.
38. On translations in general, see Marie-Térèse d'Alverny, "Translations
and Translators," *Renaissance and Renewal*, pp. 421–62, and references
given there.

in tracing out the chains of influence, it has been easy to forget that
the relationship of medieval scholars to classical learning was far from a passive one. Instead of being the product of a "renaissance" in the narrow sense of a worship of classical culture, the works translated reflect the new questions that were being asked in the schools. The English scholar Adelard of Bath did not translate Arabic science because he studied in Spain; he went to Spain because he was already interested in science. So, too, the translation of Aristotle's *Politics* came only after jurists had already begun to elaborate theories of government that broke away from Augustine by treating society and government as products of human nature.[39] This point is worth stressing because if medieval speculations had not already reached the point where they could profit from classical theories before the translations were made, it is easy to imagine the translations extinguishing rather than advancing debate.

These textbooks, translations, and finding devices, all intended for the use of subsequent generations of scholars, were the work of a stable academic community—but so had been those of the Carolingian age. The difference lay in the conception of what future scholars would do. For the men of the ninth century, knowledge had been very finite. One learned how to read Boethius or scripture just as one learned grammar and geography and for the same reason: because these were fixed for all time and beyond doubt. Thus, the works of Remi of Auxerre or Hraban Maur did not so much open up new areas of inquiry as close old ones. In contrast, the creators of the learning aids of the twelfth century provided not answers but tools potentially adaptable to many different purposes. They treated texts and information not as ends in themselves but as material to be used, rearranged, and manipulated. In short, they assumed the existence of an ongoing process of inquiry, and by making this assumption and passing it on to subsequent generations they helped to make that process a reality.

39. Gaines Post, "The Naturalness of the State and Society," in *Studies in Medieval Legal Thought* (Princeton, 1964); Brian Tierney, "*Natura id est Deus*: A Case of Juristic Pantheism?," *Journal of the History of Ideas* 24 (1963): 307–22. For a later episode of a scholar's interests leading him to undertake translations, see Alexander Murray, "Confessions as a historical source in the thirteenth century," in *The Writing of History in the Middle Ages: Essays presented to Richard William Southern*, eds. R. H. C. Davis and J. M. Wallace-Hadrill (New York, 1981); Murray shows that Robert Grosseteste made his translation of Aristotle's *Ethics* not during his years as a university scholar but when, as bishop of Lincoln, he found himself, through his pastoral responsibilities, immersed in the moral problems of everyday life.

It might be imagined (though it would be wrong to do so) that educational institutions are more susceptible than others to the influence of ideas. But other social institutions were equally transformed in the twelfth century, and through them the lives of ordinary men and women were permanently altered. My subject here is limited to the effect of the new cognitive structures on institutions of religion and law. As with the previous section it will be necessary to summarize much that could bear more detailed discussion. Also as before, however, it will be possible to observe the changes being worked on institutions not by abstract forces but by individuals endeavoring to make sense out of their traditions and society.

RELIGIOUS ORDERS

To appreciate the achievements of the twelfth century in religious organization, it is necessary first to recall what was said about early medieval monastic life. To begin with, we discussed the value placed on behavior as the measure of a monastic existence. One consequence of this emphasis was the recruitment of children too young to make an informed profession; another was the elaboration of monastic routines so time consuming that they virtually ruled out any opportunity for meditation or serious study. What both these tendencies derived from was an essential indifference to the presence of an inner spirituality. Next we looked at the attention given to the relationship between monk and abbot. Always important, by the time the Benedictine Rule was written, this hierarchical relationship had grown to the point of excluding any attention to peer relationships as part of a Christian existence. In both theory and practice, obedience replaced charity as the justification for communal existence. Finally, in following the history of monasticism through the Carolingian period, we saw how the Rule itself was treated as an inspired document above question or interpretation. The monastic ideal was taken to be conformity to the letter of the Rule, and reform could therefore mean only a return to the Rule and strict obedience to its least prescription.

Although by the last quarter of the eleventh century an enormous number of houses had grown up based on these principles, the next century and a half saw important changes in the direction and expression of religious impulses. One product of this movement was an enormous body of literature concerned with inner spiritu-

ality—a result of the reconceptualization of the relationship be-
tween monk and God to one of mutual respect. This literature, really another manifestation of the importance of intention, has found excellent historians,[40] and my focus instead is on what might be called the constitutional aspects of the reforms: the restructuring of these existing houses and the creation of new ones to express a radically different ideal.

Two distinct processes were involved. First, there was a remarkable amount of legislation at every level: the individual house, the order, the Church as a whole. For centuries people had sought to accommodate their desires to the Benedictine Rule, supplementing its precepts with rules drawn from other sources or pruning away accretions of time to return to the "true" Rule. Now, in the period we are discussing, one finds people not only legislating but doing so with the conscious intention of creating something new, and in the process displaying an attitude that regarded monastic institutions as founded in human custom. The most obvious manifestation of this spirit was the proliferation of new orders that broke with traditional Benedictine practices: the regular canons first (though these claimed as their rule a letter of St. Augustine), followed by the Cistercians, the Premonstratensians, and the Carthusians among others. No less important were the changes in traditional Benedictine houses. This willingness to innovate, to invent deliberately institutions that were meant to be different from those provided by tradition, is an expression of the new mentality no less than the meditations of Ailred of Rievaulx or the sermons of St. Bernard.

Less dramatic but equally a product of the change in mental outlook was the evolution of monastic routine which modified the character of religious communities throughout Europe. One such trend was the turn away from infant oblation, which was virtually eliminated as a means of monastic recruitment. Another was the rise in the importance of the chapter of monks as a collegial body, distinct from the abbot and often opposed to him. The fact that these were innovations may not have been fully grasped by all the people involved. But that does not mean the development did not reflect their conscious wishes, and, in fact, the changes were not always accomplished without conflict. Both trends, for example,

40. For an introduction to twelfth-century monastic spiritual literature see J. Leclercq, *The Monks and Love* (Oxford, 1979); Caroline Bynum, *Jesus as Mother* (Berkeley and Los Angeles, 1982), and the references there. Many of the basic sources have been translated in the Cistercian Fathers Series (Kalamazoo, Mich.).

may be glimpsed in a suit conducted by the community of St. Augustine's of Canterbury against its superior. Having complained that he was introducing into the monastery infants recently at nurse, the monks obtained a papal injunction against receiving boys under fifteen years of age.[41]

These two processes, the legislative and evolutionary, were not opposed but complementary. Many of the reforms put into practice by individual monasteries were later enacted into law; both the ban on oblation and the rights of the chapter were the subject of legislation at the Fourth Lateran Council. So, too, many reformers consciously intent on increasing opportunities for private devotion, for example, or on withdrawal from the world found it natural to reduce the hierarchy and ritual of the monastery as a means of accomplishing these ends. Whatever the specific means, however, the motivating impulse was the desire to live up to a new conception of religious life and a new attitude toward the role of the community in furthering the spiritual perfection of its members. In what follows I shall trace the transforming power of the new mentality in three milieus: the new orders, the reformed Benedictinism of Citeaux, and traditional Benedictine houses.

Grandmont

An example of a new order is provided by the little community of Grandmont in the Limousin.[42] Founded by the disciples of St. Stephen of Muret (d. 1124), Grandmont was dedicated to a life of absolute poverty. The brothers lived in cells, traveled rarely, kept no animals for work or food, possessed no fixed revenues, and participated in no lawsuits. Such austerity was extreme even in an age that placed a high value on rejection of worldly goods, so it is not surprising that the order was never large. But it did win an important patron in Henry II of England, who asked to be buried at Grandmont,[43] and by the end of his reign communities were scattered across his domains.

41. On both these trends see David Knowles, *The Monastic Order in England*, 2d ed. (Cambridge, 1963), pp. 411–22. The case involving St. Augustine's is discussed on p. 421. For the trend against oblation, see also Pierre Riché, "L'enfant dans la société monastique au xiie siècle," *Pierre Abélard/Pierre le Vénérable*, pp. 689–701.

42. The basic sources are all collected in *Scriptores Ordinis Grandmontensis*, ed. J. Becquet (CCCM vol. 8) (Turnhout, 1968). For Stephen Muret see the entry by Becquet in the *Dictionnaire de Spiritualité*, ed. Marcel Viller (Paris, 1932–81); and Lester K. Little, *Religious Poverty and the Profit Economy* (Ithaca, 1978), pp. 79–83.

43. W. L. Warren, *Henry II* (Los Angeles and Berkeley, 1973), p. 212.

What we know of Grandmont depends largely on a small collection of documents, all dating from the middle decades of the
twelfth century. They form a diverse miscellany: a life of St. Stephen, a collection of his sayings, a rule. Probably they were intended to support the attempts to win canonization for the founder
and papal approval for the order, both of which efforts were
brought to a successful conclusion in 1189. There is no reason to
doubt that they represent with substantial accuracy the teachings
of Stephen himself, but that question is not greatly important here.
It would be enough that they contained the views of the midcentury
brothers who led the order to its brief period of importance.

For the reader who comes to the rule after immersion in Benedictine monasticism, the most striking thing must be its sparseness of
detail. Apart from the itemized accounting of the properties monks
are not to own, the rule leaves most matters relatively undefined.
Liturgy is disposed of in a few sentences, food and clothing even
more quickly. This attitude, seen equally in the Augustinian canons
or the Carthusians, marks a turn away from the love of regulation
for its own sake typical of earlier rules and customaries. The willingness to trust to good sense had triumphed over the desire to
minimize the area where decisions had to be made by the monks or
abbots themselves.

The brevity of the rule does not however prevent us from seeing
that the community at Grandmont was thought of in terms very
different from that of a traditional Benedictine house. To begin
with, the leader's obligations as a disciplinarian were very slight,
and in recognition of this fact he was called not an abbot (a term
expressly forbidden) but pastor or prior.[44] The intention was
clearly to avoid the hierarchy of the traditional monastery, and this
is confirmed by the oath sworn by the brothers to obey each other
as well as the pastor "without murmur or hesitation."[45] This unmistakable echo of the Benedictine Rule is thus turned by the context into a rebuke of traditional monasticism.

For all the rigors of its rule, Grandmont permitted—indeed encouraged—conversation at certain hours. The collection of St. Stephen's teachings, among other sources, permits us to form an impression of what was discussed. In a twelfth-century work, it can

---

Henry also used Grandmont as a site to meet count Raymond of Toulouse
(ibid., p. 105), and Stubbs's outline itinerary lists four other occasions
when Henry was at Grandmont. *RS* 44.2.
44. *Regula*, c. 61 (CCCM 8: 97).
45. *Regula*, c. 1 (CCCM 8: 67).

come as no surprise to find that many of the lessons were concerned with the distinction between action and intention. Development of a rich interior life was obviously one of the chief purposes of Grandmont, and indeed Stephen can say, in words that Abelard could have approved, that works are good or bad only according to intention.[46] More unusual is the important teaching reported by Walter Map as a claim that Stephen "wrote his rule out of the gospels."[47] Map was not always an accurate reporter, and he was not one here, for what the Grandmontines held was that the value of any rule, not just theirs, came from the Bible. Stephen believed that there was no real need for a rule at all, and though his disciples later compiled one out of his example, they did not otherwise draw back on this point. Late in the century one finds Gerard Ithier, the seventh prior, arguing that all Christians could be regarded as monks: "In the rule of God . . . one can be saved with wife or without, which is impossible in the rule of St. Benedict; it is certainly of great perfection, but there is another of greater perfection, that is the rule of Saint Basil."[48] This praise of the rule of Basil is easily understood, for we have seen how the orientation to peer relationships brought the Grandmontines to a conception of monastic community not greatly different from Basil or Cassian. But the willingness of these severe ascetics to regard married people also as monks strikes an unusual note of toleration fully in keeping with the gentle modesty that was Grandmont's special contribution to the twelfth century.

Citeaux

Less austere than Grandmont, and vastly more successful, was the order of Citeaux, which as a follower of the Benedictine Rule lay midway between the radical foundations and traditional monasticism. Citeaux's history is a microcosm of the transformations affecting monasticism in the twelfth century. Its stated purpose, to return to the Rule of St. Benedict, reminds us of the ambition that had guided monastic reformers from the time of Charlemagne, and in its early days Citeaux differed from these earlier efforts chiefly in the rigor with which it pursued these objectives: nearly all accre-

46. "Universa opera quae fiunt, bona vel mala sunt propter intentionem." *Liber de Doctrina,* c. 55 (CCCM 8: 30).
47. "Regulas suas ex Evangelis scripsit." *De Nugis Curialium,* ed. M. R. Jones, *Anecdota Oxonensis* (Oxford, 1914), 14: 54.
48. Prologue to *Liber de Doctrina* (CCCM 8: 5–6).

tions to the Rule were discarded, physical work was insisted upon, and the monastery itself was removed from human settlements whose proximity might interfere with the objective of flight from the world. Within a few decades, however, this original intention was transformed from within, so that by the twenties and thirties of the twelfth century ascetic withdrawal was complemented by an intense fellowship and equality within the communities that fostered the leading monastic spiritual writers of the time.

For the most part this evolution is hidden from us, hidden so well, in fact, that the temptation has always been to interpret early Citeaux in light of what the order eventually became. The chief place where the changes can be observed, and there but dimly, is in the *Carta Caritatis*, the document setting forth the constitution of the whole order.[49] For a long time the *Carta Caritatis* was thought to be the work of Stephen Harding, third abbot of Citeaux, who presented it for confirmation to Pope Calixtus II in 1119, but the picture that has emerged since World War II is much more complicated than that. It now appears that the *Carta Caritatis* underwent a long development before reaching its mature form in the 1150s or 1160s, and in that development it is possible to trace the shift of the early Cistercians from one conception of their order to another.

The aim of the *Carta Caritatis* was again one which earlier reformers would have understood: to insure perfect obedience of every house to the rules of the order. Cluny had tried to achieve the same end by extending the hierarchical conception of the Rule itself: the abbot of Cluny was personally to have supreme authority over every subordinate community, each monk—at least as an ideal —was to come to Cluny to make his profession, and often a small annual tribute would be paid to the mother house. These devices did secure to the abbot of Cluny the power to impose his will everywhere, but it was a power that there was no practical means of putting into effect. The abbot could not be everywhere and know everything, yet by holding all power in his own hands he encouraged his subordinates to wait for him instead of making decisions on their own. The failure was not of men—the abbots of Cluny in these years were nearly all extraordinarily capable men—

49. The basic documents of the Cistercian order are printed in Ph. Guignard, ed., *Monuments primitifs de la Règle cistercienne* (Dijon, 1878); and J. M. Canivez, ed., *Statuta Ordinis Cisterciensis* (Louvain, 1933). For what follows on the *Carta Caritatis*, see D. Knowles, *Great Historical Enterprises* (London, 1963), pp. 187–222, who also gives an extensive bibliography of previous works on this subject.

but of conception, the same failure that had doomed the Carolingian empire to an early demise.[50]

To all appearances the early structure of the Cistercians was not greatly different from this. Citeaux from the beginning of expansion in 1114 foreswore any exactions or tribute from daughter monasteries, but Stephen Harding kept the right to oversee discipline (thus excluding the local bishop) and perhaps even to nominate abbots. This organization was certainly susceptible of extension. It would not have been difficult, for example, to have assigned visitation of each daughter house to the abbot of the mother house, and by lightening the load on any one person even this would have been an improvement on Cluny. What the Cistercians chose to do instead, however, was to move away from vertical relationships toward reliance on peer relations among the body of abbots. First, probably by 1118, there was the institution of the general chapter at which apparently abbots could accuse one another of lapses as well as receive correction from Stephen.[51] Then, after Stephen's death, provision was made for visitation of Citeaux itself by three and later by four abbots of its first daughter houses. Finally, responsibility for visitation of Citeaux is given to the general chapter, meeting annually and attended—at least in principle—by all abbots. This general trend, moreover, was accompanied by the publication of instructions limiting the power of the visiting abbot to interfere with routine (except where questions of discipline were involved) to cases in which he had the consent of the abbot and (the addition is significant) the monks of the daughter house.[52] The strength of this constitution was not, therefore, so much that it created "a single strong chain of authority from top to bottom."[53] That Cluny had done. Rather, it was that by making

50. For Cluny, see N. Hunt, *Cluny under St. Hugh, 1049–1109* (London, 1967). It is interesting to note that Cluny itself in the course of the twelfth century developed a system of general chapters that limited the power of the abbot of Cluny (cf. Knowles, *Monastic Order*, pp. 145–48), but this history has not been well studied. Guy de Valous, *Le Monachisme clunien des origines au xve siècle*, 2d ed. (Paris, 1970), is too general to be of help.

51. J. Lefebvre, a pioneer student of the development of the *Carta Caritatis*, argued that at this point there occurred a shift from a *unilateral* relationship to one that already showed "un aspect contractuel." Lefebvre, "Le veritable carta caritatis primitive et son evolution (1114–1119)." *Collectanea Ordinis Cisterciensium Reformatum.* 16 (1954): 5–29.

52. Compare the version printed by Guignard (p. 80) with the earlier version given in P. Tiburtius Hämpfner, *Exordium Cistercii cum Summa Cartae Caritatis* (Vac, 1932).

53. Southern, *Western Society and the Church in the Middle Ages* (Baltimore, 1970), p. 255.

authority come from the group and giving to all abbots the responsibility and experience of sharing in it, the Cistercians were able
to instill not just the rules themselves, but the spirit of the organization.

Something like this history must also have taken place at the
level of the individual monastery. In its early years Citeaux seems to
have been given over to austerity and physical work; certainly this,
together with literal adherence to the Rule, is the point on which all
early accounts agree. At some point, however, and one would wish
to know whether it was with Stephen Harding's abbacy or the
arrival of Bernard, the focus of many Cistercian houses shifted
from the work of the Rule to the interplay of souls in the monastery—from, one might say, obedience to charity.[54] The most significant legislation that attests to the change is the ban, sometime
before 1115, on reception of child oblates. This means of recruitment had been part of Benedictine monasticism from the very beginning; for the Cistercians (with their strong devotion to the Rule)
to do away with it argues that many of them had come consciously
to think of a monastery as a union of wills. And this impression
is confirmed by the flood of Cistercian literature, which became
abundant in the 1130s and 1140s, that portrayed the monastery as
the scene of intense friendships based on equality, affection, and
trust. In describing the monastery as a place where charitable impulses could be expressed and cultivated,[55] Cistercian writers were
returning to a conception of monasticism explicit in Basil and Cassian. Those texts had never been entirely forgotten. But the Cistercians were better able to incorporate such views into their own
ideas because they were cognitively closer to Basil and Cassian than
had been the monks of the early Middle Ages.

A thorough examination of this evidence, though it abundantly
illustrates the twelfth-century concern with intention, lies beyond
my present purpose.[56] But one letter, preserved with St. Bernard's

54. For an earlier example of the revival of charity as the central monastic
virtue, see Ivo of Chartres, Ep. 259, *PL* 162: 260–62; it is discussed by
G. Morin, "Rainaud l'ermite et Ives de Chartes: un episode de la crise du
cenobitism au XIe–XIIe siècles," *Revue Bénédictine* 40 (1928): 99–115;
and Giovanni Miccoli, *Chiesa Gregoriana* (Florence, 1966), pp. 285–88.
55. Bynum, *Jesus as Mother*, pp. 62–66. For a portrait of an early Cistercian community, see Ailred of Rievaulx's *Speculum Caritatis* (CCCM, vol.
1). For an interesting comment on the status of the abbot in the early
Cistercian monastery, see the passage quoted in the next paragraph, and
Bynum, *Jesus as Mother*, pp. 154–59, where she treats Cistercian ambiva-
lence toward the authority of the abbot.
56. In chapter 3 of *Jesus as Mother*, Bynum raises the issue of whether one

correspondence, does deserve quotation as indicative of the direction of future changes and the forces that would bring them about.
The letter was written in the name of the community of Clairvaux;
its subject is the decision by the abbot of Morimond to go on
pilgrimage to Jerusalem. There are two points of interest here
alone: that the community was acting as a community, and that it
was acting in a matter not of immediate concern to its members.
The real importance of the letter, however, lies in the way this
intervention is justified:

> If you should give assent to this project [the community wrote
> to the pope] consider how much it would be an occasion for
> the destruction of our order, for by this example any abbot
> who shall feel himself burdened by his pastoral charge will
> throw it off, since he will think that he may do so lawfully, es-
> pecially among us where there is little honor and much work.
> Furthermore, in order to complete the destruction of the
> house committed to his charge, he has taken with him the
> best and most exemplary of the brethren who were under
> him. He will declare perhaps, as we have heard, that he
> wishes to spread the observances of our order in that country,
> and that it is with that intention he has taken with him a mul-
> titude of brothers. But our order will receive the greatest det-
> riment from this action of his: since it will be made easy for
> any religious who feels like wandering over the world to un-
> dertake a pilgrimage to some country where he can claim
> there are examples to be observed.[57]

What is striking about this passage is that the community based its
appeal upon the good of the whole Cistercian order, although an

---

can describe the twelfth century as discovering the individual (as Colin
Morris does in *Discovery*) when it also discovered the group. Because
awareness of both individuality and group are cognitively related, I would
argue that both phenomena have a common origin in the cognitive shifts
that are the subjects of this and the previous chapter. The attitudes are
not opposed but intrinsically related. The whole question of whether the
twelfth century was as "individual" as the Renaissance is rather badly
posed, since the Renaissance itself was no simple phenomenon.

57. Ep. 359 (A.D. 1143), *S. Bernardi Opera*, ed. J. Leclercq and H. Rochais
(Rome, 1977) 8: 304–5. I have abbreviated the passage slightly in making
the translation. It may be observed that this argument belongs to Kohlberg's stage 4 (see appendix). The reasoning in nearly all of St. Bernard's
own letters, in contrast, belongs to stage 3, that is, they focus on interpersonal relationships instead of institutions.

equally good case could have been argued on the basis of the Rule
or the abbot's obligations to his monks. There is no mystery as to where this conception should have come from; participation in community decisions would normally produce it once a people perceived their society in terms of collective abstractions. Yet the argument strikes a note unheard since before Augustine, and it is a note that merits our attention because it was sounded increasingly loudly—and with reference to many kinds of institutions—as the twelfth century went on. Its effects in general, moreover, were those that can be observed in this letter: stronger institutions, premised now on the active loyalty of their members, and decreased latitude for individuals to depart from the expectations of their fellows for either good reasons or bad.

The Black Monks

As new institutions, the orders we have been considering had considerable freedom to devise structures that reflected their ideas about moral worth and social organization. Existing Benedictine houses had no such latitude, yet their history is, for that very reason, particularly instructive about the role of mentality as a force for institutional change. The actual process of introducing reforms, as well as their content, varied greatly depending on the situation of the monastery involved and the source of the impulse for change. Two illustrations must suffice to suggest the range of possibilities.

At Cluny the impulse for change came from its own abbot, Peter the Venerable (1122–56). In his first years a defender of Cluny's customs against the criticism they were drawing from the members of the new orders, by the 1130s Peter was a reformer himself, lecturing the superiors of his order on matters of discipline and enacting a series of statutes to apply to all Cluniac houses. Some of this legislation was aimed at abuses that had crept into Cluniac usages. But many targets of Peter's reforms were customs that were part of a monastic routine that not too long before had been widely admired and imitated.[58]

One of these was a curious custom that had grown up around the siesta on fast days during the summer. The Rule had provided for the siesta to be taken while fasting, before the main meal of the day, but in subsequent centuries sleeping on an empty stomach had come to be thought of as unhealthy. At Cluny, the solution was to

58. The text of the statutes are printed in G. Charvin, *Statuts, Chapitres généraux et visites de l'order de Cluny* (Paris, 1965), 1: 20–40. They are discussed by several essays in both *Pierre Abélard/Pierre le Vénérable*, and *Studia Anselmiana* 40 (1956).

have the monks go to the dormitory and pull up the covers as if to nap, but then, before actual sleep, to ring bells to rouse them. We are told that upon this signal the monks rose and went through all the motions of waking up: washing their hands, combing their hair. This ritual obviously had its origin in a time when the objective of monasticism was held to be adhering literally to the Rule in all its particulars. But to the twelfth century it could only seem, as Peter observed, "a laughable superstition" *(ridenda superstitio)*. He abolished it in favor of using the time for reading or private prayer.[59]

This custom was doubtless one of those Peter had in mind as *contra rationem*, against reason. Elsewhere he is obviously replying to the criticisms directed against Cluniac customs. Luxury in food was reduced, as was luxury in clothing. One of the two daily periods of conversation was abolished. A certain amount of manual work was imposed. Reception of boys below the age of 20 was abolished.[60] None of this would have satisfied a true ascetic, and Cluny did not aspire to become another Grande Chartreuse or Citeaux. But by the standards of the time they were a step in the right direction.

More complicated changes involved the liturgy, which had always been Cluny's special trademark and burden: 27 of the 76 statutes introduce reforms in this area. Some cuts are made in the liturgy to reduce tedium, while other alterations were clearly intended to increase the intellectual meaningfulness of the liturgy. Answering the criticisms of Citeaux that the monks raced unthinkingly through the prayers, Peter imposed a pause after each verse. From Abelard's design for the Paraclete, he took the idea of matching the prayer to circumstances, not having a verse about the sun at night, for example.[61] Such eclecticism is typical of his reforms, inspired as they were less by an original sense of what religious life ought to be than a desire to drag Cluny into the twelfth century.

59. Charvin, *Statuts*, c. 26. See also c. 28, where Peter condemns the *superstitio* of sprinkling water on one's shoes with the tip of the fingers to take the place of the shoe washing, required by the Rule but unnecessary for monks who spent years without leaving the cloister.
60. It is worth quoting the reason Peter gives for this: "Causa instituti huius fuit, immatura nimisque celer infantium susceptio, qui antequam aliquid rationabilis intelligentie habere possit, sacre religionis vestibus induebenter, et admixti aliis pueriis ineptiis omnes perturbatbant." Ibid., c. 36.
61. On this see J. Szövérffy, " 'False' Use of 'Unfitting' Hymns: Some Ideas Shared by Peter the Venerable, Peter Abelard and Heloise," *Revue Bénédictine* 89 (1979): 187–99.

At Cluny reform came from the top. Peter the Venerable tried to mitigate the appearance of arbitrariness by consulting with senior monks and obtaining the assent of the general chapter, but this does not alter the fact that it was he who conceived the statutes and his authority that put them into effect. At Bury St. Edmunds later in the century it was the monks themselves who took steps to alter the practices of their monastery.[62] The situation that provoked them to action arose during the reign of Abbot Hugh. As far as the discipline of the cloister went, Hugh's government was apparently adequate enough, but he was an imprudent manager and—what may have been worse—a poor judge of men. Each obedientiary, the monks in charge of certain areas of monastic administration, had his own seal, and many of Hugh's appointees used the freedom this gave them to contract debts that eventually would fall on the whole monastery to pay. The abbot himself, moreover, far from being concerned about the mounting obligations, punished those who complained and bent all his efforts to securing papal privileges that would enable him to evade oversight from ecclesiastical superiors who might be able to intervene. By the time Hugh finally died, in fall 1180, things had reached the point that there was no money left to bury him properly: only the chance of a tenant's rent falling due made it possible to provide any honors at all.

Relief did not come immediately, for on the death of Abbot Hugh the monastery fell into the king's hands, and he kept control for fifteen months. When, however, the time finally came to elect a new abbot, the monks concerted their forces to assert their own wishes. One way they did this was to prepare a list of acceptable candidates (all already monks at Bury) to be presented to the king by their delegation. Another was to swear the delegation not to accept an outsider without consulting the entire chapter. But the most important solution was to swear all likely candidates to a code of behavior should they eventually become abbot: they were to treat the convent reasonably, not change obedientiaries without the consent of the convent, and not admit a monk without the agreement of the monks. Given the magnitude of the problems Bury faced, the list is rather short, and it certainly aims at none of the spiritual objectives that had been important to Peter the Venerable. Yet it shows us the chapter in action, asserting its corporate existence and its right to control certain affairs of the monastery.

We are informed about this episode because it was recorded by Jocelin of Brakelond, a monk of Bury whose chronicle provides a

62. For what follows, see *Cronica Jocelini de Brakelonde*, ed. and trans. H. E. Butler (London, 1949).

uniquely intimate picture of domestic monastic life. But similar incidents—monks combining with their fellows to protect their common interests—must have been common by the later twelfth century, with lawsuits probably the more usual outcome. Much could be said about the effects of such aspirations on monastic life, but for the historian of mentalities their chief significance, as David Knowles remarked of Jocelin himself,[63] is in their very ordinariness. They show us men of very modest intellectual gifts putting into action ideas about the relation of authority and community that would have been virtually inconceivable only a hundred years before.

LAW AND GOVERNMENT

What we have seen in twelfth-century monasticism is the effect on religious institutions of new conceptions of social organization and moral worth. The consequences for government were slower to appear, in part because of the difference between clerical and lay culture, in part also because government never has the option of including only persons whose ideas correspond to those of the whole community. A wide consensus is necessary before there can emerge new patterns of politics, administration, or law, so in most parts of Europe these did not assume solid form until the thirteenth century. The chief exception was England. A consideration of the reasons for this precocity would take us far beyond our present concerns, though some credit must be given to the heavy hand of the Norman kings who imposed a peace in which new kinds of relationships could develop, and some to the particular genius of Henry II, a figure as protean, controversial, and original in government as Abelard was in scholarship. But precisely because English institutions developed so early, before the spread of Roman law provided models for ready imitation, they offer particularly good evidence of the way new kinds of reasoning led people to a conception of government different from that which prevailed in the early Middle Ages.

Political Styles
Patterns of interaction between rulers and their subjects, particularly those whose cooperation is essential for the proper functioning of government, can tell us much about the conceptions of the leading political actors about the nature of their society and their

63. *Monastic Order*, p. 508.

responsibilities in it. In our period, the direction of change can be
illustrated by comparing the methods of Henry II with those of his great-grandfather William I. William the Conqueror was a king very much in the mold of Charlemagne: he knew his rights and duties, and his effectiveness in pursuing both was chiefly due to a combination of personal tenacity and military ability that intimidated many potential adversaries and defeated the rest. As a young man, while still duke of Normandy, he was willing to besiege the castle of a man who betrayed him for years if necessary; and when at the end of his life his half-brother Odo pursued a policy William disliked, neither Odo's blood nor his ecclesiastical rank could save him from prison. The reputation William won by these methods had its uses. It gave real meaning to the cruel code of law he imposed on England, and England was a safer place to live because of it. Yet it afforded little scope for his subordinates except to obey his will, and even the Domesday survey, his greatest administrative achievement, has less in common with the bureaucracies of 100 years later than with Charlemagne's censuses of 300 years before.

For William the Conqueror, government was primarily a matter of loyalty and obedience. The less than seventy years that divided his reign from that of Henry II did not make these concerns less urgent, but the task of assuring them was greatly altered by an important shift in the ties between the king and the great men of his kingdom. Vassalage had begun to be rationalized, and this meant not only that the relationship was more reciprocal than it had been (a process that goes back to Fulbert) but that it was more standardized, an ideal that applied equally to simple knights and great barons.[64] Whether these ties were thereby stronger than those that had existed before may reasonably be doubted; in many cases, they were certainly weaker. But by being based on a shared ideal rather than a relationship between two specific individuals, they were more adaptable to the needs of large-scale organization and less susceptible to the disruptions inherent in the succession of generations.

This evolution made military ability less essential: it was possible for some, like Louis VII of France, to survive and even prosper

64. Henry's relationship to his lord, Louis VII of France, provides an excellent example of the process; see Warren, *Henry II*, p. 224–28; for a general overview of developments, see J. R. Strayer, "The Development of Feudal Institutions," in *Twelfth Century Europe and the Foundations of Modern Society*, ed. Marshall Clagett et al. (Madison, 1965), pp. 76–88. [repr. in *Medieval Statecraft and the Perspectives of History* (Princeton, 1971), ed. William Jordan et al., pp. 77–89].

without it. Yet military ability was too admired in the Middle Ages ever to be totally insignificant, and the secret of Henry's success lay in the fact that he combined the ability of a great captain—though he preferred the lightning unexpected stroke to the Conqueror's nutcracker-like application of superior forces—with more purely political skills, the capacity to dominate a council or debate by the force of his intelligence and personality.

We can observe Henry's technique in the reception he gave to the monks of Bury when their delegation arrived to select a successor to Abbot Hugh. Hoping to be permitted a free election, the delegates had come equipped with a list of three names, all members of the convent of Bury. Henry did not concede them their wish, but what followed was a remarkable give and take that left the monks satisfied without Henry's yielding any authority. First, when they were permitted to present their list, Henry insisted that they add three more names from the convent and then another three from other houses. Then he permitted them to strike three names. They struck off the outsiders, he struck two and so on until only two names were left. When the monks made clear their choice of the two Henry objected that he did not know the man. Yet he accepted him anyway.[65]

This meeting with the monks of St. Edmund's was well within Henry's control at all times, but he could be equally effective surrounded by those actually or potentially hostile. At Montmirail in 1169, for example, he won over (for a brief while) nearly all of Becket's supporters by the reasonableness with which he stated his own position.[66] In 1174, following the defeat of the rising led by Henry's son, he punished the former rebels with neither executions nor forfeitures, contenting himself with leveling their castles. This policy, in many ways the opposite of William the Conqueror's when faced with similar situations, speaks volumes for the change that the century had worked in politics. Fear was no longer the only means of winning obedience. It was now possible to preserve working relationships by overlooking faults without leniency being taken for weakness. In fact when Henry's sons later rebelled again they found themselves virtually without support.[67]

King and Society

Perhaps the earliest official document which reveals a new attitude toward the relationship between king and society is the charter

65. *Cronica Jocelini de Brakelonde*, pp. 21–23.
66. Warren, *Henry II*, pp. 109–10.
67. Warren, *Henry II*, p. 381.

issued by Henry I in 1100 to win support for his coronation in the confused conditions that followed the death of his brother, William II. This is a familiar document to medievalists; indeed, perhaps too familiar, for our awareness of its originality has been blunted by the over-grand claims that have sometimes been made for it. But I have it in front of me as I write, and the edition I am using provides a ready comparison in the actual oath Henry swore, an oath based on old Anglo-Saxon forms. The Anglo-Saxon oath (slightly condensed) reads as follows: "In the name of Christ I promise these three things to the Christian people subjected to me. First that the church of God and all Christian people shall enjoy a true peace; second that I will forbid all rapacities and iniquities to all ranks; third that I shall show equity and mercy in all judgments as the clement and merciful God indulges me and you by his mercy." The idea here is one we are already familiar with, the people under the king as the king himself is under God. But when we pass from the oath to the charter, which, lacking precedents, was an original composition, a different note begins to be heard. There Henry acknowledges his responsibilities to his subjects by the promise to refrain from unjust exactions "out of respect for God and the love which I have toward you all," and also by the references to the common counsel (or consent) of the barons of England that occur four times in all. The detailed provisions of the charter make it plain that the king was thinking more in terms of his relations with his individual vassals than the country as a whole, but this in itself is still new enough in 1100 to be worthy of notice.[68]

Given the circumstances of its issuance, the coronation charter of Henry I cannot be considered a free gift, though at the least it shows that the exactions of Henry's predecessor had stimulated the barons of England to conceive of their relations with the king in terms of mutually agreed upon obligations. Yet by the reign of Henry II the notion that the king was to act only after due consultation with those he governed was beginning to penetrate the daily workings of government. From the chronicle of Battle Abbey comes the story of how, when the abbot of that monastery sought confirmation of the monastery's charters, Henry refused, saying he ought not to act "except by judgment of my court." The abbot may have suspected a trick, and it is easy to imagine his anxiety as he considered his disintegrating originals. But he took the advice of the king's justiciar and asked again when the king was surrounded by his magnates, and he then found Henry willing not only to confirm

68. W. Stubbs, *Select Charters*, 9th ed., rev. by H. W. C. Davis (Oxford, 1913), pp. 116–19.

his charters but to devise a form that would be valid even if the originals disappeared.[69]

Doubtless Henry was not always so punctilious. One finds the same idea expressed in his most important enactments, however, and particularly in those that concerned the administration of law. The assize of Clarendon, for example, is described as

> made by king Henry . . . with the assent of the archbishops, bishops, abbots, earls, and barons of all England.

The assize of the Forest (1184):

> This is the assize of the lord king Henry concerning his forest and game, by the counsel and assent of archbishops, bishops, and barons, earls, and nobles of all England.

Glanvill on the Grand Assize:

> that assize is a great royal benefit, granted to the people by the clemency of the prince with the counsel of his magnates.[70]

Perhaps not all this favorable counsel was willingly given; there were not many men willing to deny Henry II his will to his face. Yet it is nonetheless significant that Henry and his advisors felt the taking of counsel important enough to mention, and within a few more decades it was to be possible for barons to tell a different king that against his advice they preferred not to change the laws of England.

These comparatively modest claims for royal authority say nothing, of course, for actual political power. Henry II could make his will felt in distant parts of his realm more effectively than the Frankish kings with their greater pretensions, and even more than the Roman emperors of the fourth century. But this is only apparently a paradox. Political power dependent on passive obedience is inherently weaker than when a ruler can rely on his or her subjects actively to commit themselves to a cause. It was this active commitment—the sense on the part of subjects that they shared in the social order, that made the kings of the later Middle Ages strong, and which provided the basis for Europe's dominance of the rest of the world after the sixteenth century.

Crime and Punishment

It is not possible to trace in such detail the development of legal doctrines for these appear with what Maitland called "marvellous

69. Warren, *Henry II*, pp. 303–4.
70. Stubbs, *Select Charters*, pp. 170, 186, 190.

suddenness" leaving no clue to their precise origin. At the beginning of the century Germanic law was still intact. Thus the *Leges
Henrici Primi* from the 1110s describes a system still based on
wergild and *wite*, on feuds and oaths and ordeals, and on all the
jurisdictional complexities of the old regime. The reign of Stephen
then imposes a break in the sources: by the time evidence becomes
abundant again, all this elaborate system has disappeared leaving
virtually not a trace. What existed instead was a law recognizably
the ancestor of our own in values as well as procedures, and it
might well be argued that the institutions themselves had their origin in a desire to enforce new standards of right and wrong.

The direction of the change in values may be suggested by the
history of two words. The first is *murdrum*. In Anglo-Saxon law
this had been the term for secret homicide, the ambush of an enemy
out of sight of witnesses, giving him no chance to defend himself. It
still had this meaning in the eleventh century when it became the
name of the fine that William the Conqueror imposed on neighbor-
hoods where were discovered the victims of such attacks. The second word is *felon*, the name for one who betrayed his lord. Both
these words carried enormous emotional impact, a sense of which
can still be gotten from the use of *felon* as an insult in the *chansons
de geste*. The important point, however, is that as values changed in
the twelfth century it was the emotional impact that survived instead of meaning, so that murder came to refer to premeditated
homicide and felony to a whole category of especially grave crimes
which too had the connotation of deliberate malice. This unconscious shift in linguistic usage, with both words changing in meaning from the worst crimes imaginable in the old mentality to the
worst in the new, provides perhaps the most eloquent testimony to
the metamorphosis of popular attitudes that underlay the transformation of English law in the twelfth century.

It was the task of the professional jurist to make this attitude into
law, and this process was proceeding apace by the end of the reign
of Henry II. The most obvious changes occurred in the law of
homicide, where around 1200 there begins the practice of excusing
children and madmen from the penalties of their acts. The idea
here was clearly that mental competence was a prerequisite to
criminal behavior, that one had to be capable of choosing rightly
before one was eligible for penalties for misbehavior.[71] But what is
perhaps most important about these judgments is that to be imple-
mented they required no refined procedures for evaluating inten-

71. See my "Evolution of Medieval Mentalities," *American Historical Review* 83 (1978): 581, 593 and references there.

tion, although these were later to be developed. In the beginning the mere willingness of the courts to consider mental states was enough to create new doctrines of law.

One area, then, where law came to enforce the values of the new mentality was in attention to intention, the *mens rea* of later law. Another was in regarding certain categories of offenses as crimes against the whole community instead of just the victim. In England this idea found its earliest expression in the assizes of Clarendon and Northampton, which established an accusing jury to denounce notorious wrongdoers to the king's justices who then took on the investigation of the accusation themselves. The ancestry of this institution is admittedly complex, including both the king's peace of Germanic law (a conception that, however, in the twelfth century ceased to be tied to an actual king) and the more specifically English device of using sworn panels to answer the queries of the government. Yet the appearance of continuity is shattered if we consider what happened in this period to the institutions that had represented the victim's interest. It is not significant that the feud itself was suppressed; the interests of public order would have required that. But though the suppression of feud by no means requires the end of private accusation or compensation of victims (both were retained by Roman law), these, too, were reduced to insignificance in medieval England: in the case of homicide all compensation to the kin was abolished. Such evolution would have been avoided if the interests of the victim weighed as heavily in the concerns of the judges as the punishment of those who offended against the peace of society.

The conservatism of the law is such that, even though the implications of these new rules were far from being spelled out by the end of our period, they stand as especially strong evidence that the influence of new cognitive structures was spreading beyond the circles of schools and the spiritual elite. Yet they are no less significant for creating structures that were to shape the experience of later generations. A later chief justice would remark that the law cannot try the mind of men.[72] But he was speaking of witchcraft; the *mens rea* was already imbedded in the common law and was routinely dealt with by the courts not just in criminal cases but civil ones as well. Nor was this influence confined to professional jurists. Juries who had to deal with questions of malice; businessmen who had to master the rudiments of contracts; landlords who had

72. Chief Justice Brian in Yearbook 7 Edward IV, f. 2, cited in Pollock and Maitland, *History of English Law*, 2: 475.

to understand the limits of their authority over their villeins: all these had to adapt themselves to the judicial structure whose foundations were laid in the twelfth century. For the law is not just an instrument of coercion. It is also a great teacher of what society does and does not value. From 1200 on the courts of England and of Europe were teaching very different lessons than they had before.

Jurisprudence

It remains to say something of the effects on law of the enhanced capabilities to arrange and intellectually manipulate complicated sets of material. To see what this meant at the theoretical level it is necessary only to read the book known as *Glanvill*.[73] In the first place, the author made a largely successful effort to consider exhaustively all the situations that might develop in actual practice. Considering the writ *praecipe*, for example, we learn not only how the action itself proceeds, but what excuses *(essoins)* are to be accepted for nonappearance of the defendant and what is to happen if the defendant neither appears nor sends an *essoiner*; concerning the grand assize, what conditions stand as an obstacle to its invocation; and for each of the petty assizes what pleas can be made in bar of the assize as well as how the recognition is to be taken. To write such a book it is necessary not only to have great practical experience but also the ability to consider what situations might arise even though in actual experience they had not—to imagine, as Piaget would have it, a universe of possibilities. What is just as important, *Glanvill* tries to make explicit where the law is in doubt, where certainty is impossible, and different opinions have to be reckoned with. Far from being a weakness, such recognition of uncertainty prepares the way for intelligent legislative or judicial action to resolve the difficulty: it is an essential component of seeing law as formed by human consensus and subject to the principles of jurisprudence.

The skillful analysis of existing law does not exhaust the twelfth-century role of this analytical ability, for it was equally important in devising the procedures that turned haphazard activity at the king's command into institutions capable of attending to common problems with a minimum of executive intervention. At first sight this may seem to be more a product of literacy narrowly defined than cognition. Writing certainly made it possible to send instruc-

73. Ed. and trans. G. D. H. Hall (London, 1965).

tions over great distances, and when added to the habit of record-keeping, permitted both a continuity of administrative memory and persistence of effort that was otherwise impossible. Yet while literacy was essential to twelfth-century government, it must be doubted that the availability of literate men was alone a cause of change. Medieval English government was always thrifty in its use of personnel, and it is not likely that Henry II employed more literate men than had Charlemagne, or than were available to Charlemagne had he wished for them. One could shift the grounds of the argument a bit and contend that what was new was not so much literacy but education of the kind taught in the schools, but even this, though it concedes the impact on government of the revolution in thought, is only part of the story. For while twelfth-century kings undoubtedly disposed of agents more capable than those of the Carolingian era, their lasting achievement lay less in delegating power to able men than in planning structures that even in the hands of those of little learning or judgment could produce useful results.

The process I have in mind can be illustrated by the series of twelfth century writs in the collection made for the Selden Society by Raoul van Caenegem.[74] All of them concern seisin, the peaceful enjoyment of property, and all were intended to put unlawfully ousted tenants back into possession. The earliest, from the reign of Henry I, are more in the manner of royal decrees than anything else: the king ordered the recipient—the disseisor himself or (presumably) the lord of the property—to reseise the disseisee. The beneficiary of these writs apparently had managed to present his case to the king himself, who seems to have then acted without hearing the other side. One assumes that if the party in seisin wished to protest, he had two options, neither of them entirely satisfactory: he could refuse to comply, putting himself technically in contempt, and hope to persuade the king later of the justice of his claim to the property; or he could hand the property over, losing its fruits for a while, and then proceed to the royal court to attempt to obtain a reversal of the judgment.

Writs from the early years of Henry II show an advance in a number of ways. The property is specified with greater precision. The details of the alleged seisin and disseisin are often given. And the writ often goes to a royal official. Of these improvements, the

74. *Royal Writs in England from the Conquest to Magna Carta* (Selden Society, 1959); see also Donald Sutherland, *The Assize of Novel Disseisin* (Oxford, 1973).

first two involve chiefly changes in draftsmanship, though important ones, while the last reflects the growing tendency of the king to
rely on his own agents, who could be supervised more readily by
the central administration. Yet the writs still left much to the good
judgment of the sheriff, who as a local landowner might well have
sympathies or interests in the dispute and who in any case could
not be expected to have the inclination or the training to master the
niceties of law.

Thus far it would be possible to say the royal government has
learned more or less directly from experience. But the last writ in
the series, the writ of *novel disseisin* itself, adds a new element of
conscious calculation, a deliberate reckoning in advance of what
kind of evidence could be had and of the limits to which the discretion of an agent ought to be pushed. It is much more limited than
earlier writs, applicable only to grievances of recent origin and to
cases where the disseisor was still in possession, but much was
gained in compensation for the lack of flexibility.

1) It avoids the ordeal or wager of battle.
2) It permits the bailiff to be summoned in place of the lord,
and neither need be present for the recognition.
3) It shares the work out among three distinct groups: the
sheriff, a sworn panel of neighbors, and a judge dispatched
from the royal court.

Of these changes, the first two are typical of the way the new
mentality was making possible a different approach to the law.
Henry's opposition to the ordeal was exceedingly early, but it is a
feature that occurs so consistently in his legislation that it is impossible to doubt he was pursuing a policy of avoiding these proofs as
untrustworthy. The summons of the bailiff testifies to the emergence of the principle of legal representation. For the old law, only
the litigant himself would do, even though this had meant the mul-
tiplication of essoins that could delay final judgment for long periods. By accepting his knowledge of the proceeding (through the
person of his agent) in place of his physical presence, the assize thus
made possible enormous economies of time and effort. But what
was just as important as these advantages was the division of responsibilities among sheriff, jury, and judge. This arrangement not
only avoided giving one agent too much discretion. It made possible great efficiencies in the use of trained personnel because it permitted judges to hear and settle many cases in little time. In the
thirteenth century, justices commonly settled well over half of the

cases of novel disseisin on the first day of hearing, and some particularly efficient justices reached totals near ninety percent.[75]

It was remembered later that Henry II and his advisers had spent
many sleepless nights devising this writ and we may well believe
that it was so. Yet effort alone does not explain the durable success
of the assize: Charlemagne and William the Conqueror, among
many others, had also been conscientious and hard-working kings,
equally dedicated to bringing justice and peace to their subjects, but
they left behind them no comparable institutions. Nor does the
revival of formal jurisprudence explain everything; *novel disseisin*,
for example, certainly owed much to the *actio spolii* of canon law,
but adaptation to English circumstances required much creative
rethinking. Instead, the important thing was the ability to group a
myriad of concrete circumstances into a few manageable categories, to treat government as a business of routine rather than of
decree. The structure that resulted was not immutable or without
quirks. But it was ceasing to be arbitrary or dependent on the
continuing initiative of the king, and this long-term stability was
perhaps the greatest contribution of the twelfth century to the security of everyday life. It is a mark of the changing values of the times
that in the areas where Henry II retained the power to be arbitrary
it was bitterly complained about.[76]

Nature

In the previous section we were chiefly concerned with expressions
of the new mentality that affected actual institutions, but had we
considered the theoretical literature on society we would have encountered the idea of nature there. The notion of society as natural
was a common theme in the twelfth century, especially in the writings of the jurists for whom it had two main implications: that the
laws of the social world were discoverable through reason; and
that society existed on a plane with its own significance, apart from
the Augustinian imputations of divine reward and punishment.
Tracing out these important ideas is beyond the scope of this book.
But they are worth mentioning because the idea of the world as
natural had the same consequences as the idea of society as natural.
It made phenomena susceptible to study. And it offered an explana-

75. Sutherland, *Novel Disseisin*, pp. 128–29.
76. Warren, *Henry II*, pp. 385–96.

tion of events that freed at least some Europeans of the sense that supernatural justice shaped the events of everyday life.

SCIENCE

The relationship between cognition and science was one of Piaget's abiding interests, and his last book, published posthumously, details the parallels between the history of science and the stages of cognitive development in children.[77] Piaget's purpose was a theoretical one: to illustrate first the interaction between cognition and reality, and then the hierarchical structure of certain ideas. "To the extent that epistemological analysis of scientific thought finds itself obliged to return to those previously constituted ... at the prescientific level, one finds oneself in the presence of structures always more unconscious and always more dependent on their own prior history."[78] Piaget thus rejected Kuhn's position that all scientific theories are logically equivalent.

For historians, the interest of a cognitive approach to science lies not in sketching parallels but seeing how specific scientists conceived the problems of their discipline, what issues forced the invention of new concepts, and how changes in concepts altered the way scientific facts and literature were understood. Medieval science makes a good subject for this kind of study. I have already had occasion to notice the role of nature in the commentaries on Genesis of Abelard and Thierry of Chartres, and, indeed, this is an idea that appears in various kinds of cosmological speculations in the twelfth century. These works, ranging from the *Philosophia Mundi* of William of Conches to the allegorical myths of Bernard Sylvestris, were not themselves scientific; they do not propose either hypotheses susceptible to verification or explanations of specific phenomena. But their central assumption, that the world is governed by regular laws, is one that must underlie any science, and in other hands we do see the resumption of scientific inquiry.

Much of this twelfth-century science was devoted to the tedious but necessary translation of Greek and Arabic science. Much of it, too, went into the steady accumulation of observations on everything from the movement of the stars to the flight of birds. Less obvious than either of these, however, but more important to my theme was the gradual formulation of concepts that future genera-

77. Piaget and Rolando Garcia, *Psychogénese et Histoire des Sciences* (Paris, 1983).
78. Ibid., pp. 290–91.

tions of scientists could use to think about scientific questions. Not theories but the building blocks of theories, these concepts have proved among the most lasting contribution of the Middle Ages to the study of the natural world.

I can illustrate what I mean by the early history of medieval kinematics. The key concept there is velocity, which to the modern scientist is the ratio of the distance covered to the time elapsed. This is a familiar idea to those of us accustomed to reading a speedometer or who learned in school the formula $v = d/t$. But cognitively, velocity is a difficult concept to master. It depends, to begin with, on concepts of distance and time as composed of or measured by equal units—seconds, for example, or meters. In Piaget's terms these are concrete-operational concepts in that they require the individual to impose an intellectual order on experience. Velocity, as a ratio of time and distance, is still further removed from experience since it requires the manipulation of ideas as well as sensory data. It is thus a formal-operational concept, though not even individuals capable of formal-operational reasoning will necessarily arrive at the concept of velocity if it is not provided by the existing culture.[79]

We can get a sense of the difficulties of reasoning about nature by considering how Aristotle dealt with the question of speed in the *Physics*. His first definition, in book six, is barely above the level of intuition. Of two moving bodies, he writes, the faster travels (1) a greater distance in an equal time, (2) an equal distance in a shorter time, and (3) a greater distance in a shorter time.[80] Of these principles, the third follows, as Aristotle notes, from the infinite divisibility of time and space; it is essentially a red herring in that it obscures the question of determining how much faster one object is moving. The other two claims transform either time or distance into a constant. They say no more than could be stated on direct observation of two runners or other moving objects, and Aristotle later shows his inability to move beyond concrete comparisons by refusing to compare curved or circular movement, as around a track, with movement in a straight line. We can understand his difficulty if we imagine one runner on a track and another running cross-country; how are we to compare their speeds by direct observation? We cannot devise a system of timers and distance markers unless we know in advance our modern definition of speed.[81]

79. These ideas are discussed in full in Piaget's books on time, space, and motion.
80. *Physics* vi.2.
81. For the ancient and medieval sources of what follows, I have used

Aristotle was not classical science's last word on motion, but the *Physics* was among the first works on motion to be translated in the twelfth century and it was where medieval scientists began. It is this circumstance that makes the first medieval work on kinematics as significant for its independence of spirit as for its genuine advances in conceptualization. Gerard of Brussels's *Liber de Motu*, written within a few decades of 1200, is chiefly devoted to the subject Aristotle had ruled out of court—comparing motion that follows differently shaped paths. In itself this had the consequence of directing attention to distance instead of path as the crucial component of speed. There had been some Greek works written for the same purpose, though Gerard does not seem to have been familiar with them. Yet this unfamiliarity ought not to be lamented. For thinking freshly on the problem of motion, with only Aristotle's naive ideas to provide guidance, Gerard was able to break away from the habit of all classical authors of comparing distances and he began to treat velocity itself as a quantity that can be compared. He was not yet able to define that quantity as the ratio of distance to time. But even his elementary conception marked a crucial break with the concreteness of classical thinking on the subject, and later scientists in the medieval tradition quickly arrived at the formal definition of velocity we still use today.

Much of medieval science seems to have been work of this kind, the hammering out of concepts by which the phenomena of nature could be thought about. One way to understand its significance is in terms of what Thomas Kuhn has taught us to regard as scientific revolutions.[82] Scientists could not but think of motion differently when they employed more exact concepts to frame their questions, and, as a result, the "Aristotelean" physics of the later Middle Ages was very different from that of Aristotle himself. Yet there is obviously more to the matter than this. For the history I have given can also be seen—and certainly Piaget would have seen it—as a shift from concrete to formal operations at the level not of the individual but of an entire discipline. The effort of imagination required to make this shift is perhaps unimaginable today to those of us who find concepts of speed ready-made and even illustrated by a moving needle in our cars. What resulted was a science whose concepts were more fully manipulable for being less tied to intu-

---

Marshall Clagett, *Mechanics in the Middle Ages* (Madison, 1959), pp. 163–98. A fuller discussion of the same material is found in Clagett's article, *"Liber de Motu* of Gerard of Brussels," *Osiris* 12 (1956): 73–175.
82. *The Structure of Scientific Revolutions* (Chicago, 1962).

itions, and more capable of giving rise to other concepts. Thus in kinematics the definition of velocity enabled a definition of acceleration. Scientists of Galileo's time thus were not only heir to ideas that had not existed before 1100. They also inherited a tradition of inquiry committed to imposing the order of the mind on the variety of nature.

MIRACLES

In the Middle Ages as today, scientific inquiry was the business of but a handful of specialists. But the idea of nature was not confined to those who made science their profession, and in the course of the twelfth century its influence can be seen in the steady decline of willingness to attribute everyday events to supernatural causes. Before exploring this phenomenon, however, it is necessary to say a few words about another concept that makes a dramatic reappearance in the twelfth century.

The classical goddess, Fortune, symbol of the role of chance in human affairs, had attracted little interest in the early Middle Ages. Pierre Courcelle found only one pictoral and three literary representations of Fortune before 1100,[83] and we have seen that despite the prominent place accorded her in the *Consolation of Philosophy*, commentators on that work paid her little attention or misunderstood her meaning as Alfred did in his translation. All this changed in the twelfth century. Not only do artists rediscover Fortune and her wheel, which would become a popular motif for a long time to come, but references to Fortune appear casually, as something to be taken entirely for granted, in nearly every kind of literary work.

Alexander Murray has recently suggested that the social mobility of the twelfth century inspired the revival of Fortune,[84] but I am not persuaded that this was the only or chief cause. In the first place, the wheel of fortune on which artists pictured kings, clerics, peasants, and others as being raised and lowered may not have referred to changes in social status. It is just as likely that it meant that all groups were equally subject to the whims of Fortune, and surely the mechanical version of the wheel—built by the abbot of Fécamp for the edification of his monks—showed kings occasionally at the bottom of the cycle instead of the crown shifting from head to head. Further, there is no obvious reason why the successes

83. La *"Consolation de Philosophie" dans la tradition littéraire* (Paris, 1967), pp. 135, 141–43.
84. *Reason and Society in the Middle Ages* (Oxford, 1978), pp. 98–101.

or failures of the twelfth century should not have been understood as the consequence of divine justice just as those of previous centuries had been. The chosenness of the successful has been an abiding theme in Western society, and John D. Rockefeller was not the only or the last capitalist to believe God had given him his money.

It is important to remember this older tradition because it gives the new one its meaning. For what Fortune really represents in the twelfth century is the absence of divine justice in human affairs, the element of chance to which all people are subject. Often indeed Fortune is mentioned in trivial connections, to refer to the ups and downs of everyday life. A typical example comes from the letter of a Parisian scholar who wrote a friend that Fortune's wheel "had raised me lately to a better state only to thrust me down to the bottommost depths of adversity."[85] But Fortune could equally be invoked to explain major historical events. It was by Orderic Vitalis to explain the Norman conquest, and by William of Malmesbury when he remarked of William Rufus that "he formed mighty plans, which he could have brought to effect, could he have spun out the tissue of fate or broken through and disengaged himself from the violence of fortune."[86] This passage, reminiscent of some in *The Prince* about Cesare Borgia, presents us with the Fortune of later tradition—capricious and inscrutable, defying human plans and understanding. For a twelfth-century cleric to have expressed such views, however, meant rejecting the temptation to see Rufus's death as punishment for his many sins.

This opposition to immanent justice provides the point of contact between the order of Nature and the randomness of Fortune: both suggested nonmiraculous explanations of events that otherwise would have been attributed to supernatural forces. I do not mean, of course, that people stopped believing in miracles. That was and remained a basic tenet of the Christian faith. What changed was not doctrine but mentality, not the belief itself but the reasoning by which it was applied to concrete circumstances. For when the natural and fortuitous had first to be ruled out, it became very much harder to prove that any specific event was a miracle.

I can illustrate this process through the growing percentage of cures in the miracle collections of the eleventh and twelfth centuries. The collection of the miracles of Ste. Foy from the early elev-

85. Andrew of St. Victor to Thomas, quoted by Beryl Smalley, *The Study of the Bible in the Middle Ages*, 2d ed. (Oxford, 1952), p. 117.
86. Quoted by Robert Hanning, *The Vision of History in Early Britain* (New York, 1966), p. 228 n. 51.

enth century can serve as a point of departure: 43 percent of 123 recorded miracles were cures, the rest consisting of apparitions and the saint's intervention on behalf of just causes or (what perhaps amounted to the same thing) her worshippers. We are here still very much in the mental world of the early Middle Ages, and I doubt that Gregory of Tours's collections or the *Dialogues* of Gregory the Great would tell a greatly different story. But from this point on the percentage of cures in collections rises, as problems of health and sickness eluded understanding and criticism longer than other kinds of miracles. In the later eleventh century collection of St. Vulfran, 75 percent of the miracles recorded are cures. In 1145, of the 112 recorded miracles of St. Gibrien 108 were cures.[87]

This series can be rounded off with the miracle collection made at the very beginning of the thirteenth century as part of the canonization of Gilbert of Sempringham.[88] Prodigies, revelations, and divine punishments by now have been almost entirely excluded: of 30 miracles in the official collection only one—a shift in winds for sailing to Normandy—was not a cure, and of 26 miracles in a supplementary collection all except a vision were cures. But no less important than the results was the manner in which the collection was made, for Innocent III had required his agents to take special care in collecting miracles and to accept only those attested by trustworthy witnesses. This rigorous scrutiny of claimed miracles exemplifies the kind of reasoning that was driving the supernatural into a smaller and smaller corner of human life.[89]

This of course was the view from the top. In 1200 probably the majority of Europeans were still untouched by this new way of thinking about the supernatural, and it was doubtless they whom Innocent III had in mind when he issued such strict orders to his commission. And even among those who shared the new mentality, there were some who felt uneasy about a world where the forces of nature and chance dealt impartially with the just and unjust. Thus it was that the twelfth century saw a revival of astrology and other occult arts that had virtually disappeared in the centuries when saints and devils accounted for the vicissitudes of life, but which had the attraction of submitting chance itself to reason. Yet to

87. I am taking my figures from P.-A. Sigal, "Maladie, Pélerinage et Guérison au XIIe siècle. Les Miracles de Saint Gibrien à Reims," *Annales: Economies. Sociétés. Civilizations.* 24 (1969): 1527 n. 1.

88. Raymonde Foreville, ed., *Un procès de canonisation a l'aube du XIIIe siècle (1201–1202): Le livre de Saint Guibert de Sempringham* (Paris, 1943).

89. For the development of canonization procedures, see E. W. Kemp, *Canonization and Authority in the Western Church* (Oxford, 1948).

concede these limitations does not make the consequences of the changes less significant. Whatever the beliefs of private individuals, when there existed people capable of raising doubts about the miraculous, as Peter the Chanter did with ordeals, the supernatural could never for long be a means of establishing broad consensus or settling public disputes. In this real, practical sense, therefore, God was just a bit more removed from human affairs in 1200 than he had been at any time since the first century A.D.

The examples I have given in the foregoing pages illustrate the interaction of cognition with society and culture in the twelfth century. But cognitive change altered medieval society in many other ways that there is no space to discuss in detail. Not all twelfth-century scholars, for example, were formed on Abelard's model. Some focussed their studies on other disciplines, others, such as Rupert of Deutz and the Victorines, pursued their activities in very different contexts, and most disagreed with one or another of Abelard's positions on specific issues. Yet underlying the differences in style and even in content was a shared conception that the task of scholars was to impose intellectual order on the materials they studied, and this attitude sets them apart from the scholars of the early Middle Ages.[90]

Some of the specific attitudes that I have discussed as expressions of the new mentality also took shapes other than those I have specifically mentioned. Concern with intention was not confined to formal works on ethics or to courts sitting on cases of homicide. It was equally expressed in knightly romances and in the intensely interior spirituality of people such as Francis of Assisi. The ideas of people who perceived social life in terms of community changed the conception of the Church as a whole as well as of the monastery,[91] of the city and guild as well as the kingdom. Awareness of nature as a system meant not just that scientists could begin to study that system. It also made it possible for theologians to conclude that homosexuality was "unnatural,"[92] and to discuss whether Mary had menstruated.[93]

90. For a recent survey of twelfth-century theology, in and out of the schools, see G. R. Evans, *Old Arts and New Theology* (Oxford, 1980).
91. For the articulation of a sense of the corporateness of the church, see Brian Tierney, *Foundations of the Conciliar Theory* (Cambridge, 1955).
92. John E. Boswell, *Christianity, Social Tolerance, and Homosexuality. Gay People in Western Europe from the Beginning of the Christian Era to the Fourteenth Century* (Chicago, 1980).
93. Charles T. Wood, "The Doctor's Dilemma: Sin, Salvation and the Menstrual Cycle in Medieval Thought," *Speculum* 56 (1981): 710–27.

The extent to which the new cognition was diffused throughout society was of course no recipe for agreement. Though Abelard in his *Ethics* and Bernard in his sermons both took intention as the touchstone of morality, as men they clashed bitterly because of differences in temperament, situation, and interests. The importance of recognizing the role of cognition, therefore, is not to homogenize the twelfth century but to understand the dynamics of its history. People articulated new ideas and formed new institutions, not just because the world was different, but because they experienced it differently.

Conclusion

Cognition and Society

*Wherever, emerging from
savage, fierce, and bestial
times, men begin to
domesticate themselves . . .
they begin, proceed, and
end by those stages which
are investigated here.*

—*The New Science, 393.*

The theme of this book has been the role of cognition in the shaping of European culture and society from the late Roman empire to the end of the twelfth century. First, we saw how changes in cognitive processes in the first centuries A.D. severed many classical traditions of thought. Magic, both Christian and pagan, reigned supreme in attitudes toward the natural world, while in social thought conceptions of peer relations began to disappear, replaced by an ideal of hierarchy and authority. This mentality, expressed in many different kinds of institutions and beliefs, was scarcely challenged from the second century to the tenth, with indeed few exceptions even worth mentioning after the death of Augustine. And it was not only scholars who were affected by these changes in reasoning. Germanic law, Benedictine monasticism, and indeed the general organization of society from the late Roman empire showed the impress of these conceptions as people structured a social world that made sense in their terms and often at the expense of traditions which they thought they were upholding.

It was in the eleventh century that we found the first evidence of a break with this early medieval mentality. The settings in which change appeared earliest—the cathedral school at Chartres under Fulbert, the lawcourt at Pavia—were remote from the pressures of the growing commercial world and remote, too, from the stirrings of eleventh-century reform that still looked toward the reestablishment of an ideal order. Yet the conditions of debate in these traditional milieus had changed in two subtle ways. The first was the result of the long-term rise in educational standards, which by increasing the number of educated people accentuated the impact of any dispute. The second was the collapse of political order in many parts of Europe that made appeal to outside authority impossible. Thrown back on their own resources, people had to learn again the skills of persuading each other, and they responded by finding more skillful ways of reading texts, by insisting upon logical consistency as a foundation of argument, and by taking more account of the views of those with whom they disagreed.

Finally, we traced the effects of this new cognition on twelfth-century society. Intellectual discourse, which had long consisted chiefly of citations from authorities, was reconstructed on the basis of logic, and this was just one of the ways in which education changed toward being a creative instead of a curatorial process. No less important were the changes worked in social institutions. Law and politics became affairs of the community and not just the king alone, while in the monasteries a similar process encouraged the religiously inclined to seek expression of their interior feelings in the company of equals. This focus on social life, moreover, was accompanied by the growing independence of human society from the action of supernatural forces. Nature became less the mirror of human life than a subject of interest on its own merits.

The importance and durability of the institutions rooted in this period need no additional emphasis. What may be less obvious, however, is that the mentality itself remained the dominant one in Europe for centuries after the terminus of this book. Only in the eighteenth century does one find both the completion of the mechanization of nature, with no room left for occult forces, and the attack on custom when contrary to principle that undermined the synthesis of logic and tradition established in Abelard's time. It is this similarity betweeen the twelfth and eighteenth centuries, both of which saw the flowering of powerful new kinds of reasoning, that led me to suggest the usefulness of thinking of the twelfth century as a kind of enlightenment in the title of part three.

Perhaps the best way to grasp the implications of all this is to consider what it does to our perception of historical periods. Traditionally the Middle Ages has been thought to run from the fifth to the fifteenth centuries, bounded on one side by the ancient world and on the other by early modern society, and though these broad periods are for purposes of research often subdivided, they still frame our way of thinking about the past. Yet what we have ended up with is two long periods which are bound together by essential continuities in cognition and attitudes toward the world, the first running from about 100 A.D. to about 1050, and the second from 1050 to about 1700. That there were changes of tradition within these periods is indisputable—the conversion to Christianity, for example, or the Reformation. But I believe they also express an essential truth about the continuities or discontinuities of human experience. For just as in everything but religion Isidore or Alcuin had more in common with a pagan sage of the fourth century than with Alan of Lille, so one need only read the debates of the Parlement of Paris during the Fronde to see the congruence between their conceptions of society and that of medieval lawyers.[1] The kinship is not one of language or even belief so much as of mentality: how they posed problems to themselves and integrated them into a broader intellectual structure.

This general outline can be modified in two ways. The first concerns what can best be described as a cultural *décalage*—beliefs originating in the reasoning of an earlier age that survived as doctrine despite changes in cognition. There had been many such doctrines in the early Middle Ages; indeed, as we saw, nearly all Christian social doctrines ran counter to the reasoning people actually used, but because these doctrines were not well understood they had been no source of anxiety. The situation in the twelfth century was different, not least because the eleventh century had been particularly fruitful in producing articles of faith that proved difficult to explain as standards of intellectual coherence rose.

The process I have in mind can be illustrated by the intellectual history of indulgences. These had had their origin in the promise Urban II made to those who went on the First Crusade—that they would be freed of penalties for their sins. Just what Urban meant by this is by no means self-evident from the sources, and it is probably wrong to attribute to him any terribly clear ideas about what he was promising or whether he had the power to do so. The popes in the Gregorian tradition, after all, took literally their powers of binding and loosing. But to the theologians of the twelfth century these were not questions that could easily be brushed aside. The whole idea of forgiving the sins of those who performed certain deeds must have been suspect to people who were beginning to stress contrition as the key element of penance, though this scruple could be dealt with by making the efficacy of the indulgence contingent on there being contrition. It was not as easy to explain how the pope could act as he did in dispensing sins (or punishments) at will. This problem, which really had to do with the nature of papal

1. See, for example, A. Lloyd Moote, *The Revolt of the Judges. The Parlement of Paris and the Fronde 1643–1652* (Princeton, 1971).

and priestly power, required much thought, and it was not until the middle of the thirteenth century that a Dominican theologian succeeded in converting the pope from a dispenser of indulgences on his own authority to the administrator on behalf of the church of a Treasury of Merits.[2]

Twelfth- and thirteenth-century scholars who dealt with issues such as these (purgatory,[3] the eucharist, and papal authority were others) had no latitude to decide whether the practices or doctrines in question were correct. That had already been settled by tradition. What they had to do was to come up with an intellectually acceptable explanation of conclusions whose surface meanings would usually be rejected by their own reasoning, and the long time needed to do this is a sign of how difficult the process was. These issues, then, were stress points between mentality and tradition. It is not by chance that these same issues recur frequently in the heresies of the later Middle Ages and ultimately in the Reformation itself.

The other limitation to be acknowledged concerns the fact that not everyone in medieval society shared the new mentality. Because cognition is an attribute of individuals and not groups, it is hardly possible that things could have been otherwise. But it is nonetheless important to pose the question to what extent the new mentality was diffused throughout society, and though the sources do not permit a detailed answer it is possible to discern the basic outlines of the situation.

We may begin with the landed aristocracy, the group about which we are best informed of all those who do not speak to us in their own words. Of the influence in their circles of the change in cognition, we have already had occasion to remark the restructuring of vassalage in the twelfth century toward greater uniformity and reciprocity. One example is the custom new in the twelfth century of awarding fiefs to simple knights who in an earlier era would have been kept as personal retainers. Another is the effort, even on the part of great lords, to display toward their lords the obedience they expected of their vassals. These are both significant trends because for many they meant sacrificing rights or properties they would have enjoyed under earlier codes of behavior.

Yet perhaps the best evidence of the new mentality among the aristocracy is the growing importance of the married couple in

2. See the discussion by R. W. Southern, *Western Society and the Church in the Middle Ages* (Baltimore, 1970), pp. 136–43.
3. J. Le Goff, *La naissance du purgatoire,* (Paris, 1981).

knightly society. In Georges Duby's impressive treatment of this
development, he has rightly stressed that much of the new emphasis on the couple came from the Church, though even there we need
to recall that the new forms of reasoning had effected a metamorphosis of the ideas of the clergy. Thus it was only in the early
twelfth century that shared intention to marry was singled out as
the essential attribute of a valid marriage. But the church cannot be
held responsible for the courtly ideal of the late twelfth-century
romances, where frankly sexual love was justified by the emotional
tie between the couple even when (as in the Tristan legend) the
couple was adulterous.[4] This ideal, both chivalric and ecclesiastical, was the domestic counterpart to the transformation that had
been worked in the relationship between lord and vassal or monk
and God. The similarity derives not from imitation but from shared
ways of thinking about social relationships, from thinking in terms
of intention and consent instead of hierarchy and obedience.

What this ideal meant at the personal level can be illustrated by
the scene at the deathbed of William the Marshal in the early
thirteenth century. It was a fortunate death in many ways. William
was very old, and the approach of his death was known sufficiently
in advance for him to be able to bid a solemn public farewell to his
retainers, his sons, but especially his wife. The comparison with,
for example, Socrates's death in the *Phaedo* is instructive; Socrates
in gathering his loved ones to him sent his wife away early in the
proceedings. But what is just as important is to realize that William
was following no set script. He was acting out of his personal desire
or—and there is no necessary contradiction—his sense of what was
socially acceptable. The closeness of the couple had become part
and parcel of the excellence as a knight and as a Christian that
William wanted to convey.[5]

This last point deserves special emphasis because it is here that
the history of mentalities touches the history of women, a subject I
have not elsewhere in this book had occasion to discuss. To the
ancients, women were clearly inferior to men, so much so that
Aristotle even used the relationship between men and women as a
paradigm to discuss the relationship between unequals. For him, as
for most Greeks, truly mutual love could exist only between men,

4. Georges Duby, *Le Chevalier, la femme, et le prêtre* (Paris, 1981).
5. The basic text is the *Histoire de Guillaume le Mareschal*, ed. Paul Meyer
(Société de l'histoire de France, 1891–1901). The inspiration for using it
here comes from hearing a talk given by Professor Duby at Brooklyn Col-
lege in 1982, though I do not claim my conclusions are the same as his.

and this attitude can still be seen flourishing in the fourth century A.D. in Augustine's casual omission from his *Confessions* of the name of the woman with whom he lived for years and who bore his son. In the centuries following the Germanic invasions, the general incomprehension of peer relationships in the early Middle Ages sapped the strength of this ideal, which survived only in the disconcertingly passionate language of some monastic correspondence, and some individual women reached positions of unheard-of prominence in the early Middle Ages. But the significance of their achievements should not be overestimated. Their independence was a bare fact, unclothed by ideology, and says little about the conditions in which most women lived. No one who reads the Germanic laws can doubt that women were seen as scarcely better than possessions, and that their fate was—in principle at least—controlled by their fathers or their husbands. Some communities even appear to have practiced female infanticide, a sure sign that female life was held to be of little value.

Thus it was that the position of women in society was an issue that had to be dealt with as part of the general rethinking of social relationships in the eleventh and twelfth centuries, and some tentative efforts to do so were quite radical. There were apparently some heretics in the eleventh century who held as part of their doctrines views favorable to women's equality, and the twelfth century saw established some double monasteries headed by women. Not all these initiatives proved enduring, of course, and sexual equality was never actually achieved. But even when the limitations are allowed for, it remains true that from the twelfth century on Western society acknowledged the humanity of women in a way it had not done before, and that the ramifications of this new attitude can be seen in everything from marriage and courtship customs to the laws regarding property-holding by women to their life expectancy, which for the first time exceeded that of men.

The evidence on marriage and vassalage, together with what was earlier said about politics, suggests that the reasoning typical of the new mentality was fairly well diffused throughout the chivalric class. The nature of the sources makes the state of affairs in other classes of society much harder to judge, but on balance it seems likely that in them egocentric cognition remained common for a long time after the twelfth century. The differences in cognition made possible not only disagreements but disagreements in which both sides unconsciously attributed different meanings to the same words and concepts. One place where this effect can be seen is in

witchcraft, where allegations that mentioned charms or incanta-
tions—usually the simplest kinds of participatory rituals—were
turned by learned judges into prosecutions for demonology.[6] Something of the same thing can be seen in the common law courts,
where juries often insisted on judging homicides solely on the basis
of premeditation, despite the judges' instructions to weigh other
evidence concerning the psychical state of the accused.[7] These cognitive differences represented an important barrier to understanding between social groups, as of course they still do where they
exist, and historians would do well to remember them when they
are tempted to write of a society's traditions and institutions as if
they meant the same thing for all they touched.

These qualifications of the general outline help to remind us of
the continuing interaction between the cognition of individuals and
the essentially social forces of tradition and class. And the fact that
there was, and is, interaction is a point worth insisting upon, especially because of the tendency today to see economics and tech-
nology as the engines that drag culture and society behind them. It
is too easily forgotten that the industrial revolution was a late arrival to the scene, that in its attitudes toward nature and society
Europe by the end of the twelfth century was already a very different place from the rest of the world, and that these differences were
only enhanced by the developments of the next several centuries.
The changes were not necessarily for the better. Too often superior
capacity for social organization meant superior capacity for war, so
that the Hundred Years' War was already a war between populations as well as armies. But while seventeenth-century Europe was,
by modern standards, economically underdeveloped, socially, po-
litically and culturally it was very sophisticated, and it was this
sophistication that made possible Europe's dominance of the rest of
the world and its own later social and economic development.

There may be some who reject this conclusion because they dis-
like its implications for modern problems. Their attitude, similar to
that of cultural relativism, is not difficult to understand. Undoubt-

6. See particularly Richard Kieckhefer, *European Witch Trials: Their
Foundation in Popular and Learned Culture 1300–1500* (London, 1976);
and for the later period, Keith Thomas, *Religion and the Decline of Magic*
(New York, 1971). My own comments on the subject can be found in
"Superstition to Science," *American Historical Review* 84 (1979): 967–68.
7. Thomas A. Green, "Societal Concepts of Criminal Liability for Homicide in Medieval England," *Speculum* 47 (1972): 669–94. It should be
added of course that the juries' attitude does mark a significant change
from the reasoning of the early Middle Ages.

edly it is easier to build steel mills and oil refineries than to change cultures, and that is why it has usually been conservatives who have seen culture as difficult to change. Yet I do not believe my conclusions are either pessimistic or conservative. For what we have seen in this book is the transformation of a culture in the space of a few generations, a change accomplished moreover without discarding essential traditions or religious heritage.[8] To be sure, this is not something that has happened often; as far as I know, only Greece of the fifth and sixth centuries B.C. offers a real parallel. But that it has happened at all, that some people do change their ways of thinking without simply borrowing ideas, and that they can rebuild their institutions to accommodate new values, does more than provide a clue to the dynamics of cultural evolution. It reminds us of the possibilities of human existence, and of the fact that it is men and women who make those possibilities realities.

8. For a discussion of contemporary problems in these terms, see Fazlur Rahman, *Islam and Modernity: Transformation of an Intellectual Tradition* (Chicago, 1983).

A Short Course in Piagetian Psychology

When men are ignorant of the natural causes producing things, and cannot explain them by analogy to similar things, they attribute their own nature to them. The vulgar, for example, say the magnet loves the iron. This axiom is embraced by the first: namely, that the human mind, because of its indefinite nature, wherever it is lost in ignorance makes itself the rule of the universe in respect of everything it does not have.
—The New Science, 181–82.

The purpose of this appendix is twofold: to introduce cognitive theory to readers who wish to know more than I have given in the text, and to indicate my reasons for choosing the questions I did for investigation. For simplicity, I have divided this material into two parts, one on thought about the natural world, the other on moral reasoning.[1]

1. The following summary of Piaget is based on these works: *The Language and Thought of the Child*, trans. Marjorie and Ruth Gabain, 3rd ed. (London, 1959; orig. pub. 1926); *The Child's Conception of the World*, trans. Joan and Andrew Tomlinson (London, 1929); *The Child's Conception of Physical Causality*, trans. Marjorie Gabain (London, 1930); *The Moral Judgment of the Child*, trans. Marjorie Gabain (New York, 1948; orig. pub. 1932); *The Origins of Intelligence in Children*, trans. Margaret Cook (New York, 1963; orig. pub. 1952); *The Child's Conception of Time*, trans. A. J. Pomerans (New York, 1971; orig. pub. 1946); *The Child's Conception of Movement and Speed*, trans. G. E. T. Holloway and

Children's earliest articulate thought—including the belief in immanent justice that we found underlying the ordeal—belongs to a world view that Piaget called egocentric because of children's inclination to assume theirs is the only way of seeing the world. Piaget observed that children were not able to take into account what another person knew when they were talking to him, to be fully aware of their own uniqueness as individuals, or to differentiate clearly between themselves and the physical world. "The child is a realist and a realist because he has not yet grasped the distinction between subject and object and the internal nature of thought."[2]

One consequence of this realism is that children tend to endow the world with qualities similar to those they possess themselves. Thus, when asked where the sun, clouds, or mountains come from, children commonly reply that they were "made" or "grew." Balloons go up "because they want to fly away." Boats float, though they are heavier than pebbles, "'because the boat is cleverer than the stone.' 'What does it mean to be clever?' 'It doesn't do what it ought not to do.'"[3] There is, in general, no intuition of the uniform and deterministic operation of physical laws; physical laws, just as moral laws, have many exceptions.

> When children between 5 and 8 are asked whether the sun could go away if it wanted to, they always answer that it could: if it does not go away it is because it "has to shine a little longer," or because "it has to lighten us during the day." Clouds cannot go because they show us the way, etc. In short, if there are natural laws at work, it is not because the bodies in question are physically determined; they could perfectly well evade the law if they wished to. It is simply that they are obedient.[4]

M. J. Mackenzie (New York, 1971; orig. pub. 1946); *Genetic Epistemology*, trans. Eleanor Duckworth (New York, 1970); *Psychology and Epistemology*, trans. Arnold Rosin (New York, 1972; orig. pub. 1970); *The Child and Reality*, trans. Arnold Rosin (New York, 1973; orig. pub. 1972); and with Bärbel Inhelder, *The Origins of the Idea of Chance in Children*, trans. L. Leake et al. (New York, 1975; orig. pub. 1951). A good introduction by Piaget and Inhelder is *The Psychology of the Child*, trans. Helen Weaver (New York, 1966). J. H. Flavell, *The Developmental Psychology of Jean Piaget* (Princeton, 1963), is also helpful.

2. *World*, p. 292.
3. *Causality*, pp. 110, 136.
4. *Causality*, p. 274.

The conception that objects act as they do because they are obedi-

ent is particularly interesting in view of the belief, common before
the revival of science in the twelfth century, that the order of nature
is due to the world's submission to God's will.

The reality attributed to thought is revealed particularly well by
children's belief that phenomena that affect them similarly coexist
or cause each other, beliefs that Piaget called "participation" after
Lévy-Bruhl's term for similar reasoning among primitives.[5] In one
experiment Piaget squeezed an inflated ball so that the children
could feel the air on their skin; the youngest children (under six)
insisted that the air came from outside through the window, although the windows and door of the room had been closed before
they entered the room. Shadows cast by hands are said to come
from night, trees, or chairs, "because it is dark under the chair."
Thought, which young children believe is produced by the mouth,
participates with the wind; memories leave the head and go into
the sky when we are not thinking them. Thoughts in general exist
at once within the body and outside it, and one intelligent seven-
year-old told Piaget one could touch thought "when the thoughts
are real."[6]

Given the external reality attributed to thought, it is not surprising that children credit the products of thought with an objective
existence. Dreams are believed to be external and real, and even
when children accept the fact that dreams arise within themselves
they continue to attribute an external existence to them—they are
"in front of the eyes." Names are believed in some way indispens-
able parts of objects, and Piaget reported the following conversation between two six-year-olds playing a building game:

> AR: "And when there weren't any names ..."
> BO: "If there weren't any names it would be very awkward
> (on serait très ennuyé). You couldn't make anything. How
> could things have been made" (if there hadn't been names for
> them).[7]

(Bilingual Swiss children, who might be expected to understand the
relativity of names, believe just as strongly in the immutability of
names as children who speak only one language.) Children of the
ages of seven or eight are less insistent that names are intrinsic to

5. Cf., for example, Lucien Lévy-Bruhl, *Les fonctions mentales dans les
sociétés inférieures* (Paris, 1910); *Primitive Mentality*, trans. Lilian A.
Clare (Boston, 1966).
6. *Causality*, pp. 3–31, 184; *World*, p. 47.
7. *World*, p. 62.

objects, but it is only after the age of ten that most children will agree that names are purely conventional signs that could easily be changed.[8]

Along with intellectual realism, the distinguishing tendency of egocentric thought is the privileged place occupied by appearances. In infants, the dependence on appearances takes extreme forms: it is not until eight or ten months that babies realize objects are permanent; before that age, they believe objects disappear when they are removed from sight and that they grow smaller when they are placed further away.[9] Until the age of five or six, moreover, older children will assume that the other side of a mountain looks the same as the one they see and will believe that water is altered in quantity if it is poured into a container of a different shape. At the age of three Sarah contradicted me immediately when I told her, in the course of answering a question, that the moon was far away. "No, it isn't," she said pointing, "it's right there!" When she was about five she commented as she was walking "The moon must like me. It follows me wherever I go." Other children have been observed to believe the clouds or the sun follow them, and they have offered similarly realist explanations.

As a consequence of their egocentric reasoning, children frequently develop beliefs that they can influence the physical world through correctly performed rituals. The belief that a person can make the clouds move by walking is a simple instance of this attitude. Other examples are beliefs that by making a shadow the child can cause night to come, and that by choosing stones of the right color and shape for the bottom of the flowerpot one can make the plant grow. Piaget points out that it is not sufficient to say that these rituals are projections of wishes, as Freud suggests and many historians assume. Such an interpretation "seems to claim that if a desire has exceptional value, belief in its necessary realization must follow," although as adults we, in fact, recognize that our desires are subjective and that external reality is full of other beings with wishes of their own and inanimate objects that cannot be bent to our will. It is necessary, therefore, to add that children's wishes are able to find their expression in magic because egocentric cognitive structures are not able to differentiate the objective and subjective. Gestures and names are real and powerful, so that while "magical actions are, to the observer, symbols . . . to the subject they are

8. *World*, pp. 88–122, 61–87.
9. *Intelligence*.

effective, precisely because they are not yet symbolic and because they participate in things."[10]

Piaget's discovery of the egocentricity of children has profound implications for our understanding of the character of all human thought. To begin with, it is apparent that many ideas are far more greatly removed from sensory impressions than is commonly supposed; as Einstein observed, "the relationship [between concepts and experience] is analogous not to that of soup to beef, but rather of check number to overcoat." Moreover, until sophisticated concepts are formed, experience is simply assimilated to other conceptual frameworks, often without any great awareness of incongruity. Melanesian villagers of the twentieth century, for example, approached the problem of obtaining manufactured goods (cargo) as an exercise in determining which European practices were effective as rituals. They began by converting to Christianity, giving up cannibalism and polygamy, and attending church. When the cargo failed to arrive, they became convinced that the missionaries had withheld from them the truly efficacious rituals and tried to guess the secret: one group put bottles with flowers in them on the table; another added bathing in hot water to their traditional fertility rites; others listened to flagpoles as though they were radio aerials, dug up geodesic markers under which the cargo was thought to be hidden, and tried to elect Lyndon Johnson as their representative to the central government. Diverse as these efforts were, they all show how western culture can be assimilated to logical schema that believe ritual is an effective means of controlling the world.[11]

The existence of egocentric thought also poses the problem of how other kinds of reasoning develop. The accumulation of experience does not in itself break down egocentricity because, as we have seen, egocentric reasoning is equally evident in matters with which children are quite familiar. Early in his career Piaget discovered that young children (ages five to eight) with siblings did not realize that they themselves were brothers and sisters, and that children who know their own right and left hands could not correctly identify the right and left hands of someone facing them. Nor can children easily be dissuaded of their ideas by counterexamples.

10. *World*, pp. 152, 162, and pp. 123–70 generally.
11. On this see the interesting article by W. Lidz, T. Lidz, and B. G. Burton-Bradley, "Culture, Personality, and Social Structure: Cargo-Cultism—A Psychosocial Study of Melanesian Millenarianism," *Journal of Nervous and Mental Diseases* 157 (1973): 370–88.

DELESD (7; 8): "What is it that makes it dark at night?" "*It is because we go to sleep.*" "If you go to sleep in the afternoon is it dark then?" "*No, Sir.*" "Then what will make it dark this evening? . . ." Despite this objection, Delesd maintained that it is because we sleep that it becomes night.[12]

Egocentric notions can even persist despite acquaintance with adult ideas through formal education, as a colleague of mine discovered when discussing clouds with her seven-year-old. The child explained that clouds were always the same, and they looked different because they moved around so that we saw different ones. He also claimed (rather to his mother's surprise because his own experience provided contradictory evidence) that there was never a cloudless day. She then asked him what he thought about the theory that clouds were formed from water vapor that rose from the ground and later fell as rain. "Yes," he said, "we learned about that in school."

Piaget's explanations of the breakdown of egocentricity evolved over the course of his career. In his earliest work he described the process as one of decentering through learning to take the viewpoints of other people into account. Thus children learn the moon does not follow them when they realize that the moon seems to follow everyone at once, including people going in different directions. And intellectual realism in general is corrected by the same means. "It is through contact with others and the practice of discussion that the mind is forced to realize its subjective nature and thus to become aware of the process of thought itself."[13] In his later work Piaget incorporated the concept of decentering into a more general theory describing the development of logical operations—Piaget's term for the ability mentally to manipulate phenomena. It is the child's construction of operatory schemes that Piaget believed to be at the center of learning, and his account of the development of operational thought is at once the cornerstone of his theory of human cognition and its least readily grasped part.

Piaget divided the period of operational thought into two stages. The first of these, concrete operations, is commonly achieved by Western children between the ages of six and eight years and consists of the ability to solve problems involving real objects. An example of concrete operations is conservation, the understanding that quantity remains the same despite changes in form. In experi-

12. *World*, p. 292.
13. *World*, p. 87.

mental situations conservation is tested by filling two identical beakers with the same amount of water, and then pouring the water from one of the beakers into a narrower or wider glass. Pre-operational children, who reason only about static configurations, will then think the amounts of water are no longer equal, that the liquid in the glass has increased or decreased in quantity. Operational children, however, will continue to assert the equality of the two containers of water, and they can explain that the water could be poured back, that it is the same water, or that nothing has been added or taken away. In these children's thought, then, the actual appearance of the water is subordinated to the transformations in appearance they can imagine. (Conservation experiments can also be performed with balls of clay rolled into different shapes or, most strikingly, with coins or other counters. A preoperational child can be shown two lines of coins of identical number and length; if the experimenter then, while the child watches, increases the space between the coins in one line so that the line is longer, the child will assert the longer line has more coins.)

In addition to conservation, concrete operations include the abilities to classify items, arrange them in order, and measure them, but these manipulations are limited to the world of real items. It is only at the age of ten or twelve that children master formal operational logic, which enables them to manipulate or combine verbal propositions such as the following:

> Carl is taller than Alice. Alice is shorter than Bob. Who is the shortest?[14]

There is nothing in this problem that a concrete operational child could not solve in the presence of Carl, Bob and Alice, but casting the problem in words alone requires the ability to think about already completed thoughts. Only when the child can think about thoughts can he or she solve problems involving several variables at once. Thus, though concrete operations suffice to measure the movement of a snail along a board, and the movement of a board along a table, formal operations are needed to calculate from these measurements the movement of the snail relative to the table. In effect, formal operational thought frees the child from the world of the concrete, for only then is a child capable of framing hypotheses, preparing an exhaustive list of possible realities, and devising strategies to test which of the possible realities is the actual one.

14. Diana Kuhn et al., "The Development of Formal Operations in Logical and Moral Judgment," *Genetic Psychology Monographs* 95 (1977): 124.

The effects of the development of operational thought can be illustrated by Piaget's study of the idea of chance. The background of this study is Piaget's discovery that everything has an explanation—a belief most obvious in the interminable series of why's known to every parent of a three or four year old. Although many of the why questions concern cases for which reasons exist, others (Why is that stick taller than you? Why are there a Big Salève and a Little Salève [mountains outside of Geneva]?) show the child's disposition to seek a meaning for every feature or occurrence however fortuitous it may in fact be.[15] And if one turns the why questions around and asks them of a child, they can answer them, as Sarah did when I asked her why the stick was taller than she.

Piaget tested the effects of operational development on the egocentric notion of order in an experiment using red and white marbles arrayed in a row along one side of a box and separated by a divider. The objective was to see whether the children could anticipate the mixing of the colors that would occur when the box was rocked so the marbles rolled back and forth. Children of four to six expected the balls would return to their original places, or that the red and white balls would switch sides in a general crisscross; when the experiment was performed and the colors began to mix the children then predicted that further rocking of the box would restore the original order. Older children, aged seven to eleven, foresaw the mixing of the marbles (although some still expected them to return to an ordered position if the box were rocked a sufficient number of times), but when asked to draw the trajectories of the marbles as they collided with each other en route to the new position they were unable to do it. Their drawings either treated the path of each marble without regard for the simultaneous movement of the other marbles—an example of the difficulty of coordinating more than one variable with concrete operational thought alone—or the trajectories simply showed a crisscross of the colors instead of the mixed position they were trying to portray. Only at about eleven or twelve, with the development of formal thought, do the children recognize the truly random nature of the mixture, and that it is based on the possible permutations of the positions of the marbles. Children of this age are able to coordinate the movements of the marbles in a sketch of the trajectories of the marbles while they mix.[16]

In another experiment on chance, Piaget used coinlike counters,

15. *Language and Thought*, chapter 5, "A Child's Questions."
16. *Chance*, pp. 1–25.

each marked with a circle on one side and a cross on the other.

Children were asked how the counters would fall if fifteen or
twenty were thrown at once, and after a few throws the experimenter surreptitiously substituted counters marked on both sides
with a cross to test the children's reaction to the counters' falling all
crosses. Though surprised by these results, the youngest children
accepted it easily and when shown the trick insisted it could happen
even with the authentic counters.

> CHAP (5; 4) thinks that the first counter will fall with the
> cross up *"because its larger* (than the circle)." "Try it." (He
> makes a toss.) *"It's the circle."* "And next?" (Experiment.)
> *"Cross."* "Now if we throw all of them together, could all of
> them turn up crosses?" *"No, they couldn't all fall crosses be-*
> *cause they turn and hit each other as they fall."* "Why?"
> *"That's the way it works; they can't fall all crosses or all cir-*
> *cles."* (False counters.) *"All crosses at the same time!"* (He is
> amazed.) "Try it yourself." *"Yes, they all fall crosses up."* "Do
> it again." *"Again all crosses."* "Again." *"That's funny, again."*
> "Why is that?" *"They all fell to that side as they came down."*
> "Don't you think there might be a trick? . . . Look at it." (We
> give him a counter.) *"A cross on both sides."* "And with the
> true counters (we show him the sack and the counters with
> crosses and circles), could they all fall with the circle up?"
> *"Yes, if we want them to."*[17]

Somewhat older children, with concrete operational abilities, instantly rejected the experiment with the false counters.

> BER (7; 2) . . . "What if I throw them all at once?" *"Both*
> *sides."* "Both equal?" *"No, many of one and few of the*
> *other."* (Experiment.) *"About the same number of each."* "Is
> there some reason for that?" *"No."* (False counters.) *"Oh,*
> *surely they are the same on both sides"* (his immediate reac-
> tion without looking). "Could the true counters have fallen
> all with the same side up?" *"No, there are too many and they*
> *are too mixed."*[18]

For these children, chance exists as an intuition that certain situations are rare, but the very rarity of these situations makes them
appear so impossible that they deny them without testing further.
But the children with formal operations (generally over eleven

17. *Chance*, p. 99.
18. *Chance*, pp. 103–4.

years of age) do recognize that the counters could, once in a long while, fall all crosses and they therefore adopt a sampling procedure to test reality.

> MUL (11; 9) claims that we cannot know the results of throwing twenty counters, whether there will be more crosses, more circles, or the same number of each because *"it's chance, it depends."* "And is it more likely to get half and half with one thousand or ten thousand throws?" *"With a million."* (False counters.) *"All crosses! You must have a trick someplace in here."* (He turns over a counter.) *"There!"* "But do they all have crosses on the other side?" *"No doubt about it."* "Would it be possible with the true ones?" *"Yes, if we did it many times."*[19]

Piaget concluded that since children "lack deductive operations and the notion of chance, everything for them is, in differing degrees, miraculous. It is only when we have a rational mind, that the question of miracle is posed because it is contrary both to natural regularities and fortuitous fluctuations. For the ancients, on the contrary, a miracle (in the etymological sense of 'marvel' or 'wonder') was a natural thing, and for the primitive everything is a miracle."[20] In general, then, children's notions of chance move from a denial of chance, to a recognition of chance either as rare events or events impossible to predict with the certainties of concrete operations, to the incorporation of chance into a logical scheme capable of analyzing all the possibilities inherent in a situation and devising a strategy to test which possibility actually exists.

The existence of this and other developmental sequences poses serious problems for traditional theories of learning.[21] Operational

19. *Chance*, p. 106.
20. *Chance*, p. 221.
21. For what follows, see *Psychology of the Child*, pp. 152–59; *Psychology and Epistemology*, pp. 45–88; *Child and Reality*, pp. 1–30, 143–62. C. R. Hallpike, *Foundations of Primitive Thought* (Oxford, 1979), discusses in detail cross-cultural research. For earlier assessments of the literature, see P. R. Dasen, "Cross-cultural Piagetian Research: A Summary," in J. W. Berry and P. R. Dasen, *Culture and Cognition: Readings in Cross-Cultural Psychology* (London, 1974), pp. 409–23. Dasen tentatively concludes that "in all cultures studied so far, some or all individuals reach the stage of concrete operations, although usually at a later age than middle-class Europeans. The fact, however, that some individuals, even of adult age, continue to show a pre-operational type of reasoning, and that some qualitative differences are being reported, indicates that environmental factors may be more important than Piaget seemed to hypothesize in his earlier

logic cannot be acquired by imitating adults or identifying with parents; otherwise, children of formal operational parents could proceed directly to formal thought without passing through the pre-operational and concrete operational stages. Nor are advanced logical structures innate patterns brought out by biological maturation, because environmental factors appear capable of advancing and retarding the attainment of concrete and formal operations. The ages I have given above are true only for European children, among whom there can be considerable variation. Of children in Iran, those schooled in Teheran mastered principles of conservation at about the same ages as European or American children, while illiterate children in the countryside were two or three years later on the same tests. The disparities are still greater for some African tribes, where conservation appears at about the age of twelve on average and where many adults lack the ability to conserve water.

Piaget concludes from this evidence that intelligence, by its nature, is active. Children learn first by manipulating the material objects of their existence, later and as adults by mentally manipulating intellectual images and concepts. Society can provide more or less stimulation. Children in a society where adults explain events as resulting from chance might become critical of their egocentric notions more quickly than those in a society where unusual events were explained as witchcraft. And social pressures can impede or reverse progress toward sophisticated notions. In Atayal society, where adults believe dreams are real, children nonetheless develop toward a subjective notion of dreams until they are about eleven years old, when they gradually return to ideas they had abandoned at an earlier age.[22] But operational thought is not simply internalized—otherwise the Atayal would not develop subjective notions of dreams that ran counter to adult teaching—but created anew by each individual. "Knowledge results from continuous construction, since in each act of understanding some degree of invention is involved; in development, the passage from one stage to the next is always characterized by the formation of new structures which did not exist before, either in the external world or in the subject's mind."[23]

---

writings" (p. 421). A somewhat differently balanced summary is that of M. Cole and S. Scribner, *Culture and Thought* (New York, 1974), esp. pp. 146–56.

22. Lawrence Kohlberg, "Stage and Sequence: The Cognitive-Developmental Approach to Socialization," in *Handbook of Socialization Theory and Research*, ed. David A. Goslin (Chicago, 1969), pp. 356–61.

23. *Genetic Epistemology*, p. 77.

In analogy to the "realism" of egocentric reasoning that attributes real or objective existence to names and other products of thought, Piaget termed the moral attitudes of young children "moral realism." According to Piaget, moral realism has three main features. First, the belief that any act showing obedience to a rule is good, and that any act not conforming to a rule is bad. The rule, moreover, is not taken as something to be judged and interpreted but is seen as given "ready made and external to the mind." Second, and related to the first, is that the letter and not the spirit of the rule is to be obeyed. Third, acts are evaluated in terms of their conformity with the rule, and not according to the motive that prompted them.

The consequence of moral realism for conceptions of rules was seen in the discussion of the game of marbles, but no less important are the attitudes revealed by Piaget's studies of how children conceived of lies. Piaget presented his subjects with paired stories. One story was about a child who, not having been examined at school, told his mother that he had received good marks and was rewarded. In the other story, a child was frightened by a dog and told his mother he was chased by "a dog as big as a cow." Young children in Piaget's sample (those under eight) typically said that the two children are equally bad or that the second child was worse; that the first child intended to deceive and the second did not was not taken into account. Instead, the crucial issue was the response of the adult: some of Piaget's subjects believed the first child had done nothing wrong because his mother believed him. Most young children also thought it was all right to tell lies to other children, since they were not capable of inflicting punishment and would believe the lie. In contrast, children over ten usually thought the first child, who had lied about the marks, was worse because he had lied to deceive his mother into rewarding him. They dismissed the lie about the dog because there was no intent to deceive and no one would believe it. Older children also thought it was as bad to lie to children as to adults or worse, because children are little and likely to be taken in.[24]

The tendency of small children to focus on objective circumstances, such as the size of the lie or the giving of rewards, was also revealed by Piaget's interrogatories on the themes of clumsiness and stealing. In one story, a child climbs into a cupboard to get some

24. *Moral Judgment*, pp. 139–74.

jam and knocks over a cup, which falls and breaks. In the other
story, a child is called to dinner. He or she opens the door to the dining room, but behind the door on a chair is a tray of cups the child could not have known about. The tray falls and fifteen cups are broken. Piaget found that most young children (six to seven) paid attention to the amount of damage—in this case they thought it was worse to break the fifteen cups—whereas older children (over ten) were interested primarily in intention. Children between seven and ten used both criteria, judging objectively at one time and subjectively according to intention at another.[25]

Piaget's studies revealed a greater role for individual cognition than other theorists of the origin of morality had suspected. Durkheim, for example, thought that society was the source of moral ideas, which the child was conditioned to accept; Freud believed that moral feelings resulted from the internalization of a parental figure as a superego. In actuality, the development of subjective morality seems to depend less on the constraint of society or the unilateral respect one feels for superiors than on experiencing the equality of relations with peers. Emotional factors do of course influence moral judgment. A person may lack the strength of character to act on his or her judgment of right and wrong, or he may persuade himself that what he wants to do is right. But the circumstances in which one experiences the feelings of conflict, and the reasoning one uses to justify one's actions, reflect the cognitive assessment one makes of a situation.[26]

Piaget's work on moral development contains all the basic elements I have used in this work, but since theory in this area has been the subject of considerable research in the last twenty-five years, it is appropriate to say a few words about what seems to me the most important body of new work, that of Lawrence Kohlberg and his associates.[27] Kohlberg's methodological innovation con-

25. *Moral Judgment*, pp. 155–56.
26. Piaget discusses these issues in the last chapter of *Moral Judgment* and in *Psychology of the Child*, pp. 122–27.
27. This discussion is based upon "Stage and Sequence," cited above; Kohlberg, "From Is to Ought: How to Commit the Naturalistic Fallacy and Get Away with it in the Study of Moral Development," in *Cognitive Development and Epistemology*, ed. T. Mischel (New York, 1971), pp. 151–235; and, with K. Kauffman et al., *The Just Community Approach to Corrections: A Manual*, pt. 2, chap. 5: "Understanding and Diagnosing Moral Stages" (Moral Education Research Foundation). Kohlberg's works are now collected in: *The Philosophy of Moral Development: Moral Stage and the Idea of Justice* (San Francisco, 1981); and *The Psychology of*

sisted of devising hypothetical dilemmas of sufficient complexity and interest that they could be used to elicit the reasoning of adolescents and adults as well as children. The classic dilemma concerns a man who steals a drug for his sick wife because he could not afford to buy it; another asks whether a boy who had earned money himself should give it to his father if his father tells him to. In giving answers to these dilemmas (and ideally, as in the Piagetian interrogatory, the interviewer is to follow up what seems to be the subject's line of thought with questions to elucidate it), people are required to discuss their ideas about the nature of obligations between people, the value of human life, the relationship between law and morality, and other questions of recurrent importance in moral thought. The material gathered by means of such interviews then made it possible for Kohlberg to describe the way different attitudes fit together into structures of reasoning.

The theory itself describes five such structures of moral reasoning, which for convenience are grouped into three "levels," the first of which is roughly equivalent to Piaget's moral realism. These are summarized in Table 1. (There were originally six structures but the sixth has been deemphasized of late for reasons that will appear below.) Kohlberg terms these structures *stages*, because according to his theory they represent a fixed developmental sequence, with all children beginning at first stage and not reaching the fourth stage, for example, without passing through the second and third. Although not everyone's reasoning fits entirely into one stage, Kohlberg claims that when mixtures of reasoning do occur it is the reasoning of adjacent stages (stages 2 and 4 for someone whose dominant reasoning is at stage 3) that will most often be utilized.

Kohlberg's theory has provoked much criticism and debate. Some of it—that which concerns details of certain stages or scoring techniques—is too technical to be of interest here because historical materials are rarely going to be susceptible to the kind of precise analyses these disagreements suppose. Of greater concern are the charges that have been made, often with some heat, that Kohlberg's theory is either ethnocentric or slanted toward a male point of view. These accusations were provoked by Kohlberg's reporting that societies, and groups within societies, differ in the frequency with

---

Moral Development: the Nature and Validity of Moral Stages (San Francisco, 1984). See also, Thomas Lickona, "Moral Development and the Problem of Evil," in *Developmental Psychology*, ed. R. M. Liebert et al. (New York, 1977), pp. 370–75.

Stage	Social Perspective	Moral Judgment

Level I (Pre-conventional)

| I | Egocentricism, not recognizing differences between one's interests and those of others, often confusing the perspective of authority with one's own. | Right is obedience to rules and authority, avoiding punishment and not doing physical harm. |
| 2 | Concrete individualism, in which society is seen from the perspective of one individual looking at other individuals. | Right is serving one's own needs and making fair deals in terms of concrete exchange. |

Level II (Conventional)

| 3 | Perspective of the individual who sees himself or herself sharing expectations or feelings with other individuals. | Right is playing an appropriate role, being concerned about other people and their feelings, keeping loyalty and trust with partners and being motivated to follow rules. |
| 4 | Perspective of the individual who sees himself or herself as a member of a group or society. | Right is doing one's duty in society, upholding the social order and the welfare of the society or group. |

Level III (Principled)

| 5 | Social-contract perspective in which the individual sees himself or herself in relation to society or the universe of all individuals. | Right is upholding rationally discoverable ethical principles or the basic values of society even when they conflict with concrete laws of the group. |

which certain stages appear in the adult population; specifically, that while most American men are at stage 4, there is a markedly higher occurrence of stage 3 among American women, and, further, that members of modern peasant societies are most often at stage 3 with a large percentage at stages 1 and 2.[28] Kohlberg's defense, that the same studies showed the existence of his developmental sequence in other societies and among women, addresses what seems to me the basic theoretical issue; and indeed, given the different opportunities of social interaction provided by industrial and peasant society and by male and female roles in American society, the results are hardly surprising. (An interesting commentary on the concerns of American academics is offered by the fact that Kohlberg's claim to have found differences across class lines aroused no particular discussion.)

Yet if part of the reaction to Kohlberg's research doubtless reflects the dogmatic denial of any real differences among humans, a doctrine I have traced to the rise of cultural relativism, part of it also is in response to some of the claims he has seemed to make that the higher the stage the more moral the person. The place where this conclusion is implied most strongly is in his assertion that stage 6 as he originally defined it, that is, orientation to universal ethical principles, constitutes an "ultimately adequate, universal, and mature conception of morality," and therefore ought to be the goal of any program of moral education. This position is extreme in omitting from consideration other aspects of personality and character that influence moral behavior, and it has been criticized for that reason. The fact that Kohlberg's theory is not as comprehensive as he sometimes asserts does not, however, mean it is not powerful within its own sphere, though obviously the next step for the study of morality as for psychology in general has to be the integration of emotional and cognitive theories into an approach capable of dealing with both aspects of personality.[29]

These criticisms aside, there are two reasons why historians will

28. "Stage and Sequence," pp. 385, 397–404. See also, Carolyn P. Edwards, "Societal Concepts and Moral Development: A Kenyan Study," *Ethos* 3 (1975): 505–28.
29. For a beginning in this direction see Laetitia Ward and John P. Wilson, "Motivation and Moral Development as Determinants of Behavioral Acquiescence and Moral Action," *Journal of Social Psychology* 112 (1980): 271–86; and Carol Gilligan, *In A Different Voice. Psychological Theory and Women's Development* (Cambridge, Mass., 1982). Gilligan does not discuss the relationship between cognition and affect, an omission that causes her analysis of some points to blur important distinctions.

find his theory repays study. The first is that Kohlberg's dilemmas,
dealing as they do more explicitly with the moral issues adults encounter, is closer to the material historians are likely to encounter than is Piaget's. Second, and related to the first, is the additional detail that Kohlberg provides about the way one aspect of moral reasoning relates to another. I have found particularly helpful, for example, his finding that each stage of moral reasoning supposes a typical perception of social relations, because in certain authors their conception of society is clear even when the basis on which they are making their moral judgments is not. In part this kind of detail means that one can often make fairly precise estimations of the stage of reasoning (in Kohlberg's sense) that a given writer uses, although to avoid burdening this book with the distractions of extra psychological terminology, I have not done this in so many words. But what is most important is that increased sensitivity to the different ways ideas can hang together can make us as historians more capable of following the thought of the people we study without forcing upon them our own standards for logical consistency. It is this sensitivity that I believe makes cognitive theory of importance even to historians who are not particularly interested in cognition as a historical issue.

Index